Oracle Certified Associate: Java SE 8 Programmer I

Practice Tests

By: Udayan Khattry

DEDICATION

This book is dedicated to my wife Neha, with love.

21-Dec-2017:   v1.00 (1st Release)
23-Mar-2019:   v2.00 (2nd Release)
21-Aug-2019:   v2.01
10-Oct-2019:   v2.02
09-Sep-2020:   v3.00 (3rd Release)
01-Nov-2021:   v3.01
11-Jun-2023:   v3.02

Author's Profile

Udayan Khattry

SCJP, SCWCD & Oracle Database SQL Certified Expert

Author has a master's degree in Computer Applications from Symbiosis International University, Pune, India and have completed following professional certifications:
- **SCJP** 1.6 (Sun Certified Programmer for J2SE 6.0)
- **SCWCD** 1.5 (Sun Certified Web Component Developer)
- **Oracle Database SQL Certified Expert**

After working as a software developer and consultant for over 9 years for various companies in India, Dubai & Singapore, he decided to follow his lifelong passion of teaching.

In the last 7 years, author has published multiple books and online courses on Java and Java certifications. He currently has 75000+ students from 140+ countries.

Audience

Anyone preparing for OCA (1Z0-808) certificate or interviews can take this book to assess his/her preparation.

Table of Content

Introduction

OCA - Java SE 8 Programmer I - Exam Information:

- **Exam Code: 1Z0-808**
- **Duration: 150 minutes**
- **Questions #: 70 (Multiple Choice / Multiple Select)**
- **Passing score: 65%**

Exam Curriculum:

- **Java Basics**
- **Working With Java Data Types**
- **Using Operators and Decision Constructs**
- **Creating and Using Arrays**
- **Using Loop Constructs**
- **Working with Methods and Encapsulation**
- **Working with Inheritance**
- **Handling Exceptions**
- **Working with Selected classes from the Java API**

All topics listed above are divided appropriately in **4 Practice Tests consisting of 70 questions each i.e., 280 questions** in total and **2 bonus tests** containing **144 questions**. These questions are designed based on real examination questions in terms of pattern and complexity.

After each Practice Test, **correct answers** are provided with **explanation** for reference and understanding. **Relevant hints and how to approach a question in real examination setting is also provided in explanation.**

Completing all the tests successfully will boost your confidence to attempt Oracle Certified Associate (OCA) examination.

More information on detailed curriculum and assumptions, to be followed for examination is available on oracle certification page.

https://education.oracle.com/pls/web_prod-plq-
dad/db_pages.getpage?page_id=5001&get_params=p_exam_id:1Z0-808

Disclaimer: These questions are not real examination questions / dumps. These questions are created to evaluate your preparation for certification exam.

For any questions / problems in above links send an email to: udayan.khattry@outlook.com.

1   Practice Test - 1

1.1   70 Questions covering all topics

1.1.1   Which of the following correctly defines class Printer?

| A. | ```java
public class Printer {

}
package com.udayan.oca;
``` |
| B. | ```java
/* Java Developer Comments. */
package com.udayan.oca;
public class Printer {

}
``` |
| C. | ```java
public class Printer {
        package com.udayan.oca;
}
``` |
| D. | ```java
import java.util.*;
package com.udayan.oca;
public class Printer {

}
``` |

1.1.2   Consider below code:

```java
//Guest.java
class Message {
    static void main(String [] args) {
        System.out.println("Welcome " + args[2] + "!");
    }
}

public class Guest {
    public static void main(String [] args) {
        Message.main(args);
    }
}
```

And the commands:

javac Guest.java

java Guest Clare Waight Keller

What is the result?

A. Welcome Clare!

B. Welcome Waight!

C. Welcome Keller!

D. ArrayIndexOutOfBoundsException is thrown at runtime

E. Some other error as main method can't be invoked manually

F. Compilation error as main method is not public in Message class

1.1.3 For the class Test, which options, if used to replace /*INSERT*/, will print "Hurrah! I passed..." on to the console? Select 2 options.

```java
public class Test {
    /*INSERT*/ {
        System.out.println("Hurrah! I passed...");
    }
}
```

A.   static public void main(String [] args)
B.   public static void main(String [] a)
C.   static public void Main(String [] args)
D.   public void main(String [] args)
E.   protected static void main(String [] args)
F.   public void static main(String [] args)

1.1.4 **Consider 3 files:**

```
//Order.java
package orders;

public class Order {

}

//Item.java
package orders.items;

public class Item {

}

//Shop.java
package shopping;

/*INSERT*/

public class Shop {
    Order order = null;
    Item item = null;
}
```

For the class Shop, which options, if used to replace /*INSERT*/, will resolve all the compilation errors? Select 2 options.

A.	`import orders.Order;` `import orders.items.Item;`	B.	`import orders.*;`
C.	`import orders.items.*;`	D.	`import orders.*;` `import orders.items.*;`
E.	`import orders.*;` `import items.*;`		

1.1.5   How many objects of Pen class are eligible for Garbage Collection at Line 4?

```java
class Pen {

}

public class TestPen {
    public static void main(String[] args) {
        new Pen(); //Line 1
        Pen p = new Pen(); // Line 2
        change(p); //Line 3
        System.out.println("About to end."); //Line 4
    }

    public static void change(Pen pen) { //Line 5
        pen = new Pen(); //Line 6
    }
}
```

A.	0	B.	1
C.	2	D.	3

1.1.6   What will be the result of compiling and executing Test class?

```java
public class Test {
    char var1;
    double var2;
    float var3;

    public static void main(String[] args) {
        Test obj = new Test();
        System.out.println(">" + obj.var1);
        System.out.println(">" + obj.var2);
        System.out.println(">" + obj.var3);
    }
}
```

A.	>null >0.0 >0.0	B.	> >0.0 >0.0
C.	> >0.0 >0.0f	D.	>null >0.0 >0.0f

1.1.7   Given the code of Test.java file:

```java
package com.udayan.oca;

class Point {
    int x;
    int y;
    void assign(int x, int y) {
        x = this.x;
        this.y = y;
    }

    public String toString() {
        return "Point(" + x + ", " + y + ")";
    }
}

public class Test {
    public static void main(String[] args) {
        Point p1 = new Point();
        p1.x = 10;
        p1.y = 20;
        Point p2 = new Point();
        p2.assign(p1.x, p1.y);
        System.out.println(p1.toString() + ";" +
p2.toString());
    }
}
```

What will be the result of compiling and executing Test class?

A. Point(10, 20);Point(10, 20)

B. Point(10, 20);Point(0, 20)

C. Point(0, 20);Point(0, 20)

D. Point(0, 20);Point(10, 20)

E. None of the other options

1.1.8 What will be the result of compiling and executing Test class?

```java
import java.util.ArrayList;
import java.util.List;

public class Test {
    public static void main(String[] args) {
        List<Integer> list = new ArrayList<>();
        list.add(100);
        list.add(200);
        list.add(100);
        list.add(200);
        list.remove(100);

        System.out.println(list);
    }
}
```

A. [200, 100, 200]

B. [100, 200, 200]

C. [200, 200]

D. [200]

E. Compilation error

F. Exception is thrown at runtime

1.1.9 What will be the result of compiling and executing Test class?

```java
public class Test {
    public static void main(String[] args) {
        Double [] arr = new Double[2];
        System.out.println(arr[0] + arr[1]);
    }
}
```

A. NullPointerException is thrown at runtime

B. 0.0

C. Compilation error

D. ClassCastException is thrown at runtime

1.1.10 What will be the result of compiling and executing Test class?

```java
public class Test {
    public static void main(String[] args) {
        System.out.println("Output is: " + 10 != 5);
    }
}
```

A. Output is: true

B. Output is: false

C. Compilation error

D. Output is: 10 != 5

1.1.11   What will be the result of compiling and executing the Test class?

```java
public class Test {
    public static void main(String[] args) {
        int grade = 60;
        if(grade = 60)
            System.out.println("You passed...");
        else
            System.out.println("You failed...");
    }
}
```

A. You passed...

B. You failed...

C. Compilation error

D. Produces no output

1.1.12   What will be the result of compiling and executing Test class?

```java
public class Test {
    public static void main(String[] args) {
        byte var = 100;
        switch(var) {
            case 100:
                System.out.println("var is 100");
                break;
            case 200:
                System.out.println("var is 200");
                break;
            default:
                System.out.println("In default");
        }
    }
}
```

A. var is 100

B. var is 200

C. In default

D. Compilation error

1.1.13 What will be the result of compiling and executing Test class?

```java
public class Test {
    public static void main(String[] args) {
        String fruit = "mango";
        switch (fruit) {
            default:
                System.out.println("ANY FRUIT WILL DO");
            case "Apple":
                System.out.println("APPLE");
            case "Mango":
                System.out.println("MANGO");
            case "Banana":
                System.out.println("BANANA");
                break;
        }
    }
}
```

A.	ANY FRUIT WILL DO	B.	MANGO
C.	MANGO BANANA	D.	ANY FRUIT WILL DO APPLE MANGO BANANA

1.1.14 For the class Test, which options, if used to replace /*INSERT*/, will print "Lucky no. 7" on to the console? Select 3 options.

```java
public class Test {
    public static void main(String[] args) {
        /*INSERT*/
        switch(var) {
            case 7:
                System.out.println("Lucky no. 7");
                break;
            default:
                System.out.println("DEFAULT");
        }
    }
}
```

A. char var = '7';

B. char var = 7;

C. Integer var = 7;

D. Character var = '7';

E. Character var = 7;

1.1.15 What will be the result of compiling and executing Test class?

```
import java.time.LocalTime;

public class Test {
    public static void main(String[] args) {
        LocalTime time = LocalTime.of(16, 40);
        String amPm = time.getHour() >= 12 ?
                (time.getHour() == 12) ? "PM" : "AM";
        System.out.println(amPm);
    }
}
```

A. PM

B. AM

C. Compilation error

D. An exception is thrown at runtime

1.1.16 What will be the result of compiling and executing Test class?

```
public class Test {
    public static void main(String [] args) {
        int a = 100;
        System.out.println(-a++);
    }
}
```

A. Compilation error

B. -100

C. -101

D. 99

E. -99

1.1.17 Which of the following is not a valid array declaration?

```
A.    int [] arr1 = new int[8];
B.    int [][] arr2 = new int[8][8];
C.    int [] arr3 [] = new int[8][];
D.    int arr4[][] = new int[][8];
```

1.1.18 Given code:

```
public class Test {
    public static void main(String[] args) {
        String [] arr = {"I", "N", "S", "E", "R", "T"};
        for(/*INSERT*/) {
            if (n % 2 == 0) {
                continue;
            }
            System.out.print(arr[n]); //Line n1
        }
    }
}
```

And below options:

```
1. int n = 0; n < arr.length; n += 1
2. int n = 0; n <= arr.length; n += 1
3. int n = 1; n < arr.length; n += 2
4. int n = 1; n <= arr.length; n += 2
```

How many above options can be used to replace /*INSERT*/, such that on execution, code will print NET on to the console?

A. Only one option

B. Only two options

C. Only three options

D. All four options

E. None of the other options

1.1.19 Given Code:

```
public class Test {
    public static void main(String[] args) {
        /*INSERT*/
        arr[1] = 5;
        arr[2] = 10;
        System.out.println("[" + arr[1] + ", "
                             + arr[2] + "]"); //Line n1
    }
}
```

And below statements:
```
1. short arr [] = new short[2];
2. byte [] arr = new byte[10];
3. short [] arr; arr = new short[3];
4. short [2] arr;
5. short [3] arr;
6. int [] arr = new int[]{100, 100};
7. int [] arr = new int[]{0, 0, 0, 0};
8. short [] arr = {};
9. short [] arr = new short[2]{5, 10};
```

How many above statements can be used to replace /*INSERT*/, such that on execution, code will print [5, 10] on to the console?

A. Only one option

B. Only two options

C. Only three options

D. Only four options

E. None of the given options

F. More than four options

1.1.20 What will be the result of compiling and executing Test class?

```
public class Test {
    public static void main(String[] args) {
        double [] arr = new int[2]; //Line 3
        System.out.println(arr[0]); //Line 4
    }
}
```

A. 0

B. 0.0

C. Line 3 causes compilation error

D. Line 4 causes runtime exception

1.1.21 Which of the following statement is correct about below code?

```java
public class Test {
    public static void main(String[] args) {
        do {
            System.out.println(100);
        } while (false);

        System.out.println("Bye");
    }
}
```

A.	Compiles successfully and prints "Bye"	B.	Compiles successfully and prints 100 in infinite loop
C.	Unreachable code compilation error	D.	100 Bye

1.1.22 What will be the result of compiling and executing Test class?

```java
import java.util.ArrayList;
import java.util.List;

public class Test {
    public static void main(String[] args) {
        String[] names = { "Smith", "Brown",
                    "Thomas", "Taylor", "Jones" };
        List<String> list = new ArrayList<>();
        for (int x = 0; x < names.length; x++) {
            list.add(names[x]);
            switch (x) {
                case 2:
                    continue;
            }
            break;
        }
        System.out.println(list.size());
    }
}
```

A. 0

B. 1

C. 2

D. 3

E. 4

F. 5

G. None of the other options

1.1.23 What will be the result of compiling and executing Test class?

```java
public class Test {
    public static void main(String[] args) {
        int [] arr = {2, 1, 0};
        for(int i : arr) {
            System.out.println(arr[i]);
        }
    }
}
```

A.	2 1 0	B.	0 1 2
C.	Compilation error	D.	ArrayIndexOutOfBoundsException is thrown at runtime

1.1.24 What will be the result of compiling and executing Test class?

```java
class Message {
    String msg = "Happy New Year!";

    public void print() {
        System.out.println(msg);
    }
}

public class Test {
    public static void change(Message m) {
        m = new Message();
        m.msg = "Happy Holidays!";
    }

    public static void main(String[] args) {
        Message obj = new Message();
        obj.print();
        change(obj);
        obj.print();
```

```
    }
}
```

A.	Happy New Year! Happy Holidays!	B.	Happy Holidays! Happy Holidays!
C.	Happy New Year! Happy New Year!	D.	null Happy New Year!

1.1.25 What will be the result of compiling and executing Test class?

```java
public class Test {
    public static void main(String[] args) {
        double price = 90000;
        String model;
        if(price > 100000) {
            model = "Tesla Model X";
        } else if(price <= 100000) {
            model = "Tesla Model S";
        }
        System.out.println(model);
    }
}
```

A. Tesla Model X

B. Tesla Model S

C. null

D. Compilation Error

1.1.26 Consider the following class:

```java
public class Employee {
    public int passportNo;  //line 2
}
```

Which of the following is the correct way to make the variable 'passportNo' read only for any other class?

A. Make 'passportNo' private.

B. Make 'passportNo' private and provide a public method getPassportNo() which will return its value.

C. Make 'passportNo' static and provide a public static method getPassportNo() which will return its value.

D. Remove 'public' from the 'passportNo' declaration. i.e., change line 2 to int passportNo;

1.1.27 What will be the result of compiling and executing Test class?

```java
public class Test {
    private static void m(int x) {
        System.out.println("int version");
    }

    private static void m(char x) {
        System.out.println("char version");
    }

    public static void main(String [] args) {
        int i = '5';
        m(i);
        m('5');
    }
}
```

A.	int version int version	B.	char version char version
C.	int version char version	D.	char version int version
E.	Compilation error		

1.1.28 _____ uses access modifiers to protect variables and hide them within a class.

Which of the following options accurately fill in the blanks above?

A. Polymorphism

B. Inheritance

C. Encapsulation

D. Abstraction

1.1.29 What will be the result of compiling and executing Test class?

```java
public class Test {
    public static void main(String[] args) {
        short [] args = new short[]{50, 50};
        args[0] = 5;
        args[1] = 10;
        System.out.println("[" + args[0] + ", "
                + args[1] + "]");
    }
}
```

A. Compilation error

B. An exception is thrown at runtime

C. [50, 50]

D. [5, 10]

1.1.30 What will be the result of compiling and executing Test class?

```java
//Test.java
package com.udayan.oca;

class Student {
    String name;
    int marks;

    Student(String name, int marks) {
        this.name = name;
        this.marks = marks;
    }
}

public class Test {
    public static void main(String[] args) {
        Student student = new Student("James", 25);
        int marks = 25;
        review(student, marks);
        System.out.println(marks + "-" + student.marks);
    }

    private static void review(Student stud, int marks) {
        marks = marks + 10;
        stud.marks+=marks;
    }
}
```

A. 25-25

B. 35-25

C. 35-60

D. 25-60

1.1.31 **What will be the result of compiling and executing Test class?**

```java
public class Test {
    public static void main(String[] args) {
        int x = 1;
        while(checkAndIncrement(x)) {
            System.out.println(x);
        }
    }

    private static boolean checkAndIncrement(int x) {
        if(x < 5) {
            x++;
            return true;
        } else {
            return false;
        }
    }
}
```

A.	2 3 4 5	B.	1 2 3 4
C.	1 2 3 4 5	D.	Infinite loop

1.1.32 Consider the code of Test.java file:

```
package com.udayan.oca;

class Student {
    String name;
    int age;

    void Student() {
        Student("James", 25);
    }

    void Student(String name, int age) {
        this.name = name;
        this.age = age;
    }
}

public class Test {
    public static void main(String[] args) {
        Student s = new Student();
        System.out.println(s.name + ":" + s.age);
    }
}
```

What will be the result of compiling and executing Test class?

A. Compilation error

B. null:0

C. James:25

D. An exception is thrown at runtime

1.1.33 Which of these access modifiers can be used for a top level interface?

A. private

B. protected

C. public

D. All of the other options

1.1.34 **What will be the result of compiling and executing Test class?**

```java
//Test.java
package com.udayan.oca.test;

abstract class Animal {
    private String name;

    Animal(String name) {
        this.name = name;
    }

    public String getName() {
        return name;
    }
}

class Dog extends Animal {
    private String breed;

    Dog(String breed) {
        this.breed = breed;
    }

    Dog(String name, String breed) {
        super(name);
        this.breed = breed;
    }

    public String getBreed() {
        return breed;
    }
}

public class Test {
    public static void main(String[] args) {
        Dog dog1 = new Dog("Beagle");
        Dog dog2 = new Dog("Bubbly", "Poodle");
        System.out.println(dog1.getName() + ":"
                + dog1.getBreed() + ":" + dog2.getName()
                + ":" + dog2.getBreed());
    }
}
```

A. Compilation error for Animal Class

B. Compilation error for Animal(String) constructor

C. Compilation error for Dog(String) constructor

D. Compilation error for Dog(String, String) constructor

E. null:Beagle:Bubbly:Poodle

F. :Beagle:Bubbly:Poodle

1.1.35 Consider below code fragment:

```java
interface Printable {
    public void setMargin();
    public void setOrientation();
}

abstract class Paper implements Printable { //Line 7
    public void setMargin() {}
    //Line 9
}

class NewsPaper extends Paper { //Line 12
    public void setMargin() {}
    //Line 14
}
```

Above code is currently giving compilation error. Which 2 modifications, done independently, enable the code to compile?

A. Replace the code at Line 7 with: class Paper implements Printable {

B. Insert at Line 9: public abstract void setOrientation();

C. Replace the code at Line 12 with: abstract class NewsPaper extends Paper {

D. Insert at Line 14: public void setOrientation() {}

1.1.36 Consider code below:

```
package com.udayan.oca;

class PenDrive {
    int capacity;
    PenDrive(int capacity) {
        this.capacity = capacity;
    }
}
class OTG extends PenDrive {
    String type;
    String make;
    OTG(int capacity, String type) {
        /*INSERT-1*/
    }
    OTG(String make) {
        /*INSERT-2*/
        this.make = make;
    }
}
public class Test {
    public static void main(String[] args) {
        OTG obj = new OTG(128, "TYPE-C");
        System.out.println(obj.capacity +
                            ":" + obj.type);
    }
}
```

Currently above code causes compilation error.

Which of the options can successfully print 128:TYPE-C on to the console?

A.	Replace /*INSERT-1*/ with:
	super(capacity);
	Replace /*INSERT-2*/ with:
	super(128);
		B.	Replace /*INSERT-1*/ with:
			super.capacity = capacity;
			this.type = type;
			Replace /*INSERT-2*/ with:
			super(128);

C.	Replace /*INSERT-1*/ with:
	super(capacity);
	this.type = type;
	Replace /*INSERT-2*/ with:
	super(0);
		D.	Replace /*INSERT-1*/ with:
			this.type = type;
			super(capacity);
			Replace /*INSERT-2*/ with:
			super(128);

E.	None of the other options		

1.1.37 Consider codes below:

```
//A.java
package com.udayan.oca;

public class A {
    public int i1 = 1;
    protected int i2 = 2;
}

//B.java
package com.udayan.oca.test;

        import com.udayan.oca.A;

public class B extends A {
    public void print() {
        A obj = new A();
        System.out.println(obj.i1);  //Line 8
        System.out.println(obj.i2);  //Line 9
        System.out.println(this.i2);  //Line 10
        System.out.println(super.i2);  //Line 11
    }

    public static void main(String [] args) {
        new B().print();
    }
}
```

One of the statements inside print() method is causing compilation failure. Which of the below solutions will help to resolve compilation error?

A. Comment the statement at Line 8

B. Comment the statement at Line 9

C. Comment the statement at Line 10

D. Comment the statement at Line 11

1.1.38   Consider codes below:

```java
//A.java
package com.udayan.oca;

public class A {
    public void print() {
        System.out.println("A");
    }
}

//B.java
package com.udayan.oca;

public class B extends A {
    public void print() {
        System.out.println("B");
    }
}

//Test.java
package com.udayan.oca.test;

import com.udayan.oca.*;

public class Test {
    public static void main(String[] args) {
        A obj1 = new A();
        B obj2 = (B)obj1;
        obj2.print();
    }
}
```

What will be the result of compiling and executing Test class?

A. A

B. B

C. Compilation error

D. ClassCastException is thrown at runtime

1.1.39   What will be the result of compiling and executing Test class?

```
import java.io.FileNotFoundException;
import java.io.IOException;

abstract class Super {
    public abstract void m1() throws IOException;
}

class Sub extends Super {
    @Override
    public void m1() throws IOException {
        throw new FileNotFoundException();
    }
}

public class Test {
    public static void main(String[] args) {
        Super s = new Sub();
        try {
            s.m1();
        } catch (FileNotFoundException e) {
            System.out.print("M");
        } finally {
            System.out.print("N");
        }
    }
}
```

A. MN

B. N

C. Compilation error

D. Program ends abruptly

1.1.40 Which of the following is a checked Exception?

A. ClassCastException

B. FileNotFoundException

C. ExceptionInInitializerError

D. RuntimeException

1.1.41 What will be the result of compiling and executing Test class?

```java
public class Test {
    public static void main(String[] args) {
        try {
            main(args);
        } catch (Exception ex) {
            System.out.println("CATCH-");
        }
        System.out.println("OUT");
    }
}
```

A. CATCH-OUT

B. OUT

C. None of the System.out.println statements are executed

D. Compilation error

1.1.42 What will be the result of compiling and executing Test class?

```
public class Test {
    public static void main(String[] args) {
        m1(); //Line 3
    }

    private static void m1() throws Exception { //Line 6
        System.out.println("NOT
                    THROWING ANY EXCEPTION");//Line 7
    }
}
```

A. Compilation error at Line 3

B. Compilation error at Line 6

C. Compilation error at Line 7

D. NOT THROWING ANY EXCEPTION

1.1.43 Consider below code:

```
public class Test {
    static {
        System.out.println(1/0);
    }

    public static void main(String[] args) {
        System.out.println("HELLO");
    }
}
```

On execution, does Test class print "HELLO" on to the console?

A. Yes, HELLO is printed on to the console

B. No, HELLO is not printed on the console

1.1.44 Fill in the blanks for the definition of java.lang.Error class:

```
public class java.lang.Error extends _____
{...}
```

On execution, does Test class print "HELLO" on to the console?

A. RuntimeException

B. Exception

C. Throwable

1.1.45 What will be the result of compiling and executing Test class?

```
public class Test {
    public static void main(String[] args) {
        String str1 = new String("Core");
        String str2 = new String("CoRe");
        System.out.println(str1 = str2);
    }
}
```

A. true

B. false

C. Core

D. CoRe

1.1.46 What will be the result of compiling and executing Test class?

```
//Test.java
package com.udayan.oca;

public class Test {
    public static void main(String[] args) {
        String s1 = "OCAJP";
        String s2 = "OCAJP" + "";
        System.out.println(s1 == s2);
    }
}
```

A. OCAJP

B. true

C. false

D. Compilation error

1.1.47 A bank's swift code is generally of 11 characters and used in international money transfers.

An example of swift code: ICICINBBRT4

ICIC: First 4 letters for bank code

IN: Next 2 letters for Country code

BB: Next 2 letters for Location code

RT4: Next 3 letters for Branch code

Which of the following code correctly extracts country code from the swift code referred by String reference variable swiftCode?

A. swiftCode.substring(4, 6);

B. swiftCode.substring(5, 6);

C. swiftCode.substring(5, 7);

D. swiftCode.substring(4, 5);

1.1.48 What will be the result of compiling and executing Test class?

```
public class Test {
    public static void main(String[] args) {
        String str = "java";
        StringBuilder sb = new StringBuilder("java");

        System.out.println(str.equals(sb) + ":"
                + sb.equals(str));
    }
}
```

A. Compilation error

B. false:false

C. false:true

D. true:false

E. true:true

1.1.49 What will be the result of compiling and executing Test class?

```
public class Test {
    public static void main(String[] args) {
        StringBuilder sb = new StringBuilder("Java");
        String s1 = sb.toString();
        String s2 = sb.toString();

        System.out.println(s1 == s2);
    }
}
```

A. Compilation error

B. true

C. false

D. An exception is thrown at runtime

1.1.50 Consider below code:

```
//Test.java
package com.udayan.oca;

public class Test {
    public static void main(String[] args) {
        StringBuilder sb = new StringBuilder(100);
        System.out.println(sb.length() + ":" +
                                sb.toString().length());
    }
}
```

What will be the result of compiling and executing Test class?

A. 100:100

B. 100:0

C. 16:16

D. 16:0

E. 0:0

1.1.51 What will be the result of compiling and executing Test class?

```
package com.udayan.oca;

public class Test {
    public static void main(String[] args) {
        StringBuilder sb = new StringBuilder();
        System.out.println(sb.append(null).length());
    }
}
```

A. 1

B. 4

C. Compilation error

D. NullPointerException is thrown at runtime

1.1.52 Consider below code:

```java
//Test.java
package com.udayan.oca;

class SpecialString {
    String str;
    SpecialString(String str) {
        this.str = str;
    }
}

public class Test {
    public static void main(String[] args) {
        Object [] arr = new Object[4];
        for(int i = 1; i <=3; i++) {
            switch(i) {
                case 1:
                    arr[i] = new String("Java");
                    break;
                case 2:
                    arr[i] = new StringBuilder("Java");
                    break;
                case 3:
                    arr[i] = new SpecialString("Java");
                    break;
            }
        }
        for(Object obj : arr) {
            System.out.println(obj);
        }
    }
}
```

What will be the result of compiling and executing Test class?

A.	Java	B.	Java
	Java		Java
	Java		<Some text containing @ symbol>
C.	Java	D.	null
	<Some text containing @ symbol>		Java
	<Some text containing @ symbol>		Java
			Java

E.	null Java Java \<Some text containing @ symbol>	F.	null Java \<Some text containing @ symbol> \<Some text containing @ symbol>
G.	Java Java Java null	H.	Java Java \<Some text containing @ symbol> null
I.	Java \<Some text containing @ symbol> \<Some text containing @ symbol> null		

1.1.53 Consider below code:

```
//Test.java
import java.time.LocalDate;

public class Test {
    public static void main(String [] args) {
        LocalDate date = LocalDate.of(2020, 9, 31);
        System.out.println(date);
    }
}
```

What will be the result of compiling and executing Test class?

A. Compilation error

B. An exception is thrown at runtime

C. 2020-10-01

D. 2020-09-30

1.1.54 Consider below code:

```java
//Test.java
import java.time.LocalDate;

public class Test {
    public static void main(String [] args) {
        LocalDate newYear = LocalDate.of(2018, 1, 1);
        LocalDate christmas = LocalDate.of(2018, 12, 25);
        boolean flag1 = newYear.isAfter(christmas);
        boolean flag2 = newYear.isBefore(christmas);
        System.out.println(flag1 + ":" + flag2);
    }
}
```

What will be the result of compiling and executing Test class?

A. false:true

B. true:false

C. An exception is thrown at runtime

D. Compilation error

1.1.55 Consider below code:

```java
//Test.java
import java.time.LocalDate;

class MyLocalDate extends LocalDate {
    @Override
    public String toString() {
        return super.getDayOfMonth() + "-"
                + super.getMonthValue() + "-"
                + super.getYear();
    }
}

public class Test {
    public static void main(String [] args) {
        MyLocalDate date = LocalDate.parse("1980-03-16");
        System.out.println(date);
    }
}
```

What will be the result of compiling and executing Test class?

A. 1980-03-16

B. 16-03-1980

C. 16-3-1980

D. An exception is thrown at runtime

E. Compilation error

1.1.56   Consider below code:

```java
//Test.java
import java.time.LocalDate;
import java.time.Period;
import java.time.format.DateTimeFormatter;

public class Test {
    public static void main(String [] args) {
        LocalDate date = LocalDate.of(2012, 1, 11);
        Period period = Period.ofMonths(2);
        DateTimeFormatter formatter =
                DateTimeFormatter.ofPattern("MM-dd-yy");

System.out.print(formatter.format(date.minus(period)));
    }
}
```

What will be the result of compiling and executing Test class?

A. 11-11-12

B. 01-11-11

C. 01-11-12

D. 11-11-11

E. Runtime exception

1.1.57   Consider below code:

```
//Test.java
import java.time.Period;

public class Test {
    public static void main(String [] args) {
        Period period = Period.of(0, 0, 0);
        System.out.println(period);
    }
}
```

What will be the result of compiling and executing Test class?

A. P0Y0M0D

B. p0y0m0d

C. P0D

D. p0d

1.1.58   Consider below code:

```
//Test.java
import java.time.LocalDateTime;

public class Test {
    public static void main(String [] args) {
        LocalDateTime obj = LocalDateTime.now();
        System.out.println(obj.getSecond());
    }
}
```

Which of the following statement is correct?

A. Code fails to compile

B. Code compiles successfully but throws Runtime exception

C. It will print any int value between 0 and 59

D. It will print any int value between 1 and 60

1.1.59 Consider below code:

```
//Test.java
import java.time.LocalDate;
import java.time.LocalTime;

public class Test {
    public static void main(String [] args) {
        LocalDate date = LocalDate.parse("1947-08-14");
        LocalTime time = LocalTime.MAX;
        System.out.println(date.atTime(time));
    }
}
```

What will be the result of compiling and executing Test class?

A. 1947-08-14T23:59:59

B. 1947-08-14T23:59:59.999

C. 1947-08-14T23:59:59.999999999

D. 1947-08-14T23:59:59.0

1.1.60 Consider below code:

```java
//Test.java
package com.udayan.oca.test;

import java.util.ArrayList;
import java.util.List;

class Student {
    private String name;
    private int age;

    Student(String name, int age) {
        this.name = name;
        this.age = age;
    }

    public String toString() {
        return "Student[" + name + ", " + age + "]";
    }
}

public class Test {
    public static void main(String[] args) {
        List<Student> students = new ArrayList<>();
        students.add(new Student("James", 25));
        students.add(new Student("James", 27));
        students.add(new Student("James", 25));
        students.add(new Student("James", 25));

        students.remove(new Student("James", 25));

        for(Student stud : students) {
            System.out.println(stud);
        }
    }
}
```

What will be the result of compiling and executing Test class?

A.	Student[James, 27] Student[James, 25] Student[James, 25]	B.	Student[James, 25] Student[James, 27] Student[James, 25]
C.	Student[James, 27]	D.	Student[James, 25] Student[James, 27] Student[James, 25] Student[James, 25]

1.1.61 Consider below code:

```java
//Test.java
import java.util.ArrayList;
import java.util.Iterator;
import java.util.List;


public class Test {
    public static void main(String[] args) {
        List<String> dryFruits = new ArrayList<>();
        dryFruits.add("Walnut");
        dryFruits.add("Apricot");
        dryFruits.add("Almond");
        dryFruits.add("Date");

        Iterator<String> iterator = dryFruits.iterator();
        while(iterator.hasNext()) {
            String dryFruit = iterator.next();
            if(dryFruit.startsWith("A")) {
                dryFruits.remove(dryFruit);
            }
        }

        System.out.println(dryFruits);
    }
}
```

What will be the result of compiling and executing Test class?

A. [Walnut, Apricot, Almond, Date]

B. [Walnut, Date]

C. An exception is thrown at runtime

D. Compilation error

1.1.62 Consider below code:

```
//Test.java
import java.util.ArrayList;
import java.util.List;

public class Test {
    public static void main(String[] args) {
        String s = new String("Hello");
        List<String> list = new ArrayList<>();
        list.add(s);
        list.add(new String("Hello"));
        list.add(s);
        s.replace("l", "L");

        System.out.println(list);
    }
}
```

What will be the result of compiling and executing Test class?

A. [Hello, Hello, Hello]

B. [HeLLo, Hello, Hello]

C. [HeLLo, Hello, HeLLo]

D. [HeLLo, HeLLo, HeLLo]

1.1.63 Consider below code:

```java
//Test.java
import java.util.ArrayList;
import java.util.List;

public class Test {
    public static void main(String[] args) {
        List<String> list1 = new ArrayList<>();
        list1.add("A");
        list1.add("D");

        List<String> list2 = new ArrayList<>();
        list2.add("B");
        list2.add("C");

        list1.addAll(1, list2);

        System.out.println(list1);
    }
}
```

What will be the result of compiling and executing Test class?

A. [A, B, C, D]

B. [A, D, B, C]

C. [A, D]

D. [A, B, C]

1.1.64 Consider below code:

```java
//Test.java
import java.util.ArrayList;

class Counter {
    int count;
    Counter(int count) {
        this.count = count;
    }

    public String toString() {
        return "Counter-" + count;
    }
}

public class Test {
    public static void main(String[] args) {
        ArrayList<Counter> original = new ArrayList<>();
        original.add(new Counter(10));

        ArrayList<Counter> cloned =
                (ArrayList<Counter>) original.clone();
        cloned.get(0).count = 5;

        System.out.println(original);
    }
}
```

What will be the result of compiling and executing Test class?

A. [Counter-5]

B. [Counter-10]

C. Compilation error

D. An exception is thrown at runtime

1.1.65 For the given code snippet:

```
List<String> list = new /*INSERT*/();
```

Which of the following options, if used to replace /*INSERT*/, compiles successfully?
Select 2 options.

A. List<String>

B. List<>

C. ArrayList<String>

D. ArrayList<>

1.1.66 Consider code of Test.java file:

```
import java.util.ArrayList;
import java.util.List;

public class Test {
    public static void main(String[] args) {
        List<Character> list = new ArrayList<>();
        list.add(0, 'V');
        list.add('T');
        list.add(1, 'E');
        list.add(3, 'O');

        if(list.contains('O')) {
            list.remove('O');
        }

        for(char ch : list) {
            System.out.print(ch);
        }
    }
}
```

What will be the result of compiling and executing Test class?

A. Compilation error

B. Runtime exception

C. VET

D. VTE

E. VTEO

F. VETO

1.1.67 Below is the code of Test.java file:

```java
import java.util.ArrayList;
import java.util.List;

public class Test {
    public static void main(String [] args) {
        List<Integer> list = new ArrayList<Integer>();
        list.add(new Integer(2));
        list.add(new Integer(1));
        list.add(new Integer(0));

        list.remove(list.indexOf(0));

        System.out.println(list);
    }
}
```

What will be the result of compiling and executing Test class?

A. Compilation error

B. An exception is thrown at runtime

C. [1, 0]

D. [2, 1]

1.1.68 Consider below code:

```java
//Test.java
import java.util.ArrayList;
import java.util.Iterator;
import java.util.List;
import java.util.function.Predicate;

class Employee {
    private String name;
    private int age;
    private double salary;

    public Employee(String name, int age, double salary) {
        this.name = name;
        this.age = age;
        this.salary = salary;
    }

    public String getName() {
        return name;
    }

    public int getAge() {
        return age;
    }

    public double getSalary() {
        return salary;
    }

    public String toString() {
        return name;
    }
}

public class Test {
    public static void main(String [] args) {
        List<Employee> list = new ArrayList<>();
        list.add(new Employee("James", 25, 15000));
        list.add(new Employee("Lucy", 23, 12000));
        list.add(new Employee("Bill", 27, 10000));
        list.add(new Employee("Jack", 19, 5000));
        list.add(new Employee("Liya", 20, 8000));

        process(list, /*INSERT*/);
```

```
        System.out.println(list);
    }

    private static void process(List<Employee> list,
                                Predicate<Employee>
predicate) {
        Iterator<Employee> iterator = list.iterator();
        while(iterator.hasNext()) {
            if(predicate.test(iterator.next()))
                iterator.remove();
        }
    }
}
```

Which of the following lambda expressions, if used to replace /*INSERT*/, prints [Jack, Liya] on to the console? Select 2 options.

A.   (Employee e) -> { **return** e.getSalary() >= 10000; }
B.   (e) -> { e.getSalary() >= 10000; }
C.   e -> { e.getSalary() >= 10000 }
D.   e -> e.getSalary() >= 10000
E.   e - > e.getSalary() >= 10000

1.1.69 **What will be the result of compiling and executing Test class?**

```java
import java.util.function.Predicate;

public class Test {
    public static void main(String[] args) {
        String [] arr = {"A", "ab", "bab", "Aa",
                        "bb", "baba", "aba", "Abab"};

        Predicate<String> p = s ->
            s.toUpperCase().substring(0,1).equals("A");

        processStringArray(arr, p);
    }

    private static void processStringArray(
            String [] arr, Predicate<String> predicate) {
        for(String str : arr) {
            if(predicate.test(str)) {
                System.out.println(str);
            }
        }
    }
}
```

A.	Compilation error	B.	Runtime exception
C.	A Aa Abab	D.	ab aba
E.	A ab Aa aba Abab		

1.1.70 **What will be the result of compiling and executing Test class?**

```java
import java.time.LocalDate;
import java.time.Month;
import java.util.ArrayList;
import java.util.List;

public class Test {
    public static void main(String[] args) {
        List<LocalDate> dates = new ArrayList<>();
        dates.add(LocalDate.parse("2018-07-11"));
        dates.add(LocalDate.parse("1919-02-25"));
        dates.add(LocalDate.of(2020, 4, 8));
        dates.add(LocalDate.of(1980, Month.DECEMBER, 31));

        dates.removeIf(x -> x.getYear() < 2000);

        System.out.println(dates);
    }
}
```

A. [2018-07-11, 1919-02-25, 2020-04-08, 1980-12-31]

B. [1919-02-25, 1980-12-31]

C. [2018-07-11, 2020-04-08]

D. Runtime exception

1.2 Answers of Practice Test - 1 with Explanation

1.1.1 Answer: B

Reason:
If package is used then it should be the first statement, but javadoc and developer comments are not considered as java statements so a class can have developer and javadoc comments before the package statement.
If import and package both are available, then correct order is package, import, class declaration.

1.1.2 Answer: C

Reason:
Class Guest has special main method but main method defined in Message class is not public and hence it can't be called by JVM. But there is no issue with the syntax hence no compilation error.
java Guest Clare Waight Keller passes new String [] {"Clare", "Waight", "Keller"} to args of Guest.main method.
Guest.main method invokes Message.main method with the same argument: new String [] {"Clare", "Waight", "Keller"}. args[2] is "Keller" hence "Welcome Keller!" gets printed on to the console.

1.1.3 Answer: A,B

Reason:
As System.out.println needs to be executed on executing the Test class, this means special main method should replace /*INSERT*/.
Special main method's name should be "main" (all characters in lower case), should be static, should have public access specifier and it accepts argument of String [] type.
String [] argument can use any identifier name, even though in most of the cases you will see "args" is used.
Position of static and public can be changed but return type must come just before the method name.

1.1.4   Answer: A,D

Reason:
If you check the directory structure, you will find that directory "orders" contains "items", but orders and orders.items are different packages.
import orders.*; will only import all the classes in orders package but not in orders.items package.

You need to import Order and Item classes.

To import Order class, use either import orders.Order; OR import orders.*; and to import Item class, use either import orders.items.Item; OR import orders.items.*;

1.1.5   Answer: C

Reason:
Object created at Line 1 becomes eligible for Garbage collection after Line 1 only, as there are no references to it. So We have one object marked for GC.
Object created at Line 6 becomes unreachable after change(Pen) method pops out of the STACK, and this happens after Line 3.
So at Line 4, we have two Pen objects eligible for Garbage collection: Created at Line 1 and Created at Line 6.

1.1.6   Answer: B

Reason:
Primitive type instance variables are initialized to respective zeros (byte: 0, short: 0, int: 0, long: 0L, float: 0.0f, double: 0.0, boolean: false, char: \u0000).
When printed on the console; byte, short, int & long prints 0, float & double print 0.0, boolean prints false and char prints nothing or non-printable character (whitespace).
Reference type instance variables are initialized to null.

1.1.7   Answer: B

Reason:
HINT: First check if members are accessible or not.

All the codes are in same file Test.java, and Point class & variable x, y are declared with default modifier hence these can be accessed within the same package.

Class Test belongs to same package so no issues in accessing Point class and instance variables of Point class.

Make use of pen and paper to draw the memory diagrams (heap and stack). It will be pretty quick to reach the result.

Point p1 = new Point(); means p1.x = 0 and p1.y = 0 as instance variable are initialized to respective zeros.

p1.x = 10; means replace 0 with 10 in p1.x,

p1.y = 20; means replace 0 with 20 in p1.y,

Point p2 = new Point(); means p2.x = 0 and p2.y = 0 as instance variable are initialized to respective zeros.

p2.assign(p1.x, p1.y); invokes the assign method, parameter variable x = 10 and y = 20. As assign is invoked on p2 reference variable hence this and p2 refers to same Point object.

x = this.x; means assign 0 to parameter variable x, no changes in this.y, which means p2.x is unchanged.

this.y = y; means assign 20 to this.y, which means p2.y is now 20

So after assign method is invoked and control goes back to main method: p1.x = 10, p1.y = 20, p2.x = 0 and p2.y = 20.

Output is: Point(10, 20);Point(0, 20)

1.1.8   Answer: F

Reason:

List cannot accept primitives, it can accept objects only. So, when 100 and 200 are added to the list, then auto-boxing feature converts these to wrapper objects of Integer type.

So, 4 items get added to the list. One can expect the same behavior with remove method as well that 100 will be auto-boxed to Integer object.

But remove method is overloaded in List interface: remove(int) => Removes the element from the specified position in this list and remove(Object) => Removes the first occurrence of the specified element from the list.

As remove(int) version is available, which perfectly matches with the call remove(100); hence compiler does not do auto-boxing in this case.

But at runtime remove(100) tries to remove the element at 100th index and this throws IndexOutOfBoundsException.

1.1.9   Answer: A

Reason:
Array elements are initialized to their default values. arr is referring to an array of Double type, which is reference type and hence both the array elements are initialized to null.

To calculate arr[0] + arr[1], java runtime converts the expression to arr[0].doubleValue() + arr[1].doubleValue(). As arr[0] and arr[1] are null hence calling doubleValue() method throws NullPointerException.

1.1.10   Answer: C

Reason:
Binary plus (+) has got higher precedence than != operator. Let us group the expression.
"Output is: " + 10 != 5
= ("Output is: " + 10) != 5
[!= is binary operator, so we have to evaluate the left side first. + operator behaves as concatenation operator.]
= "Output is: 10" != 5
Left side of above expression is String, and right side is int. But String can't be compared to int hence compilation error.

1.1.11   Answer: C

Reason:
Following are allowed in boolean expression of if statement:
1. Any expression whose result is either true or false. e.g. age > 20
2. A boolean variable. e.g. flag
3. A boolean literal: true or false
4. A boolean assignment. e.g. flag = true

boolean expression in this case is: (grade = 60), which is an int assignment and not boolean assignment. Hence Compilation error.

1.1.12 Answer: D

Reason:
case values must evaluate to the same type / compatible type as the switch expression can use.
switch expression can accept following:
char or Character
byte or Byte
short or Short
int or Integer
An enum only from Java 6
A String expression only from Java 7

In this case, switch expression [switch (var)] is of byte type.
byte range is from -128 to 127. But in case expression [case 200], 200 is outside byte range and hence compilation error.

1.1.13 Answer: D

Reason:
"mango" is different from "Mango", so there is no matching case available. default block is executed, "ANY FRUIT WILL DO" is printed on to the screen.
No break statement inside default, hence control enters in fall-through and executes remaining blocks until the break; is found or switch block ends.
So in this case, it prints APPLE, MANGO, BANANA one after another and break; statement takes control out of switch block. main method ends and program terminates successfully.

1.1.14 Answer: B,C,E

Reason:
switch can accept primitive types: byte, short, int, char; wrapper types: Byte, Short, Integer, Character; String and enums.

In this case, all are valid values but only 3 executes "case 7:". case is comparing integer value 7. NOTE: character seven, '7' is different from integer value seven, 7.
So "char var = '7';" and "Character var = '7';" will print DEFAULT on to the console.

1.1.15 Answer: C

Reason:
This question is on ternary operator (?:). If an expression has multiple ternary operators then number of ? and : should match. Given expression contains 2 ? and 1 : and hence Compilation Error.

1.1.16 Answer: B

Reason:
First add parenthesis (round brackets) to the given expression: -a++.
There are 2 operators involved. unary minus and Postfix operator. Let's start with expression and value of a.

-a++; [a = 100].
-(a++); [a = 100] Postfix operator has got higher precedence than unary operator.
-(100); [a = 101] Use the value of a (100) in the expression and after that increase the value of a to 101.
-100; [a = 101] -100 is printed on to the console.

1.1.17 Answer: D

Reason:
1st array dimension must be specified at the time of declaration. new int[][8]; causes compilation error as 1st dimension is not specified.

1.1.18 Answer: D

Reason:
From the given array, if you print the elements at 1st, 3rd and 5th indexes, then you will get expected output.

Also note that, for values of n = 0, 2, 4, 6; Line n1 would not be executed, which means even if the value of n is 6, above code will not throw ArrayIndexOutOfBoundsException.

For 1st option [int n = 0; n < arr.length; n += 1], values of n used: 0, 1, 2, 3, 4, 5 and because of continue; statement, Line n1 will not execute for 0, 2 & 4 and it will execute only for 1, 3 & 5 and therefore NET will be printed.

For 2nd option [int n = 0; n <= arr.length; n += 1], values of n used: 0, 1, 2, 3, 4, 5, 6 and because of continue; statement, Line n1 will not execute for 0, 2, 4 & 6 and it will execute only for 1, 3 & 5 and therefore NET will be printed.

For 3rd option [int n = 1; n < arr.length; n += 2], values of n used: 1, 3, 5 and therefore NET will be printed.

For 4th option [int n = 1; n <= arr.length; n += 2], values of n used: 1, 3, 5 and therefore NET will be printed.

Hence, all the 4 options are valid.

1.1.19 Answer: C

Reason:
Let's check all the statements one by one:

1. short arr [] = new short[2]; => X You can declare one-dimensional array by using either "short arr []" or "short [] arr". 'arr' refers to a short array object of 2 elements. arr[2] will throw ArrayIndexOutOfBoundsException at runtime.

2. byte [] arr = new byte[10]; => ✓ 'arr' refers to a byte array object of 10 elements, where 0 is assigned to each array element. But later on element at 1st and 2nd indexes have been re-initialized. Line n1 successfully prints [5, 10] on to the console.

3. short [] arr; arr = new short[3]; => ✓ You can create an array object in the same statement or next statement. 'arr' refers to a short array object of 3 elements, where 0 is assigned to each array element. Later on element at 1st and 2nd indexes have been re-initialized. Line n1 successfully prints [5, 10] on to the console.

4. short [2] arr; X Array size cannot be specified at the time of declaration, so short [2] arr; causes compilation error.

5. short [3] arr; X Array size cannot be specified at the time of declaration, so short [3] arr; causes compilation error.

6. int [] arr = new int[]{100, 100}; => X 'arr' refers to an int array object of size 2 and both array elements have value 100. arr[2] will throw ArrayIndexOutOfBoundsException at runtime.

7. int [] arr = new int[]{0, 0, 0, 0}; => ✓ 'arr' refers to an int array object of size 4 and all array elements have value 0. Later on element at 1st and 2nd indexes have been re-initialized. Line n1 successfully prints [5, 10] on to the console.

8. short [] arr = {}; => ✗ 'arr' refers to a short array object of 0 size. so arr[1] will throw ArrayIndexOutOfBoundsException at runtime.

9. short [] arr = new short[2]{5, 10}; => ✗ Array's size can't be specified, if you use {} to assign values to array elements.

Hence, out of the given 9 statements, only 3 will print [5, 10] on to the console.

1.1.20 Answer: C

Reason:
int variable can easily be assigned to double type but double [] and int [] are not compatible. In fact, both are siblings and can't be assigned to each other, so Line 3 causes compilation failure.

1.1.21 Answer: D

Reason:
As do-while loop executes at least once, hence none of the code is unreachable in this case.
Java runtime prints 100 to the console, then it checks boolean expression, which is false.
Hence control goes out of do-while block. Java runtime executes 2nd System.out.println statement to print "Bye" on to the console.

1.1.22 Answer: B

Reason:
break; and continue; are used inside for-loop, hence no compilation error.
In 1st iteration, x = 0. "Smith" is added to the list. There is no matching case found, hence control just goes after the switch-case block and executes break; statement, which takes the control out of the for loop. `System.out.println(list.size());` is executed and this prints 1 on to the console.

1.1.23 Answer: B

Reason:
Inside enhanced for loop, System.out.println(arr[i]); is used instead of
System.out.println(i);
When loop executes 1st time, i stores the first array element, which is 2 but
System.out.println statement prints arr[2] which is 0. Loop executes in this manner
and prints 0 1 2 on to the console.

1.1.24 Answer: C

Reason:
It is pass-by-reference scheme.
Initially, msg = "Happy New Year!"
Call to method change(Message) doesn't modify the msg property of passed object
rather it creates another Message object and modifies the msg property of new object
to "Happy Holidays!"
So, the instance of Message referred by obj remains unchanged.
Hence in the output, you get:
Happy New Year!
Happy New Year!

1.1.25 Answer: D

Reason:
In this case "if - else if" block is used and not "if - else" block.
90000 is assigned to variable 'price' but you can assign parameter value or call some
method returning double value, such as:
'double price = currentTemp();'.
In these cases compiler will not know the exact value until runtime, hence Java
Compiler is not sure which boolean expression will be evaluated to true and so
variable model may not be initialized.

Usage of LOCAL variable, 'model' without initialization causes compilation error.
Hence, System.out.println(model); causes compilation error.

1.1.26 Answer: B

Reason:

'passportNo' should be read-only for any other class.

This means make 'passportNo' private and provide public getter method. Don't provide public setter as then 'passportNo' will be read-write property.

If passportNo is declared with default scope, then other classes in the same package will be able to access passportNo for read-write operation.

1.1.27 Answer: C

Reason:

Method m is overloaded. Which overloaded method to invoke is decided at compile time. m(i) is tagged to m(int) as i is of int type and m('5') is tagged to m(char) as '5' is char literal.

1.1.28 Answer: C

Reason:

Encapsulation is all about having private instance variable and providing public getter and setter methods.

1.1.29 Answer: A

Reason:

main method's parameter variable name is "args" and it is a local to main method. So, same name "args" can't be used directly within the curly brackets of main method. short [] args = new short[]{50, 50}; causes compilation error for using same name for local variable.

1.1.30 Answer: D

Reason:

This question checks your knowledge of pass-by-value and pass-by-reference schemes. In below statements: student<main> means student inside main method.

On execution of main method: student<main> --> {"James", 25}, marks<main> = 25.
On execution of review method: stud<review> --> {"James", 25} (same object referred by student<main>), marks<review> = 25 (this marks is different from the marks defined in main method). marks<review> = 35 and stud.marks = 60. So at the end of review method: stud<review> --> {"James", 60}, marks<review> = 35.
Control goes back to main method: student<main> --> {"James", 60}, marks<main> = 25. Changes done to reference variable are visible in main method but changes done to primitive variable are not reflected in main method.

1.1.31 Answer: D

Reason:
This is an example of pass-by-value scheme. x of checkAndIncrement method contains the copy of variable x defined in main method. So, changes done to x in checkAndIncrement method are not reflected in the variable x of main. x of main remains 1 as code inside main is not changing its value.

Every time checkAndIncrement method is invoked with argument value 1, so true is returned always and hence while loop executed indefinitely.

1.1.32 Answer: B

Reason:
Methods can have same name as the class. Student() and Student(String, int) are methods and not constructors of the class, note the void return type of these methods.
As no constructors are provided in the Student class, java compiler adds default no-argument constructor. That is why the statement Student s = new Student(); doesn't cause any compilation error.

Default values are assigned to instance variables, hence null is assigned to name and 0 is assigned to age.

In the output, null:0 is displayed.

1.1.33   Answer: C

Reason:
A top level interface can be declared with either public or default modifiers.
public interface is accessible across all packages but interface declared with default
modifier and be accessed in the defining package only.

1.1.34   Answer: C

Reason:
abstract class can have constructors and it also possible to have abstract class without
any abstract method. So, there is no issue with Animal class.

Java compiler adds super(); as the first statement inside constructor, if call to another
constructor using this(...) or super(...) is not available.

Inside Animal class Constructor, compiler adds super(); => Animal(String name) {
super(); this.name = name; }, super() in this case invokes the no-argument constructor
of Object class and hence no compilation error here.

Compiler changes Dog(String) constructor to: Dog(String breed) { super(); this.breed =
breed; }. No-argument constructor is not available in Animal class and as another
constructor is provided, java compiler doesn't add default constructor. Hence
Dog(String) constructor causes compilation error.

There is no issue with Dog(String, String) constructor.

1.1.35   Answer: C,D

Reason:
First you should find out the reason for compilation error. Methods declared in
Printable interface are implicitly abstract, no issues with Printable interface.

class Paper is declared abstract and it implements Printable interface, it overrides
setMargin() method but setOrientation() method is still abstract. No issues with class
Paper as it is an abstract class and can have 0 or more abstract methods.

class NewsPaper is concrete class and it extends Paper class (which is abstract). So class NewsPaper must override setOrientation() method OR it must be declared abstract.

Replacing Line 9 with 'public abstract void setOrientation();' is not necessary and it will not resolve the compilation error in NewsPaper class.

Replacing Line 7 with 'class Paper implements Printable {' will cause compilation failure of Paper class as it inherits abstract method 'setOrientation'.

1.1.36 Answer: C

Reason:
Java compiler adds super(); as the first statement inside constructor, if call to another constructor using this(...) or super(...) is not available.
Compiler adds super(); as the first line in OTG's constructor: OTG(int capacity, String type) { super(); } but PenDrive class doesn't have a no-arg constructor and that is why OTG's constructor causes compilation error.
For the same reason, OTG(String make) constructor also causes compilation error.
To correct these compilation errors, parent class constructor should be invoked by using super(int); This would resolve compilation error.
Remember: Constructor call using this(...) or super(...) must be the first statement inside the constructor.

In the main(String[]) method, OTG(int, String) constructor is invoked, which means, we OTG(String) constructor will not be executed. So, to solve the compilation error in OTG(String) constructor, super(0); or super(128); both will work and these will not affect the expected output.

We have to make changes in OTG(int, String) constructor such that on execution, output is 128:TYPE-C.
super(capacity); will only assign value to capacity property, to assign value to type another statement is needed.
this.type = type; must be the 2nd statement.
So, /*INSERT-1*/ must be replaced with:
super(capacity);
this.type = type;

1.1.37 Answer: B

Reason:
class A is declared public and defined in com.udayan.oca package, there is no problem in accessing class A outside com.udayan.oca package.
class B is defined in com.udayan.oca.test package, to extend from class A either use import statement "import com.udayan.oca.A;" or fully qualified name of the class com.udayan.oca.A. No issues with this class definition as well.

Variable i1 is declared public in class A, so Line 8 doesn't cause any compilation error. Variable i2 is declared protected so it can only be accessed in subclass using using inheritance but not using object reference variable. obj.i2 causes compilation failure.

class B inherits variable i2 from class A, so inside class B it can be accessed by using either this or super. Line 10 and Line 11 don't cause any compilation error.

1.1.38 Answer: D

Reason:
Class A and B are declared public and inside same package com.udayan.oca. Method print() of class A has correctly been overridden by B.
print() method is public so no issues in accessing it anywhere.

Let's check the code inside main method.
A obj1 = new A(); => obj1 refers to an instance of class A.
B obj2 = (B)obj1; => obj1 is of type A and it is assigned to obj2 (B type), hence explicit casting is necessary. obj1 refers to an instance of class A, so at runtime obj2 will also refer to an instance of class A. sub type can't refer to an object of super type so at runtime B obj2 = (B)obj1; will throw ClassCastException.

1.1.39 Answer: C

Reason:
Even though an instance of FileNotFoundException is thrown by method m1() at runtime, but method m1() declares to throw IOException.
Reference variable s is of Super type and hence for compiler, call to s.m1(); is to method m1() of Super, which throws IOException.

And as IOException is checked exception hence calling code should handle it.

As calling code doesn't handle IOException or its super type, so s.m1(); causes compilation error.

1.1.40 Answer: B

Reason:
ClassCastException extends RuntimeException (unchecked exception),
FileNotFoundException extends IOException, IOException extends Exception (checked exception),
ExceptionInInitializerError is from Error family and is thrown by an static initializer block,
RuntimeException and all its sub classes are unchecked exceptions.

1.1.41 Answer: C

Reason:
main(args) method is invoked recursively without specifying any exit condition, so this code ultimately throws java.lang.StackOverflowError. StackOverflowError is a subclass of Error type and not Exception type, hence it is not handled. Stack trace is printed to the console and program ends abruptly.

Java doesn't allow to catch specific checked exceptions if these are not thrown by the statements inside try block.
catch(java.io.FileNotFoundException ex) {} will cause compilation error in this case as main(args); will never throw FileNotFoundException. But Java allows to catch Exception type, hence catch (Exception ex) {} doesn't cause any compilation error.

1.1.42 Answer: A

Reason:
If a method declares to throw Exception or its sub-type other than RuntimeException types, then calling method should follow handle or declare rule. In this case, as method m1() declares to throw Exception, so main method should either declare the

same exception or its super type in its throws clause OR m1(); should be surrounded by try-catch block.

Line 3 in this case causes compilation error.

1.1.43 Answer: B

Reason:
To invoke the special main method, JVM loads the class in the memory. At that time, static initializer block is invoked. 1/0 throws a RuntimeException and as a result static initializer block throws an instance of java.lang.ExceptionInInitializerError.

1.1.44 Answer: C

Reason:
An Error is a subclass of Throwable class.

1.1.45 Answer: D

Reason:
System.out.println(str1 = str2) has assignment(=) operator and not equality(==) operator.
After the assignment, str1 refers to "CoRe" and System.out.println prints "CoRe" to the console.

1.1.46 Answer: B

Reason:
Please note that Strings computed by concatenation at compile time, will be referred by String Pool during execution. Compile time String concatenation happens when both of the operands are compile time constants, such as literal, final variable etc.

For the statement, String s2 = "OCAJP" + "";, `"OCAJP" + ""` is a constant expression as both the operands "OCAJP" and "" are String literals, which means the expression `"OCAJP" + ""` is computed at compile-time and results in String literal "OCAJP".

So, during compilation, Java compiler translates the statement
String s2 = "OCAJP" + "";
to
String s2 = "OCAJP";

As "OCAJP" is a String literal, hence at runtime it will be referred by String Pool.

When Test class is executed,
s1 refers to "OCAJP" (String Pool object).
s2 also refers to same String pool object "OCAJP".
s1 and s2 both refer to the same String object and that is why s1 == s2 returns true.

Please note that Strings computed by concatenation at run time (if the resultant expression is not constant expression) are newly created and therefore distinct.
For below code snippet:
String s1 = "OCAJP";
String s2 = s1 + "";
System.out.println(s1 == s2);

Output is false, as s1 is a variable and `s1 + ""` is not a constant expression, therefore this expression is computed only at runtime and a new non-pool String object is created.

1.1.47 Answer: A

Reason:
substring(int beginIndex, int endIndex) is used to extract the substring. The substring begins at "beginIndex" and extends till "endIndex - 1".
Country code information is stored at index 4 and 5, so the correct substring method to extract country code is: swiftCode.substring(4, 6);

1.1.48 Answer: B

Reason:
equals method declared in Object class has the declaration: public boolean equals(Object). Generally, equals method is used to compare different instances of

same class but if you pass any other object, there is no compilation error. Parameter type is Object so it can accept any Java object.

str.equals(sb) => String class overrides equals(Object) method but as "sb" is of StringBuilder type so this returns false.

StringBuilder class doesn't override equals(Object) method. So Object version is invoked which uses == operator, hence sb.equals(str) returns false as well.

false:false is printed on to the console.

1.1.49 Answer: C

Reason:
toString() method defined in StringBuilder class doesn't use String literal rather uses the constructor of String class to create the instance of String class.

So both s1 and s2 refer to different String instances even though their contents are same. s1 == s2 returns false.

1.1.50 Answer: E

Reason:
`new StringBuilder(100);` creates a StringBuilder instance, whose internal char array's length is 100 but length() method of StringBuilder object returns the number of characters stored in the internal array and in this case it is 0. So, `sb.length()` returns 0.
sb.toString() is the String representation of StringBuilder instance and in this case as there are no characters inside the StringBuilder object, hence sb.toString() returns an empty String "", so `sb.toString().length()` also returns 0.
Output is 0:0.

1.1.51 Answer: C

Reason:
'append' method is overloaded in StringBuilder class: append(String), append(StringBuffer) and append(char[]) etc. In this case compiler gets confused as to which method `append(null)` can be tagged because String, StringBuffer and char[] are not related to each other in multilevel inheritance. Hence `sb.append(null)` causes compilation error.

1.1.52 Answer: E

Reason:
Variable 'arr' refers to an Object array of size 4 and null is assigned to all 4 elements of this array.
for-loop starts with i = 1, which means at 1st index String instance is stored, at 2nd index StringBuiler instance is stored and at 3rd index SpecialString instance is stored. null is stored at 0th index.
So, first null will be printed on to the console.
String and StringBuilder classes override toString() method, which prints the text stored in these classes. SpecialString class doesn't override toString() method and hence when instance of SpecialString is printed on to the console, you get: <fully qualified name of SpecialString class>@<hexadecimal representation of hashcode>.
Therefore output will be:
null
Java
Java
<Some text containing @ symbol>

1.1.53 Answer: B

Reason:
LocalDate.of(...) method first validates year, then month and finally day of the month. September can't have 31 days so LocalDate.of(...) method throws an instance of java.time.DateTimeException class.

1.1.54 Answer: A

Reason:

isAfter and isBefore method can be interpreted as:

Does 1st Jan 2018 come after 25th Dec 2018? No, false. Does 1st Jan 2018 come before 25th Dec 2018? Yes, true.

1.1.55 Answer: E

Reason:

LocalDate is a final class so cannot be extended.

1.1.56 Answer: D

Reason:

date --> {2012-01-11}, period --> {P2M}, date.minus(period) --> {2011-11-11} [subtract 2 months period from {2012-01-11}, month is changed to 11 and year is changed to 2011].

formatter -> {MM-dd-yy}, when date {2011-11-11} is formatter in this format 11-11-11 is printed on to the console.

1.1.57 Answer: C

Reason:

Period.of(0, 0, 0); is equivalent to Period.ZERO. ZERO period is displayed as P0D, other than that, Period components (year, month, day) with 0 values are ignored.

toString()'s result starts with P, and for non-zero year, Y is appended; for non-zero month, M is appended; and for non-zero day, D is appended. P,Y,M and D are in upper case.

NOTE: Period.parse(CharSequence) method accepts the String parameter in "PnYnMnD" format, over here P,Y,M and D can be in any case.

1.1.58 Answer: C

Reason:
LocalDateTime stores both date and time parts. LocalDateTime.now(); retrieves the current date and time from the system clock. obj.getSecond() can return any value between 0 and 59.

1.1.59 Answer: C

Reason:
LocalTime.MIN --> {00:00}, LocalTime.MAX --> {23:59:59.999999999}, LocalTime.MIDNIGHT --> {00:00}, LocalTime.NOON --> {12:00}.

date.atTime(LocalTime) method creates a LocalDateTime instance by combining date and time parts.

toString() method of LocalDateTime class prints the date and time parts separated by T in upper case.

1.1.60 Answer: D

Reason:
Before you answer this, you must know that there are 5 different Student object created in the memory (4 at the time of adding to the list and 1 at the time of removing from the list). This means these 5 Student objects will be stored at different memory addresses.

remove(Object) method removes the first occurrence of matching object and equals(Object) method decides whether 2 objects are equal or not. equals(Object) method defined in Object class uses == operator to check the equality and in this case as 5 Student objects are stored at different memory location, hence not equal.

Nothing is removed from the students list, all the 4 Student objects are printed in the insertion order.

Answer: C

Reason:
ConcurrentModificationException exception may be thrown for following condition:
1. Collection is being iterated using Iterator/ListIterator or by using for-each loop.
And
2. Execution of Iterator.next(), Iterator.remove(), ListIterator.previous(), ListIterator.set(E) & ListIterator.add(E) methods. These methods may throw java.util.ConcurrentModificationException in case Collection had been modified by means other than the iterator itself, such as Collection.add(E) or Collection.remove(Object) or List.remove(int) etc.

For the given code, 'dryFruits' list is being iterated using the Iterator<String>. hasNext() method of Iterator has following implementation:
public boolean hasNext() {
    return cursor != size;
}
Where cursor is the index of next element to return and initially it is 0.

1st Iteration: cursor = 0, size = 4, hasNext() returns true. iterator.next() increments the cursor by 1 and returns "Walnut".
2nd Iteration: cursor = 1, size = 4, hasNext() returns true. iterator.next() increments the cursor by 1 and returns "Apricot". As "Apricot" starts with "A", hence dryFruits.remove(dryFruit) removes "Apricot" from the list and hence reducing the list's size by 1, size becomes 3.
3rd Iteration: cursor = 2, size = 3, hasNext() returns true. iterator.next() method throws java.util.ConcurrentModificationException.

If you want to remove the items from ArrayList, while using Iterator or ListIterator, then use Iterator.remove() or ListIterator.remove() method and NOT List.remove(...) method. Using List.remove(...) method while iterating the list (using the Iterator/ListIterator or for-each) may throw java.util.ConcurrentModificationException.

1.1.62   Answer: A

Reason:
ArrayList's 1st and 3rd items are referring to same String instance referred by s [s -->
"Hello"] and 2nd item is referring to another instance of String.

String is immutable, which means s.replace("l", "L"); creates another String instance
"HeLLo" but s still refers to "Hello" [s --> "Hello"].

[Hello, Hello, Hello] is printed in the output.

1.1.63   Answer: A

Reason:
list1 --> [A, D],
list2 --> [B, C],
list1.addAll(1, list2); is almost equal to list1.add(1, [B, C]); => Inserts B at index 1, C
takes index 2 and D is moved to index 3. list1 --> [A, B, C, D]

1.1.64   Answer: A

Reason:

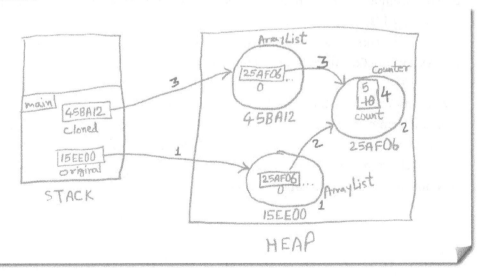

Let's see what is happening during execution:
main(String [] args) method goes on to the top of the STACK.

1. ArrayList<Counter> original = new ArrayList<>(); => It creates an ArrayList object [suppose at memory location 15EE00] and variable 'original' refers to it.
2. original.add(new Counter(10)); => It creates a Counter object [suppose at memory location 25AF06] and adds it as a first element of the ArrayList. This means element at 0th index of the ArrayList instance refers to Counter object at the memory location 25AF06.
3. ArrayList<Counter> cloned = (ArrayList<Counter>) original.clone(); => original.clone() creates a new array list object, [suppose at memory location 45BA12] and then it will copy the contents of the ArrayList object stored at [15EE00]. So, cloned contains memory address of the same Counter object.
In this case, original != cloned, but original.get(0) == cloned.get(0). This means both the array lists are created at different memory location but refer to same Counter object.
4. cloned.get(0).count = 5; => cloned.get(0) returns the Counter object stored at the memory location 25AF06 and .count = 5 means change the value of count variable of the Counter object (stored at memory location 25AF06) to 5.
5. System.out.println(original); Prints the element of ArrayList original, which is: {25AF06} and toString() method prints: [Counter-5] as Counter object referred by [25AF06] is [Counter object (5)].

1.1.65   Answer: C, D

Reason:
List is an interface so its instance can't be created using new keyword. List<String> and List<> will cause compilation failure.
ArrayList implements List interface, so it can be it can be used to replace /*INSERT*/.
List<String> list = new ArrayList<String>(); compiles successfully.

Starting with JDK 7, Java allows to not specify type while initializing the ArrayList. Type is inferred from the left side of the statement.

So List<String> list = new ArrayList<>(); is a valid syntax starting with JDK 7.

1.1.66   Answer: B

Reason:
list.add(0, 'V'); => char 'V' is converted to Character object and stored as the first element in the list. list --> [V].
list.add('T'); => char 'T' is auto-boxed to Character object and stored at the end of the list. list --> [V,T].
list.add(1, 'E'); => char 'E' is auto-boxed to Character object and inserted at index 1 of the list, this shifts T to the right. list --> [V,E,T].
list.add(3, 'O'); => char 'O' is auto-boxed to Character object and added at index 3 of the list. list --> [V,E,T,O].
list.contains('O') => char 'O' is auto-boxed to Character object and as Character class overrides equals(String) method this expression returns true. Control goes inside if-block and executes: list.remove('O');.

remove method is overloaded: remove(int) and remove(Object). char can be easily assigned to int so compiler tags remove(int) method. list.remove(<ASCCI value of 'O'>); ASCCI value of 'A' is 65 (this everybody knows) so ASCII value of 'O' will be more than 65.

list.remove('O') throws runtime exception, as it tries to remove an item from the index greater than 65 but allowed index is 0 to 3 only.

1.1.67   Answer: D

Reason:
remove method of List interface is overloaded: remove(int) and remove(Object). indexOf method accepts argument of Object type, in this case list.indexOf(0) => 0 is auto-boxed to Integer object so no issues with indexOf code. list.indexOf(0) returns 2 (index at which 0 is stored in the list). So list.remove(list.indexOf(0)); is converted to list.remove(2);

remove(int) version is matched, it's a direct match so compiler doesn't do auto-boxing in this case. list.remove(2) removes the element at index 2, which is 0.

Hence in the output, you get [2, 1].

1.1.68 Answer: A,D

Reason:
Jack's salary is 5000 and Liya's salary is 8000. If Employee's salary is >= 10000 then that Employee object is removed from the list.

Allowed lambda expression is:
(Employee e) -> { return e.getSalary() >= 10000; },
Can be simplified to: (e) -> { return e.getSalary() >= 10000; } => type can be removed from left side of the expression.
Further simplified to: e -> { return e.getSalary() >= 10000; } => if there is only one parameter in left part, then round brackets (parenthesis) can be removed.
Further simplified to: e -> e.getSalary() >= 10000 => if there is only one statement in the right side then semicolon inside the body, curly brackets and return statement can be removed. But all 3 [return, {}, ;] must be removed together.

NOTE: there should not be any space between - and > of arrow operator.

1.1.69 Answer: E

Reason:
Let us suppose test string is "aba".
Lambda expression s.toUpperCase().substring(0,1).equals("A"); means:
"aba".toUpperCase().substring(0,1).equals("A"); => "ABA".substring(0,1).equals("A");
=> "A".equals("A"); => true.

This lambda expression returns true for any string starting with a (in lower or upper case). Based on the lambda expression, 5 array elements passes the Predicate's test and are printed on to the console.

1.1.70 Answer: C

Reason:
LocalDate objects can be created by using static method parse and of.
removeIf(Predicate) method was added as a default method in Collection interface in JDK 8 and it removes all the elements of this collection that satisfy the given predicate.

Predicate's test method returns true for all the LocalDate objects with year less than 2000. So all the LocalDate objects with year value less than 2000 are removed from the list. Remaining LocalDate objects are printed in their insertion order.

2   Practice Test - 2

2.1   70 Questions covering all topics

2.1.1   Which of the following correctly defines class Printer?

A.	```package com.udayan.oca;
package com.udayan.ocp;
public class Printer {

}``` | B. | ```package com.udayan.oca;
package com.udayan.ocp;
import java.io.*
public class Printer {

}``` |
| C. | ```package com.udayan.oca;
import java.util.*;
public class Printer {

}``` | D. | ```public class Printer {
    package com.udayan.oca;
}``` |

2.1.2   What will be the result of executing Test class using below command?
java Test good morning everyone

```
private class Test
{
    public static void main(String args[])
    {
        System.out.println(args[1]);
    }
}
```

A. Compilation Error

B. good

C. morning

D. everyone

2.1.3   Consider below code:

```
//Guest.java
class Message {
    public static void main(String [] args) {
        System.out.println("Welcome " + args[0] + "!");
    }
}

public class Guest {
    public static void main(String [] args) {
        Message.main(args);
    }
}
```

And the commands:

javac Guest.java

java Guest James Gosling

What is the result?

A. Welcome James!

B. Welcome Gosling!

C. ArrayIndexOutOfBoundsException is thrown at runtime

D. Some other error as main method can't be invoked manually

2.1.4   Consider codes below:

```
//A.java
package com.udayan.oca;

public class A {
    public int i1;
    protected int i2;
    int i3;
    private int i4;
}

//TestA.java
package com.udayan.oca.test;

        import com.udayan.oca.A; //Line 3

public class TestA {
    public static void main(String[] args) {
        A obj = new A(); //Line 7
        System.out.println(obj.i1); //Line 8
        System.out.println(obj.i2); //Line 9
        System.out.println(obj.i3); //Line 10
        System.out.println(obj.i4); //Line 11
    }
}
```

Which of the following 3 statements are true?

A. Line 3 causes compilation error

B. Line 7 causes compilation error

C. Line 8 causes compilation error

D. Line 9 causes compilation error

E. Line 10 causes compilation error

F. Line 11 causes compilation error

2.1.5   How can you force JVM to run Garbage Collector?

    A. By calling: Runtime.getRuntime().gc();

    B. By calling: System.gc();

    C. By setting the reference variable to null.

    D. JVM cannot be forced to run Garbage Collector.

2.1.6   What will be the result of compiling and executing Test class?

```java
public class Test {
    public static void main(String[] args) {
        Boolean b1 = new Boolean("tRuE");
        Boolean b2 = new Boolean("fAlSe");
        Boolean b3 = new Boolean("abc");
        Boolean b4 = null;
        System.out.println(b1 + ":" + b2 +
                              ":" + b3 + ":" + b4);
    }
}
```

    A. false:false:false:null

    B. true:false:false:null

    C. false:false:true:null

    D. Compilation error

2.1.7 **What will be the result of compiling and executing Test class?**

```java
import java.util.ArrayList;
import java.util.List;

public class Test {
    public static void main(String[] args) {
        List<Integer> list = new ArrayList<>();
        list.add(100);
        list.add(200);
        list.add(100);
        list.add(200);
        list.remove(new Integer(100));

        System.out.println(list);
    }
}
```

A. [200, 100, 200]

B. [100, 200, 200]

C. [200, 200]

D. [200]

E. Compilation error

F. Exception is thrown at runtime

2.1.8   What will be the result of compiling and executing Test class?

```
public class Test {

    private static void add(double d1, double d2) {
        System.out.println("double version: " +
                                        (d1 + d2));
    }

    private static void add(Double d1, Double d2) {
        System.out.println("Double version: " +
                                        (d1 + d2));
    }

    public static void main(String[] args) {
        add(10.0, null);
    }

}
```

A. Compilation error

B. double version: 10.0

C. Double version: 10.0

D. An exception is thrown at runtime

2.1.9   Consider below code:

```
public class Test {
    public static void main(String[] args) {
        char c = 'Z';
        long l = 100_001;
        int i = 9_2;
        float f = 2.02f;
        double d = 10_0.35d;
        l = c + i;
        f = c * l * i * f;
        f = l + i + c;
        i = (int)d;
        f = (long)d;
    }
}
```

Does above code compile successfully?

A. Yes

B. No

2.1.10   What will be the result of compiling and executing Test class?

```java
public class Test {
    public static void main(String[] args) {
        System.out.println(new Boolean("ture"));
    }
}
```

A. true

B. false

C. An exception is thrown at runtime

D. Compilation error

2.1.11   What will be the result of compiling and executing Test class?

```java
public class Test {
    public static void main(String[] args) {
        System.out.println("Output is: " + (10 != 5));
    }
}
```

A. Output is: true

B. Output is: false

C. Compilation error

D. Output is: (10 != 5)

2.1.12 **What will be the result of compiling and executing the Test class?**

```java
public class Test {
    public static void main(String[] args) {
        int grade = 75;
        if(grade > 60)
            System.out.println("Congratulations");
            System.out.println("You passed");
        else
            System.out.println("You failed");

    }
}
```

A.	Congratulations	B.	You failed
C.	Compilation error	D.	Congratulations You passed

2.1.13   What will be the result of compiling and executing Test class?

```
public class Test {
    public static void main(String[] args) {
        int score = 60;
        switch (score) {
            default:
                System.out.println("Not a valid score");
            case score < 70:
                System.out.println("Failed");
                break;
            case score >= 70:
                System.out.println("Passed");
                break;
        }
    }
}
```

A.	Compilation error	B.	Failed
C.	Not a valid score Failed	D.	Passed

2.1.14 What will be the result of compiling and executing Test class?

```java
public class Test {
    public static void main(String[] args) {
        String fruit = "mango";
        switch (fruit) {
            case "Apple":
                System.out.println("APPLE");
            case "Mango":
                System.out.println("MANGO");
            case "Banana":
                System.out.println("BANANA");
                break;
            default:
                System.out.println("ANY FRUIT WILL DO");
        }
    }
}
```

A.	MANGO	B.	ANY FRUIT WILL DO
C.	MANGO BANANA	D.	MANGO ANY FRUIT WILL DO
E.	MANGO BANANA ANY FRUIT WILL DO		

2.1.15 For the class Test, which options, if used to replace /*INSERT*/, will print TEN on to the console? Select 4 options.

```
public class Test {
    public static void main(String[] args) {
        /*INSERT*/
        switch(var) {
            case 10:
                System.out.println("TEN");
                break;
            default:
                System.out.println("DEFAULT");
        }
    }
}
```

A.	byte var = 10;	B.	long var = 10;
C.	Short var = 10;	D.	Integer var = 10;
E.	char var = 10;	F.	double var = 10;

2.1.16 Consider below code:

```
//Test.java
public class Test {
    private static boolean flag = !true;

    public static void main(String [] args) {
        System.out.println(!flag ? args[0] : args[1]);
    }
}
```

What will be the result of compiling and executing Test class using below commands?

javac Test.java

java Test AM PM

A. AM

B. PM

C. ExceptionInInitializerError is thrown while loading the Test class

D. Compilation error

90

2.1.17 What will be the result of compiling and executing Test class?

```
public class Test {
    public static void main(String [] args) {
        int a = 2;
        boolean res = false;
        res = a++ == 2 || --a == 2 && --a == 2;
        System.out.println(a);
    }
}
```

A. 2

B. 3

C. 1

D. Compilation error

2.1.18 Which of the following array declarations and initializations is NOT legal?

```
A.   char [] arr1 [] = new char[5][];
B.   int [] arr2 = {1, 2, 3, 4, 5};
C.   int [] arr3 = new int[3]{10, 20, 30};
D.   byte [] val = new byte[10];
```

2.1.19 **What will be the result of compiling and executing Test class?**

```
public class Test {
    public static void main(String[] args) {
        String [] arr = new String[7];
        System.out.println(arr);
    }
}
```

A. NullPointerException

B. Compilation Error

C. null

D. Some String containing @ symbol

2.1.20 **What is the output if below program is run with the command line:**
java Test

```
public class Test {
    public static void main(String[] args) {
        System.out.println(args.length);
    }
}
```

A. 0

B. NullPointerException

C. ArrayIndexOutOfBoundsException

D. 1

2.1.21 **What will be the result of compiling and executing Test class?**

```java
public class Test {
    public static void main(String[] args) {
        String[][] arr = { { "7", "6", "5" },
                           { "4", "3" }, { "2", "1" }
};
        for (int i = 0; i < arr.length; i++) { //Line n1
            for (int j = 0;
                    j < arr[i].length; j++) {//Line n2
                switch (arr[i][j]) { //Line n3
                    case "2":
                    case "4":
                    case "6":
                        break; //Line n4
                    default:
                        continue; //Line n5
                }
                System.out.print(arr[i][j]); //Line n6
            }
        }
    }
}
```

A. 6

B. 64

C. 642

D. 7

E. 75

F. 753

G. 7531

H. 7654321

2.1.22 What will be the result of compiling and executing Test class?

```java
public class Test {
    public static void main(String[] args) {
        int x = 5;
        while (x < 10)
            System.out.println(x);
        x++;
    }
}
```

A.	Compilation error	B.	5 6 7 8 9
C.	It will go in an infinite loop	D.	Produces no output

2.1.23 Consider given code:

```java
public class Test {
    public static void main(String[] args) {
        String [][] fruits = {{"apple", "mango"},
                    {"orange", "grape"}};
        /*INSERT*/
    }
}
```

For the class Test, which options, if used to replace /*INSERT*/, will print "apple mango orange grape " on to the console? Select 2 options.

A.
```java
for(int i = 0; i < fruits.length; i++)
    for(int j = 0; j < fruits[i].length ; j++)
        System.out.print(fruits[i][j] + " ");
```

B.
```java
for(int i = 1; i <= fruits.length; i++)
    for(int j = 1; j <= fruits[i].length ; j++)
        System.out.print(fruits[i][j] + " ");
```

C.
```java
for(int i = 1; i < fruits.length; i++)
    for(int j = 1; j < fruits[i].length ; j++)
        System.out.print(fruits[i][j] + " ");
```

D.
```java
for(String [] arr : fruits)
    for(String fruit : arr)
        System.out.print(fruit + " ");
```

2.1.24 What will be the result of compiling and executing Test class?

```java
public class Test {
    public static void main(String[] args) {
        int [] arr = {3, 2, 1};
        for(int i : arr) {
            System.out.println(arr[i]);
        }
    }
}
```

A.	3 2 1	B.	1 2 3
C.	Compilation error	D.	ArrayIndexOutOfBoundsException is thrown at runtime

2.1.25 What will be the result of compiling and executing Test class?

```java
public class Test {
    public String name;
    public void Test() {
        name = "James";
    }

    public static void main(String [] args) {
        Test obj = new Test();
        System.out.println(obj.name);
    }
}
```

A. James

B. Compilation error

C. null

D. None of the above

2.1.26 **What will be the result of compiling and executing Test class?**

```
class Message {
    String msg = "Happy New Year!";

    public void print() {
        System.out.println(msg);
    }
}

public class Test {
    public static void change(Message m) {
        m.msg = "Happy Holidays!";
    }

    public static void main(String[] args) {
        Message obj = new Message();
        obj.print();
        change(obj);
        obj.print();
    }
}
```

A.	null Happy Holidays!	B.	Happy Holidays! Happy Holidays!
C.	null null	D.	Happy New Year! Happy Holidays!

2.1.27 Following statement in a Java program compiles successfully:

```
student.report(course);
```

What can you say for sure?

A. student is the reference variable name

B. student is the class name

C. report is the method name

D. course must be of String type

2.1.28 Choose the options that meets the following specification:
Create a well encapsulated class Clock with one instance variable model. The value of model should be accessible and modifiable outside Clock.

A.
```
public class Clock {
    public String model;
}
```

B.
```
public class Clock {
    public String model;
    public String getModel() { return model; }
    public void setModel(String val) { model = val; }
}
```

C.
```
public class Clock {
    private String model;
    public String getModel() { return model; }
    public void setModel(String val) { model = val; }
}
```

D.
```
public class Clock {
    public String model;
    private String getModel() { return model; }
    private void setModel(String val) { model = val; }
}
```

2.1.29 Consider code of Test.java file:

```java
public class Test {
    public static void main(String [] args) {
        int [] arr = {0, 1, 2, 3, 4, 5, 6, 7, 8, 9};
        String str = process(arr, 3, 8); //Line 5
        System.out.println(str);
    }

    /*INSERT*/
}
```

Line 5 is giving compilation error as process method is not found.

Which of the following method definitions, if used to replace /*INSERT*/, will resolve the compilation error?

A.
```java
private static int[] process(int [] arr, int start, int end) {
    return null;
}
```

B.
```java
private static String process(int [] arr, int start, int end) {
    return null;
}
```

C.
```java
private static int process(int [] arr, int start, int end) {
    return null;
}
```

D.
```java
private static String[] process(int [] arr, int start, int end) {
    return null;
}
```

2.1.30 What will be the result of compiling and executing Test class?

```java
//Test.java
package com.udayan.oca;

class Point {
    static int x;
    int y, z;

    public String toString() {
        return "Point(" + x + ", " + y +
                                  ", " + z + ")";
    }
}

public class Test {
    public static void main(String[] args) {
        Point p1 = new Point();
        p1.x = 17;
        p1.y = 35;
        p1.z = -1;

        Point p2 = new Point();
        p2.x = 19;
        p2.y = 40;
        p2.z = 0;

        System.out.println(p1); //Line n1
        System.out.println(p2); //Line n2
    }
}
```

A.	Point(17, 35, -1) Point(19, 40, 0)	B.	Point(19, 35, -1) Point(19, 40, 0)
C.	Point(17, 35, -1) Point(17, 40, 0)	D.	Point(19, 40, 0) Point(19, 40, 0)
E.	Point(17, 35, -1) Point(17, 35, -1)	F.	Point(19, 35, -1) Point(19, 35, -1)
G.	Compilation error		

2.1.31 What will be the result of compiling and executing Test class?

```java
public class Test {

    private static void add(double d1, double d2) {
        System.out.println("double version: " +
                                      (d1 + d2));
    }

    private static void add(Double d1, Double d2) {
        System.out.println("Double version: " +
                                      (d1 + d2));
    }

    public static void main(String[] args) {
        add(10.0, new Integer(10));
    }

}
```

A. Compilation error

B. double version: 20.0

C. Double version: 20.0

D. An exception is thrown at runtime

2.1.32 Consider the code of Test.java file:

```java
package com.udayan.oca.test;

class Student {
    String name;
    int age;

    Student() {
        Student("James", 25);
    }

    Student(String name, int age) {
        this.name = name;
        this.age = age;
    }
}

public class Test {
    public static void main(String[] args) {
        Student s = new Student();
        System.out.println(s.name + ":" + s.age);
    }
}
```

What will be the result of compiling and executing Test class?

A. Compilation error

B. null:0

C. James:25

D. An exception is thrown at runtime

2.1.33 Which of these keywords can be used to prevent inheritance of a class?

A. constant

B. super

C. final

D. class

2.1.34 Which is not a valid statement based on given code?

```
class A{}
class B extends A{}
```

A. B b = new A();

B. A a = new B();

C. B a = new B();

D. A a = new A();

2.1.35 What will be the result of compiling and executing Test class?

```
class Vehicle {
    public int getRegistrationNumber() {
        return 1;
    }
}

class Car {
    public int getRegistrationNumber() {
        return 2;
    }
}

public class Test {
    public static void main(String[] args) {
        Vehicle obj = new Car();
        System.out.println(obj.getRegistrationNumber());
    }
}
```

A. 1

B. 2

C. An exception is thrown at runtime

D. Compilation error

2.1.36 **What will be the result of compiling and executing Test class?**

```java
//Test.java
package com.udayan.oca.test;

class Parent {
    int i = 10;
    Parent(int i) {
        super();
        this.i = i;
    }
}

class Child extends Parent {
    int j = 20;

    Child(int j) {
        super(0);
        this.j = j;
    }

    Child(int i, int j) {
        super(i);
        this(j);
    }

}

public class Test {
    public static void main(String[] args) {
        Child child = new Child(1000, 2000);
        System.out.println(child.i + ":" + child.j);
    }
}
```

A. Compilation error for Parent(int) constructor

B. Compilation error for Child(int) constructor

C. Compilation error for Child(int, int) Constructor

D. Compilation error for Test class

E. 1000:2000

F. 1000:0

2.1.37 Given code of LogHelper.java file:

```java
package com.udayan.oca;

abstract class Helper {
    int num = 100;
    String operation = null;

    protected abstract void help();

    void log() {
        System.out.println("Helper-log");
    }
}

public class LogHelper extends Helper {
    private int num = 200;
    protected String operation = "LOGGING";

    void help() {
        System.out.println("LogHelper-help");
    }

    void log() {
        System.out.println("LogHelper-log");
    }

    public static void main(String [] args) {
        new LogHelper().help();
    }
}
```

Which of the following changes, done independently, allows the code to compile and on execution prints LogHelper-help?

Select ALL that apply.

A. Remove the private modifier from the num variable of LogHelper class

B. Remove the protected modifier from the operation variable of LogHelper class

C. Remove the protected modifier from the help() method of Helper class

D. Add the protected modifier to the log() method of Helper class

E. Add the protected modifier to the help() method of LogHelper class

F. Add the public modifier to the help() method of LogHelper class

G. Add the public modifier to the log() method of LogHelper class

H. Add the protected modifier to the log() method of LogHelper class

2.1.38 Consider below code:

```
//Test.java
package com.udayan.oca.test;

class Parent {
    public String toString() {
        return "Inner ";
    }
}

class Child extends Parent {
    public String toString() {
        return super.toString().concat("Peace!");
    }
}

public class Test {
    public static void main(String[] args) {
        System.out.println(new Child());
    }
}
```

What will be the result of compiling and executing Test class?

A. Inner

B. Peace!

C. Inner Peace!

D. Compilation error

2.1.39 What will be the result of compiling and executing the following program?

```java
import java.io.FileNotFoundException;
import java.io.IOException;

abstract class Super {
    public abstract void m1() throws IOException;
}

class Sub extends Super {
    @Override
    public void m1() throws IOException {
        throw new FileNotFoundException();
    }
}

public class Test {
    public static void main(String[] args) {
        Super s = new Sub();
        try {
            s.m1();
        } catch (IOException e) {
            System.out.print("A");
        } catch (FileNotFoundException e) {
            System.out.print("B");
        } finally {
            System.out.print("C");
        }
    }
}
```

A. AC

B. BC

C. class Sub causes compilation error

D. class Test causes compilation error

2.1.40 Which of the following keywords is used to manually throw an exception?

A. throw

B. throws

C. thrown

D. catch

2.1.41 What will be the result of compiling and executing Test class?

```
public class Test {
    private static void m1() throws Exception {
        throw new Exception();
    }

    public static void main(String[] args) {
        try {
            m1();
        } finally {
            System.out.println("A");
        }
    }
}
```

A. A is printed to the console and program ends normally.

B. A is printed to the console, stack trace is printed and then program ends normally.

C. A is printed to the console, stack trace is printed and then program ends abruptly.

D. Compilation error.

2.1.42 Consider the following interface declaration:

```
public interface I1 {
    void m1() throws java.io.IOException;
}
```

Which of the following incorrectly implements interface I1?

A.
```
public class C1 implements I1 {
    public void m1() {}
}
```

B.
```
public class C2 implements I1 {
    public void m1() throws
java.io.FileNotFoundException{}
}
```

C.
```
public class C3 implements I1 {
    public void m1() throws java.io.IOException{}
}
```

D.
```
public class C4 implements I1 {
    public void m1() throws Exception{}
}
```

2.1.43 Which of the following are Java Exception classes? Select 3 options.

A. ClassCastException

B. NullException

C. NumberFormatException

D. IllegalArgumentException

E. ArrayIndexException

2.1.44 What will be the result of compiling and executing Test class?

```java
public class Test {
    public static void main(String[] args) {
        String s1 = "OcA";
        String s2 = "oCa";
        System.out.println(s1.equals(s2));
    }
}
```

A. true

B. false

C. Compilation error

D. None of the other options

2.1.45 What will be the result of compiling and executing Test class?

```java
import java.util.ArrayList;
import java.util.List;

public class Test {
    public static void main(String[] args) {
        List<String> list = new ArrayList<>();
        list.add("X");
        list.add("Y");
        list.add("X");
        list.add("Y");
        list.add("Z");
        list.remove(new String("Y"));
        System.out.println(list);
    }
}
```

A. [X, X, Y, Z]

B. [X, X, Z]

C. [X, Z]

D. [X, Y, Z]

E. Compilation error

F. Exception is thrown at runtime

2.1.46 What will be the result of compiling and executing Test class?

```java
public class Test {
    public static void main(String[] args) {
        StringBuilder sb = new StringBuilder("Java");
        String s1 = sb.toString();
        String s2 = "Java";

        System.out.println(s1 == s2);
    }
}
```

A. Compilation error

B. true

C. false

D. An exception is thrown at runtime

2.1.47 What will be the result of compiling and executing Test class?

```java
public class Test {
    public static void main(String[] args) {
        String str1 = " ";
        boolean b1 = str1.isEmpty();
        System.out.println(b1);
        str1.trim();
        b1 = str1.isEmpty();
        System.out.println(b1);
    }
}
```

A.	false true	B.	false false
C.	true false	D.	true true

2.1.48 Consider below code:

```
//Test.java
package com.udayan.oca;

public class Test {
    public static void main(String[] args) {
        final String fName = "James";
        String lName = "Gosling";
        String name1 = fName + lName;
        String name2 = fName + "Gosling";
        String name3 = "James" + "Gosling";
        System.out.println(name1 == name2);
        System.out.println(name2 == name3);
    }
}
```

What will be the result of compiling and executing Test class?

A.	true true	B.	true false
C.	false false	D.	false true

2.1.49 What will be the result of compiling and executing Test class?

```
package com.udayan.oca;
public class Test {
    public static void main(String[] args) {
        StringBuilder sb
            = new StringBuilder("Hurrah! I Passed...");
        sb.delete(0, 100);
        System.out.println(sb.length());
    }
}
```

A. 19

B. 0

C. 16

D. StringIndexOutOfBoundsException is thrown at runtime

2.1.50 What will be the result of compiling and executing Test class?

```
package com.udayan.oca;

public class Test {
    public static void main(String[] args) {
        m1(null);
    }

    static void m1(CharSequence s) {
        System.out.println("CharSequence");
    }

    static void m1(String s) {
        System.out.println("String");
    }

    static void m1(Object s) {
        System.out.println("Object");
    }
}
```

A. Compilation Error

B. CharSequence

C. String

D. Object

2.1.51 What will be the result of compiling and executing Test class?

```java
package com.udayan.oca;
import java.util.ArrayList;
import java.util.List;
public class Test {
    public static void main(String[] args) {
        List<String> list = new ArrayList<>();
        list.add(null);
        list.add(null);
        list.add(null);
        System.out.println(list.remove(0) + ":"
                                   + list.remove(null));
    }
}
```

A. true:true

B. true:false

C. null:true

D. null:null

E. NullPointerException is thrown at runtime

2.1.52 Consider below code:

```java
//Test.java
import java.time.LocalDate;

public class Test {
    public static void main(String [] args) {
        LocalDate date = LocalDate.parse("2018-1-01");
        System.out.println(date);
    }
}
```

What will be the result of compiling and executing Test class?

A. 2018-01-01

B. 2018-1-1

C. 2018-1-01

D. An exception is thrown at runtime

2.1.53 Consider below code:

```
//Test.java
import java.time.LocalDate;

public class Test {
    public static void main(String [] args) {
        LocalDate newYear = LocalDate.of(2018, 1, 1);
        LocalDate eventDate = LocalDate.of(2018, 1, 1);
        boolean flag1 = newYear.isAfter(eventDate);
        boolean flag2 = newYear.isBefore(eventDate);
        System.out.println(flag1 + ":" + flag2);
    }
}
```

What will be the result of compiling and executing Test class?

A. false:false

B. true:true

C. false:true

D. true:false

2.1.54 Consider below code:

```
//Test.java
import java.time.LocalDate;

public class Test {
    public static void main(String [] args) {
        LocalDate date = LocalDate.parse("1980-03-16");
        System.out.println(date.minusYears(-5));
    }
}
```

What will be the result of compiling and executing Test class?

A. 1975-03-16

B. 1985-03-16

C. Compilation error

D. Runtime exception

2.1.55 Consider below code:

```java
//Test.java
import java.time.LocalDate;
import java.time.Period;
import java.time.format.DateTimeFormatter;

public class Test {
    public static void main(String [] args) {
        LocalDate date = LocalDate.of(2012, 1, 11);
        Period period = Period.ofMonths(2);
        DateTimeFormatter formatter =
                DateTimeFormatter.ofPattern("mm-dd-yy");

System.out.print(formatter.format(date.minus(period)));
    }
}
```

What will be the result of compiling and executing Test class?

A. 11-11-12

B. 01-11-11

C. 01-11-12

D. 11-11-11

E. Runtime exception

2.1.56 Consider below code:

```java
//Test.java
import java.time.Period;

public class Test {
    public static void main(String [] args) {
        Period period = Period.
                of(2, 1,
0).ofYears(10).ofMonths(5).ofDays(2);
        System.out.println(period);
    }
}
```

What will be the result of compiling and executing Test class?

A. P12Y6M2D

B. P2Y1M0D

C. P2Y1M

D. P2D

2.1.57 Consider below code:

```java
//Test.java
import java.time.LocalDate;

public class Test {
    public static void main(String [] args) {
        LocalDate d1 = LocalDate.parse("1999-09-09");
        LocalDate d2 = LocalDate.parse("1999-09-09");
        LocalDate d3 = LocalDate.of(1999, 9, 9);
        LocalDate d4 = LocalDate.of(1999, 9, 9);
        System.out.println((d1 == d2) + ":" + (d2 == d3)
                + ":" + (d3 == d4));
    }
}
```

What will be the result of compiling and executing Test class?

A. true:false:true

B. false:false:true

C. true:true:true

D. false:false:false

2.1.58 Consider below code:

```java
//Test.java
import java.time.LocalDate;
import java.time.Period;

public class Test {
    public static void main(String [] args) {
        LocalDate date = LocalDate.parse("2000-01-01");
        Period period = Period.ofYears(-3000);
        System.out.println(date.plus(period));
    }
}
```

What will be the result of compiling and executing Test class?

A. Compilation error

B. Runtime exception

C. 1000-01-01

D. -1000-01-01

E. 5000-01-01

2.1.59 Consider below code:

```java
//Test.java
package com.udayan.oca.test;

import java.util.ArrayList;
import java.util.List;

class Student {
    private String name;
    private int age;

    Student(String name, int age) {
        this.name = name;
        this.age = age;
    }

    public String toString() {
        return "Student[" + name + ", " + age + "]";
    }

    public boolean equals(Object obj) {
        if(obj instanceof Student) {
            Student stud = (Student)obj;
            if(this.name.equals(stud.name) &&
                            this.age == stud.age) {
                return true;
            }
        }
        return false;
    }
}

public class Test {
    public static void main(String[] args) {
        List<Student> students = new ArrayList<>();
        students.add(new Student("James", 25));
        students.add(new Student("James", 27));
        students.add(new Student("James", 25));
        students.add(new Student("James", 25));

        students.remove(new Student("James", 25));

        for(Student stud : students) {
            System.out.println(stud);
        }
    }
}
```

What will be the result of compiling and executing Test class?

A.	Student[James, 27] Student[James, 25] Student[James, 25]	B.	Student[James, 25] Student[James, 27] Student[James, 25]
C.	Student[James, 27]	D.	Student[James, 25] Student[James, 27] Student[James, 25] Student[James, 25]

2.1.60 Consider below code:

```java
//Test.java
import java.util.ArrayList;
import java.util.List;
import java.util.ListIterator;


public class Test {
    public static void main(String[] args) {
        List<String> dryFruits = new ArrayList<>();
        dryFruits.add("Walnut");
        dryFruits.add("Apricot");
        dryFruits.add("Almond");
        dryFruits.add("Date");

        ListIterator<String> iterator =
                        dryFruits.listIterator();
        while(iterator.hasNext()) {
            if(iterator.next().startsWith("A")) {
                iterator.remove();
            }
        }

        System.out.println(dryFruits);
    }
}
```

What will be the result of compiling and executing Test class?

A. [Walnut, Apricot, Almond, Date]

B. [Walnut, Date]

C. An exception is thrown at runtime

D. Compilation error

2.1.61 Consider below code:

```
//Test.java
import java.util.ArrayList;
import java.util.List;

public class Test {
    public static void main(String[] args) {
        List<String> list = new ArrayList<>();
        list.add("ONE");
        list.add("TWO");
        list.add("THREE");
        list.add("THREE");

        if(list.remove(2)) {
            list.remove("THREE");
        }

        System.out.println(list);
    }
}
```

What will be the result of compiling and executing Test class?

A. [ONE, TWO, THREE, THREE]

B. [ONE, TWO, THREE]

C. [ONE, TWO]

D. Compilation error

E. An exception is thrown at runtime

2.1.62 Consider below code:

```java
//Test.java
import java.util.ArrayList;
import java.util.List;

public class Test {
    public static void main(String[] args) {
        List<String> list = new ArrayList<>();
        list.add(0, "Array");
        list.add(0, "List");

        System.out.println(list);
    }
}
```

What will be the result of compiling and executing Test class?

A. [Array]

B. [List]

C. [Array, List]

D. [List, Array]

E. An exception is thrown at runtime

2.1.63 Consider below code:

```java
//Test.java
import java.util.ArrayList;

public class Test {
    public static void main(String[] args) {
        ArrayList<Integer> original = new ArrayList<>();
        original.add(new Integer(10));

        ArrayList<Integer> cloned =
                (ArrayList<Integer>) original.clone();
        Integer i1 = cloned.get(0);
        ++i1;

        System.out.println(cloned);
    }
}
```

What will be the result of compiling and executing Test class?

A. [11]

B. [10]

C. Compilation error

D. An exception is thrown at runtime

2.1.64 Consider below code:

```java
import java.util.ArrayList;
import java.util.List;

public class Test {
    public static void main(String[] args) {
        List<StringBuilder> days = new ArrayList<>();
        days.add(new StringBuilder("Sunday"));
        days.add(new StringBuilder("Monday"));
        days.add(new StringBuilder("Tuesday"));

        if(days.contains(new StringBuilder("Sunday"))) {
            days.add(new StringBuilder("Wednesday"));
        }

        System.out.println(days.size());
    }
}
```

What will be the result of compiling and executing Test class?

A. 4

B. 3

C. Compilation error

D. Runtime exception

2.1.65 Consider the code snippet:

```java
import java.util.ArrayList;
import java.util.List;

public class Test {
    List list1 = new ArrayList<String>(); //Line 5
    List<String> list2 = new ArrayList(); //Line 6
    List<> list3 = new ArrayList<String>(); //Line 7
    List<String> list4 = new ArrayList<String>(); //Line 8
    List<String> list5 = new ArrayList<>(); //Line 9
}
```

Which of the following statements compile without any warning? Select 2 options.

A. Line 5

B. Line 6

C. Line 7

D. Line 8

E. Line 9

2.1.66 Below is the code of Test.java file:

```
import java.util.ArrayList;
import java.util.List;

public class Test {
    public static void main(String [] args) {
        List<Integer> list = new ArrayList<Integer>();

        list.add(27);
        list.add(27);

        list.add(new Integer(27));
        list.add(new Integer(27));

        System.out.println(list.get(0) == list.get(1));
        System.out.println(list.get(2) == list.get(3));
    }
}
```

What will be the result of compiling and executing Test class?

A.	false false	B.	false true
C.	true true	D.	true false

2.1.67 Consider below code:

```java
//Test.java
import java.util.ArrayList;
import java.util.Iterator;
import java.util.List;
import java.util.function.Predicate;

class Employee {
    private String name;
    private int age;
    private double salary;

    public Employee(String name, int age, double salary) {
        this.name = name;
        this.age = age;
        this.salary = salary;
    }

    public String getName() {
        return name;
    }

    public int getAge() {
        return age;
    }

    public double getSalary() {
        return salary;
    }

    public String toString() {
        return name;
    }
}

public class Test {
    public static void main(String [] args) {
        List<Employee> list = new ArrayList<>();
        list.add(new Employee("James", 25, 15000));
        list.add(new Employee("Lucy", 23, 12000));
        list.add(new Employee("Bill", 27, 10000));
        list.add(new Employee("Jack", 19, 5000));
        list.add(new Employee("Liya", 20, 8000));

        process(list, e -> e.getAge() > 20);
    }
```

```
    private static void process(List<Employee> list,
                        Predicate<Employee> predicate) {
        Iterator<Employee> iterator = list.iterator();
        while(iterator.hasNext()) {
            Employee e = iterator.next();
            if(predicate.test(e))
                System.out.print(e + " ");
        }
    }
}
```

What will be the result of compiling and executing Test class?

A. James Lucy Bill Jack Liya

B. James Lucy Bill

C. Jack Liya

D. Compilation error

2.1.68 Consider below code:

```
import java.util.function.Predicate;

public class Test {
    public static void main(String[] args) {
        String [] arr = {"A", "ab", "bab", "Aa", "bb",
                                    "baba", "aba",
"Abab"};

        processStringArray(arr, /*INSERT*/);
    }

    private static void processStringArray(String [] arr,
                            Predicate<String>
predicate) {
        for(String str : arr) {
            if(predicate.test(str)) {
                System.out.println(str);
            }
        }
    }
}
```

Which of the following options can replace /*INSERT*/ such that on executing Test class all the array elements are displayed in the output? Select All that apply.

A. `p -> true`
B. `p -> !false`
C. `p -> p.length() >= 1`
D. `p -> p.length() < 10`

2.1.69 What will be the result of compiling and executing Test class?

```
import java.time.LocalDate;
import java.time.Month;
import java.util.ArrayList;
import java.util.List;

public class Test {
    public static void main(String[] args) {
        List<LocalDate> dates = new ArrayList<>();
        dates.add(LocalDate.parse("2018-7-11"));
        dates.add(LocalDate.parse("1919-10-25"));
        dates.add(LocalDate.of(2020, 4, 8));
        dates.add(LocalDate.of(1980, Month.DECEMBER, 31));

        dates.removeIf(x -> x.getYear() < 2000);

        System.out.println(dates);
    }
}
```

A. [2018-07-11, 1919-02-25, 2020-04-08, 1980-12-31]

B. [1919-02-25, 1980-12-31]

C. [2018-07-11, 2020-04-08]

D. Runtime exception

2.1.70 What will be the result of compiling and executing Test class?

```java
import java.util.function.Predicate;

public class Test {
    public static void main(String[] args) {
        String [] arr = {"*", "**", "***",
                                "****", "*****"};
        Predicate pr1 = s -> s.length() < 4;
        print(arr, pr1);
    }

    private static void print(String [] arr,
                    Predicate<String> predicate) {
        for(String str : arr) {
            if(predicate.test(str)) {
                System.out.println(str);
            }
        }
    }
}
```

A.	Compilation error	B.	* ** ***
C.	* ** *** ****	D.	* ** *** **** *****

2.2 Answers of Practice Test - 2 with Explanation

2.1.1 Answer: C

Reason:
If package is used then it should be the first statement, but javadoc and developer comments are not considered as java statements so a class can have developer and javadoc comments before the package statement.
If import and package both are available, then correct order is package, import, class declaration. Multiple package statements are not allowed.

2.1.2 Answer: A

Reason:
Top level class can have two access modifiers: public and default.
Over here Test class has private modifier and hence compilation error.

2.1.3 Answer: A

Reason:
Both the classes contain special main method. No compilation error with the code: file is correctly names as Guest.java (name of public class).
java Guest James Gosling passes new String [] {"James", "Gosling"} to args of Guest.main method. Apart from being special main method, Message.main is static method so Guest.main method invokes Message.main method with the same argument: new String [] {"James", "Gosling"}.
args[0] is "James" hence "Welcome James!" gets printed on to the console.

2.1.4 Answer: D,E,F

Reason:
class A is declared public and defined in com.udayan.oca package, there is no problem in accessing class A outside com.udayan.oca package.

class TestA is defined in com.udayan.oca.test package, to use class A either use import statement "import com.udayan.oca.A;" or fully qualified name of the class com.udayan.oca.A. No issues at Line 3 and Line 7.

As TestA is in different package so it can only access public members of class A using object reference. Line 8 compiles successfully.
protected, default and private members are not accessible outside com.udayan.oca package using object reference.

NOTE: protected members can be accessed outside but only through inheritance and not object reference.

2.1.5   Answer: D

Reason:
Both Runtime.getRuntime().gc(); and System.gc(); do the same thing, these make a request to JVM to run Garbage Collector.
JVM makes the best effort to run Garbage Collector but nothing is guaranteed.

Setting the reference variable to null will make the object eligible for Garbage Collection, if there are no other references to this object. But this doesn't force JVM to run the Garbage Collector. Garbage Collection cannot be forced.

2.1.6   Answer: B

Reason:
Boolean class code uses equalsIgnoreCase method to validate the passed String, so if passed String is "true" ('t', 'r', 'u' and 'e' can be in any case), then boolean value stored in Boolean object is true otherwise false.

b1 stores true, b2 stores false, b3 stores false and as b4 is of reference type, hence it can store null as well.
Output is: true:false:false:null

2.1.7 Answer: A

Reason:
List cannot accept primitives, it can accept objects only. So, when 100 and 200 are added to the list, then auto-boxing feature converts these to wrapper objects of Integer type.

So, 4 items get added to the list: [100, 200, 100, 200]. list.remove(new Integer(100)); removes the first occurrence of 100 from the list, which means the 1st element of the list.
After removal list contains: [200, 100, 200].

NOTE: String class and all the wrapper classes override equals(Object) method, hence at the time of removal when another instance is passes[new Integer(100)], there is no issue in removing the matching item.

2.1.8 Answer: D

Reason:
add(10.0, null); => Compiler can't convert null to double primitive type, so 2nd argument is tagged to Double reference type. So to match the method call, 10.0 is converted to Double object by auto-boxing and add(10.0, null); is tagged to add(Double, Double); method.

But at the time of execution, d2 is null so System.out.println("Double version: " + (d1 + d2)); throws NullPointerException.

2.1.9 Answer: A

Reason:
For readability purpose underscore (_) is used to separate numeric values. This is very useful in representing big numbers such as credit card numbers (1234_7654_9876_0987). long data can be suffixed by l, float by f and double by d. So first 5 variable declaration and assignment statements inside main(String []) method don't cause any compilation error.

Let's check rest of the statements:

l = c + i; => Left side variable 'l' is of long type and right side expression evaluates to an int value, which can easily be assigned to long type. No compilation error here.

f = c * l * i * f; => Left side variable 'f' is of float type and right side expression evaluates to float value, which can easily be assigned to float type. Hence, it compiles successfully.

f = l + i + c; => Left side variable 'f' is of float type and right side expression evaluates to long value, which can easily be assigned to float type. Hence, no issues here.

i = (int)d; => double can't be assigned to int without explicit casting, right side expression `(int)d;` is casting double to int, so no issues.

f = (long)d; => double can't be assigned to float without explicit casting, right side expression `(long)d;` is casting double to long, which can easily be assigned to float type. It compiles successfully.

2.1.10 Answer: B

Reason:
Boolean class code uses equalsIgnoreCase method to validate the passed String, so if passed String is "true" ('t', 'r', 'u' and 'e' can be in any case), then boolean value stored in Boolean object is true otherwise false.

In this question passed String is "ture" and not "true" and that is why false is printed on to the console.

2.1.11 Answer: A

Reason:
"Output is: " + (10 != 5) [Nothing to evaluate at left side, so let's evaluate the right side of +, 10 != 5 is true.]
= "Output is: " + true [+ operator behaves as concatenation operator]
= "Output is: true"

2.1.12 Answer: C

Reason:
As there is no brackets after if, hence only one statement is part of if block and other is outside.

Above code can be written as below:
if(grade > 60) {
    System.out.println("Congratulations");
}
System.out.println("You passed");
else
    System.out.println("You failed");

There should not be anything between if-else block but in this case,
System.out.println("You passed"); is between if-else and thus Compilation error.

2.1.13 Answer: A

Reason:
case values must evaluate to the same type / compatible type as the switch expression
can use.
switch expression can accept following:
char or Character,
byte or Byte,
short or Short,
int or Integer,
An enum only from Java 6,
A String expression only from Java 7.

In this case, switch expression [switch (score)] is of int type.
But case expressions, score < 70 and score >= 70 are of boolean type and hence
compilation error.

2.1.14 Answer: B

Reason:
"mango" is different from "Mango", so there is no matching case available. default
block is executed and as it is the last block inside switch hence after printing "ANY
FRUIT WILL DO" control goes out of switch block, main method ends and program
terminates successfully.

2.1.15 Answer: A,C,D,E

Reason:
switch can accept primitive types: byte, short, int, char; wrapper types: Byte, Short, Integer, Character; String and enums.
In this case long and double are invalid values to be passed in switch expression. char uses 16 bits (2 Bytes) and its range is 0 to 65535 (no signed bit reserved) so it can easily store value 10.

2.1.16 Answer: A

Reason:
There is no compilation error. When Test class is loaded by JVM to invoked main(String []) method, static variable declaration and initialization statement is executed and false is assigned to flag as !true is false.

As java Test AM PM command is used, so args[0] --> "AM" and args[1] --> "PM".

In ternary operator, boolean expression is evaluated first, !flag evaluates to true and therefore agrs[0] is returned.

AM is printed on to the console.

2.1.17 Answer: B

Reason:
a++ == 2 || --a == 2 && --a == 2; [Given expression].
(a++) == 2 || --a == 2 && --a == 2; [Postfix has got higher precedence than other operators].
(a++) == 2 || (--a) == 2 && (--a) == 2; [After postfix, precedence is given to prefix].
((a++) == 2) || ((--a) == 2) && ((--a) == 2); [== has higher precedence over && and ||].
((a++) == 2) || (((--a) == 2) && ((--a) == 2)); [&& has higher precedence over ||].
Let's start solving it:
((a++) == 2) || (((--a) == 2) && ((--a) == 2)); [a=2, res=false].
(2 == 2) || (((--a) == 2) && ((--a) == 2)); [a=3, res=false].
true || (((--a) == 2) && ((--a) == 2)); [a=3, res=false]. || is a short-circuit operator, hence no need to evaluate expression on the right.

res is true and a is 3.

2.1.18 Answer: C

Reason:
You can't specify size at the time of initializing with data, hence new int[3]{10, 20, 30}; causes compilation error.

2.1.19 Answer: D

Reason:
Variable arr refers to an array object of String of 7 elements.
Variable arr contains the memory address of String array object.
arr is of reference type, hence it prints some String Containing @ symbol.

2.1.20 Answer: A

Reason:
We have not passed any command-line arguments, hence args refers to an array object of Size 0.
args.length prints 0. args is not null and hence no NullPointerException.

Also we are not accessing array element so no question of ArrayIndexOutOfBoundsException as well.

2.1.21 Answer: C

Reason:
case values must evaluate to the same type / compatible type as the switch expression can use.
switch expression can accept following:
char or Character,
byte or Byte,
short or Short,
int or Integer,

An enum only from Java 6,
A String expression only from Java 7.

In this case, switch expression [switch (arr[i][j])] is of String type.
Please note that break; statement at Line n4 takes the control to Line n6 (outside switch-case block) and not out of the inner for loop, where as, continue; statement at Line n5 takes the control to the update expression (j++) of Line n2.
arr.length is 3, so outer loop executes 3 times.
1st iteration of outer loop, i=0.
 -1st iteration of inner loop, i=0, j=0 and arr[0].length = 3. 0 < 3 evaluates to true.
  arr[0][0] = "7", Line n5 is executed, and it takes the control to j++ (j = 1). 1 < 3 evaluates to true.
 -2nd iteration of inner loop
  arr[0][1] = "6", Line n4 is executed, and it takes the control to Line n6. 6 is printed on to the console. Control goes to j++ (j = 2). 2 < 3 evaluates to true.
 -3rd iteration of inner loop
  arr[0][2] = "5", Line n5 is executed, and it takes the control to j++ (j = 3). As 3 < 3 evaluates to false, control exits inner loop and goes to i++.
You must have noticed that 1st iteration of outer loop prints the even number of 1st array { "7", "6", "5" }

Similarly, 2nd iteration of outer loop prints the even number of 2nd array { "4", "3" }, which is 4
and 3rd iteration of outer loop prints the even number of 3rd array { "2", "1" }, which is 2.

Therefore, the output is: 642.

2.1.22   Answer: C

Reason:
while loop doesn't have curly bracket over here, so only System.out.println(x) belongs to while loop.

Above syntax can be written as follows:
int x = 5;
while (x < 10) {
    System.out.println(x);

```
}
x++;
```

As x++; is outside loop, hence value of x is always 5 within loop, 5 < 10 is true for all the iterations and hence infinite loop.

2.1.23 Answer: A,D

Reason:
Easy question on iterating through 2-dimensional array. Starting index should be 0 and not 1. Enhanced for loop syntax is correct.
As for loops contain 1 statement, hence curly brackets can be ignored.

2.1.24 Answer: D

Reason:
Inside enhanced for loop, System.out.println(arr[i]); is used instead of System.out.println(i);
When loop executes 1st time, i stores the first array element, which is 3 but System.out.println statement prints arr[3] and this causes java runtime to throw the instance of ArrayIndexOutOfBoundsException.

2.1.25 Answer: C

Reason:
public void Test() is method and not constructor, as return type is void.
method can have same name as the class name, so no issues with Test() method declaration.

As there are no constructors available for this class, java compiler adds following constructor.
public Test() {}

Test obj = new Test(); invokes the default constructor but it doesn't change the value of name property (by default null is assigned to name property)

System.out.println(obj.name); prints null.

2.1.26 Answer: D

Reason:
It is pass-by-reference scheme.
Initially, msg = "Happy New Year!"
Call to method change(Message) modifies msg property of passed object to "Happy Holidays!"
Hence in the output, you get:
Happy New Year!
Happy Holidays!

2.1.27 Answer: C

Reason:
It is good practice to have first character of class name in upper case, but it is not mandatory.
student can be either class name or reference variable name.

Syntax to invoke static method is: Class_Name.method_name(<arguments>); OR
reference_variable_name.method_name(<arguments>);
Syntax to invoke instance method is:
reference_variable_name.method_name(<arguments>);
If student represents class_name or refernce_variable_name, then report might be the static method of the class.
If student represents reference_variable_name, then report is the instance method of the class.
In both the cases, report must be the method name.

Type of argument cannot be found out by looking at above syntax.

2.1.28 Answer: C

Reason:
Encapsulation is all about having private instance variable and providing public getter and setter methods.

2.1.29 Answer: B

Reason:
It is clear from Line 5 that, method name should be process, it should be static method, it should accept 3 parameters (int[], int, int) and its return type must be String.

2.1.30 Answer: B

Reason:
Point class correctly overrides the toString() method. Even though variable x is static, but it can be easily accessed by instance method toString().
Variables x, y and z are declared with default scope, so can be accessed in same package. There is no compilation error in the code.
There is only one copy of static variable for all the instances of the class. Variable x is shared by p1 and p2 both.
p1.x = 17; sets the value of static variable x to 17, p2.x = 19; modifies the value of static variable x to 19. As there is just one copy of x, hence p1.x = 19

Please note: p1.x and p2.x don't cause any compilation error but as this syntax creates confusion, so it is not a good practice to access the static variables or static methods using reference variable, instead class name should be used. Point.x is the preferred syntax.

Each object has its own copy of instance variables, so just before executing Line n1,
p1.y = 35 & p1.z = -1 AND p2.y = 40 & p2.z = 0
Output is:
Point(19, 35, -1)
Point(19, 40, 0)

2.1.31 Answer: B

Reason:
int can be converted to double but Integer type can't be converted to Double type as Integer and Double are siblings (both extends from Number class) so can't be casted to each other.

add(10.0, new Integer(10)); => 1st parameter is tagged to double primitive type and 2nd parameter is converted to int, is tagged to double primitive type as well. So, add(double, double); method is invoked.

2.1.32 Answer: A

Reason:
A constructor can call another constructor by using this(...) and not the constructor name. Hence Student("James", 25); causes compilation error.

2.1.33 Answer: C

Reason:
Class declared as final can't be inherited. Examples are: String, Integer, System etc.

2.1.34 Answer: A

Reason:
B b = new A(); -> child class reference cannot refer to parent class object. This will cause compilation error.
A a = new B(); -> parent class reference can refer to child class object. This is Polymorphism.
B a = new B(); -> No issues at all.
A a = new A(); -> No issues at all.

2.1.35 Answer: D

Reason:

class Car doesn't extend from Vehicle class, this means Vehicle is not super type of Car.

Hence, Vehicle obj = new Car(); causes compilation error.

2.1.36 Answer: C

Reason:

super(); inside Parent(int) constructor invokes the no-argument constructor of Object class and hence no compilation error for Parent(int) constructor.

super(0); inside Child(int) constructor invokes Parent(int) constructor, which is available and hence no issues.

Child(int, int) constructor has both super(i) and this(j) statements. A constructor should have super(...) or this(...) but not both. Hence Child(int, int) causes compilation failure.

As all the classes are defined in Test.java file under com.udayan.oca.test package, hence child.i and child.j don't cause compilation error. i and j are declared with package scope.

2.1.37 Answer: C, E, F

Reason:

Let us first find out the issue:

As instance variables are hidden by subclasses and not overridden, hence overriding rules are not for the instance variables. There are no issues with variables 'num' and 'operation'.

log() method is declared with default modifier in both the classes, hence no issue with log() method as well.

abstract method help() is declared with protected modifier in Helper class and in LogHelper class, it is overridden with default modifier and this causes compilation error. So below solutions to resolved this issue:

1. Remove the protected modifier from the help() method of Helper class: Both the overridden and overriding methods will have same default modifier, which is allowed
OR
2. Add the protected modifier to the help() method of LogHelper class: Both the overridden and overriding methods will have same protected modifier, which is allowed
OR
3. Add the public modifier to the help() method of LogHelper class: Overridden method will have protected modifier and overriding method will have public modifier, which is allowed

2.1.38 Answer: C

Reason:
System.out.println(new Child()); invokes the toString() method on Child's instance.

Parent class's method can be invoked by super keyword. super.toString() method returns "Inner " and "Inner ".concat("Peace!") returns "Inner Peace!".

2.1.39 Answer: D

Reason:
FileNotFoundException extends IOException and hence catch block of FileNotFoundException should appear before the catch block of IOException. Therefore, class Test causes compilation error.

2.1.40 Answer: A

Reason:
catch is for catching the exception and not throwing it.
thrown is not a java keyword.
throws is used to declare the exceptions a method can throw.
To manually throw an exception, throw keyword is used. e.g., throw new Exception();

2.1.41 Answer: D

Reason:
Method m1() throws Exception (checked) and it declares to throw it, so no issues with method m1().
But main() method neither provides catch handler nor throws clause and hence main method causes compilation error.
Handle or Declare rule should be followed for checked exception if you are not re-throwing it.

2.1.42 Answer: D

Reason:
NOTE: Question is asking for "incorrect" implementation and not "correct" implementation.

According to overriding rules, if super class / interface method declares to throw a checked exception, then overriding method of sub class / implementer class has following options:
1. May not declare to throw any checked exception,
2. May declare to throw the same checked exception thrown by super class / interface method,
3. May declare to throw the sub class of the exception thrown by super class / interface method,
4. Cannot declare to throw the super class of the exception thrown by super class / interface method

2.1.43 Answer: A,C,D

Reason:
ClassCastException, NumberFormatException and IllegalArgumentException are Runtime exceptions. There are no exception classes in java with the names: NullException and ArrayIndexException.

2.1.44 Answer: B

Reason:
equals(String str) method of String class matches two String objects and it takes character's case into account while matching.

Alphabet A in upper case and alphabet a in lower case are not equal according to this method. As String objects referred by s1 and s2 have different cases, hence output is false.

2.1.45 Answer: A

Reason:
After all the add statements are executed, list contains: [X, Y, X, Y, Z].
list.remove(new String("Y")); removes the first occurrence of "Y" from the list, which means the 2nd element of the list. After removal list contains: [X, X, Y, Z].

NOTE: String class and all the wrapper classes override equals(Object) method, hence at the time of removal when another instance is passes [new String("Y")], there is no issue in removing the matching item.

2.1.46 Answer: C

Reason:
toString() method defined in StringBuilder class doesn't use String literal rather uses the constructor of String class to create the instance of String class.

So both s1 and s2 refer to different String instances even though their contents are same. s1 == s2 returns false.

2.1.47 Answer: B

Reason:
str1 refers to single space character and isEmpty() method of String returns true if no characters are there in the String. As str1 contains single space, hence b1 is false. false is first printed on to the console.

str1.trim(); => creates an empty string "" but str1 still refers to single space string " ".
b1 = str1.isEmpty(); assigns false to b1 and last System.out.println statement prints
false on to the console. So output is:
false
false

2.1.48 Answer: D

Reason:
Please note that Strings computed by concatenation at compile time, will be referred
by String Pool during execution. Compile time String concatenation happens when
both of the operands are compile time constants, such as literal, final variable etc.
Whereas, Strings computed by concatenation at run time (if the resultant expression is
not constant expression) are newly created and therefore distinct.

fName is a constant variable and lName is a non-constant variable.

`fName + lName` is not a constant expression and hence the expression will be
computed at run-time and the resultant String object "JamesGosling" will not be
referred by String Pool.

As fName is constant variable and "Gosling" is String literal, hence the expression
`fName + "Gosling"` is a constant expression, therefore expression is computed at
compile-time and results in String literal "JamesGosling".
So, during compilation, Java compiler translates the statement
String name2 = fName + "Gosling";
to
String name2 = "JamesGosling";

As "JamesGosling" is a String literal, hence at runtime it will be referred by String Pool.

So, at runtime name1 and name2 refer to different String object and that is why
name1 == name2 returns false.

`"James" + "Gosling"` is also a constant expression and hence Java compiler translates
the statement
String name3 = "James" + "Gosling";

to

String name3 = "JamesGosling";

This means at runtime, variable 'name3' will refer to the same String pool object "JamesGosling", which is referred by variable 'name3'.

So, name2 and name3 refer to same String object and that is why name2 == name3 returns true.

2.1.49   Answer: B

Reason:
'delete' method accepts 2 parameters: delete(int start, int end), where start is inclusive and end is exclusive.
This method throws StringIndexOutOfBoundsException for following scenarios:
A. start is negative
B. start is greater than sb.length()
C. start is greater than end

If end is greater than the length of StringBuilder object, then StringIndexOutOfBoundsException is not thrown and end is set to sb.length().
So, in this case, `sb.delete(0, 100);` is equivalent to `sb.delete(0, sb.length());` and this deletes all the characters from the StringBuilder object.
Hence, System.out.println(sb.length()); prints 0 on to the console.

2.1.50   Answer: C

Reason:
Method m1 is overloaded to accept 3 different parameters: String, CharSequence and Object.
String implements CharSequence and Object is the super Parent class in Java. There is no conflict among the overloaded methods for the call m1(null) as it is mapped to the class lowest in hierarchy, which is String class. Hence, output will be "String".

Now if you add one more overloaded method, `static void m1(StringBuilder s) {...}` in the Test class, then `m1(null);` would cause compilation error as it would match to both m1(StringBuilder) and m1(String) methods. So m1(null) in that case would be ambiguous call and would cause compilation error.

For the same reason, System.out.println(null); causes compilation error as println method is overloaded to accept 3 reference types Object, String and char [] along with primitive types.
System.out.println(null); matches to both println(char[]) and println(String), so it is an ambiguous call and hence the compilation error.

2.1.51 Answer: C

Reason:
It is possible to add null to ArrayList instant.
Initially list has 3 elements: [null, null, null].
remove(int) returns the deleted member of the list. In this case `list.remove(0);` returns null as null was deleted from the 0th index. So, list is left with 2 elements: [null, null].
remove(Object) returns true if deletion was successful otherwise false. In this case `list.remove(null)` removes first null from the list and returns true and list is left with just one element: [null].
Hence, the output is: 'null:true'.

2.1.52 Answer: D

Reason:
LocalDate.parse(CharSequence) method accepts String in "9999-99-99" format only. Single digit month and day value are padded with 0 to convert it to 2 digits.
To represent 9th June 2018, format String must be "2018-06-09". If correct format string is not passed then an instance of java.time.format.DateTimeParseException is thrown.

2.1.53 Answer: A

Reason:
isAfter and isBefore method can be interpreted as:

Does 1st Jan 2018 come after 1st Jan 2018? No, false. Does 1st Jan 2018 come before 1st Jan 2018? No, false.

2.1.54   Answer: B

Reason:
minusYears, minusMonths, minusWeeks, minusDays methods accept long parameter so you can pass either positive or negative value. If positive value is passed, then that specified value is subtracted and if negative value is passed, then that specified value is added. I think you still remember: minus minus is plus.

Similarly plusYears, plusMonths, plusWeeks, plusDays methods work in the same manner. If positive value is passed, then that specified value is added and if negative value is passed, then that specified value is subtracted.

2.1.55   Answer: E

Reason:
While working with dates, programmers get confused with M & m and D & d. Easy way to remember is that Bigger(Upper case) letters represent something bigger. M represents month & m represents minute, D represents day of the year & d represents day of the month.

LocalDate's object doesn't have time component, mm represents minute and not months so at runtime format method throws exception.

2.1.56   Answer: D

Reason:
of and ofXXX methods are static methods and not instance methods.
Period.of(2, 1, 0) => returns an instance of Period type. static methods can be invoked using class_name or using reference variable.
In this case ofYears(10) is invoked on period instance but compiler uses Period's instance to resolve the type, which is period. A new Period instance {P10Y} is created, after that another Period instance {P5M} is created and finally Period instance {P2D} is

created. This instance is assigned to period reference variable and hence P2D is printed on to the console.

2.1.57 Answer: D

Reason:
"parse" and "of" methods create new instances, so in this case you get 4 different instance of LocalDate stored at 4 different memory addresses.

2.1.58 Answer: D

Reason:
The minimum supported LocalDate is: {-999999999-01-01} and maximum supported LocalDate is: {+999999999-12-31}. If period of -3000 years is added to 1st Jan 2000, then result is 1st Jan -1000.

2.1.59 Answer: A

Reason:
Before you answer this, you must know that there are 5 different Student object created in the memory (4 at the time of adding to the list and 1 at the time of removing from the list). This means these 5 Student objects will be stored at different memory addresses.

remove(Object) method removes the first occurrence of matching object and equals(Object) method decides whether 2 objects are equal or not. equals(Object) method has been overridden by the Student class and equates the object based on their name and age.

3 matching Student objects are found in the list and 1st list element is removed from the list. Remaining 3 list elements are printed in the insertion order.

2.1.60 Answer: B

Reason:
If you want to remove the items from ArrayList, while using Iterator or ListIterator, then use Iterator.remove() or ListIterator.remove() method and NOT List.remove() method.

In this case ListIterator.remove() method is used. startsWith("A") returns true for "Apricot" and "Almond" so these elements are removed from the list. In the output, [Walnut, Date] is displayed.

2.1.61 Answer: D

Reason:
list.remove(Object) method returns boolean result but list.remove(int index) returns the removed item from the list, which in this case is of String type and not Boolean type and hence if(list.remove(2)) causes compilation error.

2.1.62 Answer: D

Reason:
list.add(0, "Array"); means list --> [Array],
list.add(0, "List"); means insert "List" to 0th index and shift "Array" to right. So after this operation, list --> [List, Array]. In the console, [List, Array] is printed.

2.1.63 Answer: B

Reason:

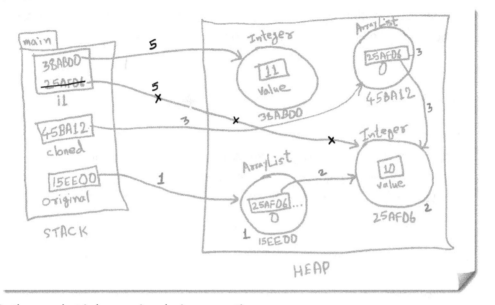

Let's see what is happening during execution:

main(String [] args) method goes on to the top of the STACK.

1. ArrayList<Integer> original = new ArrayList<>(); => It creates an ArrayList object [suppose at memory location 15EE00] and variable 'original' refers to it.

2. original.add(new Integer(10)); => It creates an Integer object [suppose at memory location 25AF06] and adds it as a first element of the ArrayList. This means element at 0th index of the ArrayList instance refers to Integer object at the memory location 25AF06.

3. ArrayList<Integer> cloned = (ArrayList<Integer>) original.clone(); => original.clone() creates a new array list object, [suppose at memory location 45BA12] and then it will copy the contents of the ArrayList object stored at [15EE00]. So, cloned contains memory address of the same Integer object.

In this case, original != cloned, but original.get(0) == cloned.get(0). This means both the array lists are created at different memory location but refer to same Integer object.

4. Integer i1 = cloned.get(0); => cloned.get(0) returns the Integer object stored at the memory location 25AF06 and variable 'i1' refers to it.

5. ++i1; => As Integer object is immutable, hence ++i1; creates a new Integer object with value 11 and suppose this newly created Integer object is stored at memory location 38AB00. This means variable 'i1' stops referring to Integer object at the

memory location 25AF06 and starts referring to Integer object at the memory location 38AB00.

Cloned list stays intact and still refers to Integer object at memory location 25AF06.

6. System.out.println(cloned); => Prints [10] on to the console as cloned contains an element which refers to Integer object containing value 10.

2.1.64 Answer: B

Reason:
StringBuilder class doesn't override equals(Object) method and hence days.contains(new StringBuilder("Sunday")) returns false. Code inside if-block is not executed and days.size() returns 3.

2.1.65 Answer: D,E

Reason:
Line 8's syntax was added in JDK 5 and it compiles without any warnings.

Line 9's syntax was added in JDK 7, in which type parameter can be ignored from right side of the statement, it is inferred from left side, so Line 9 also compiles without any warning.

Type parameter can't be removed from declaration part, hence Line 7 causes compilation error.

Both Line 5 and Line 6 are mixing Generic type with Raw type and hence warning is given by the compiler.

2.1.66 Answer: D

Reason:
This is bit tricky. Just remember this:
Two instances of following wrapper objects, created through auto-boxing will always be same, if their primitive values are same:
Boolean,
Byte,

Character from \u0000 to \u007f (7f equals to 127),
Short and Integer from -128 to 127.

For 1st statement, list.add(27); => Auto-boxing creates an integer object for 27.
For 2nd statement, list.add(27); => Java compiler finds that there is already an Integer object in the memory with value 27, so it uses the same object.

That is why System.out.println(list.get(0) == list.get(1)); returns true.

new Integer(27) creates a new Object in the memory, so System.out.println(list.get(2) == list.get(3)); returns false.

2.1.67 Answer: B

Reason:
process(List, Predicate) method prints all the records passing the Predicate's test and test is to process the records having age greater than 20. There are 3 records with age > 20 and these are printed in the insertion order.

NOTE: toString() method just returns the name.

2.1.68 Answer: A,B,C,D

Reason:
p -> true means test method returns true for the passed String.
p -> !false means test method returns true for the passed String.
p -> p.length() >= 1 means test method returns true if passed String's length is greater than or equal to 1 and this is true for all the array elements.
p -> p.length() < 10 means test method returns true if passed String's length is less than 10 and this is true for all the array elements.

2.1.69 Answer: D

Reason:
LocalDate.parse(CharSequence text) method accepts String in "9999-99-99" format only, in which month and day part in the passed object referred by text should be of 2

digits, such as to represent MARCH, use 03 and not 3 & to represent 4th day of the month, use 04 and not 4. Single digit month and day value are not automatically padded with 0 to convert it to 2 digits.

To represent 9th June 2018, format String must be "2018-06-09". If you pass "2018-6-9" or "2018-06-9" or "2018-6-09" (not in correct formats), then an instance of java.time.format.DateTimeParseException will be thrown.

In this question, LocalDate.parse("2018-7-11") throws an exception at runtime as JULY is represented as 7, whereas it should be represented as 07.

2.1.70   Answer: A

Reason:

Though Predicate is a generic interface but raw type is also allowed. Type of the variable in lambda expression is inferred by the generic type of Predicate<T> interface.

In this case, Predicate pr1 = s -> s.length() < 4; Predicate is considered of Object type so variable "s" is of Object type and Object class doesn't have length() method. So, s.length() causes compilation error.

3   Practice Test - 3

3.1   70 questions covering all topics

3.1.1   Does below code compile successfully?

```
public class Test {
    public static void main(String [] args) {
        System.out.println("Hello");;;;;;;;;
    }
}
```

A. Yes

B. No

3.1.2   Which of the following correctly imports Animal class from com.masaimara package?

A. Import com.masaimara.Animal;

B. import com.masaimara;

C. import com.masaimara.*;

D. Import com.masaimara.Animal;

3.1.3   Consider following code snippet:

```
package com.udayan.test;
public class Exam {
    public static void main(String [] args) {
        System.out.println("All the best!");
    }
}
```

Location of Exam.java file:

```
D:.
└──WORK
    └──QUIZ
        └──SEC07
            ├──classes
            └──src
                └──com
                    └──udayan
                        └──test
                            Exam.java
```

You are currently at Sec07 folder.

```
D:\WORK\Quiz\Sec07>
```

Which of the following javac command, typed from above location, will generate Exam.class file structure under classes directory?

```
D:.
└──WORK
    └──QUIZ
        └──SEC07
            ├──classes
            │   └──com
            │       └──udayan
            │           └──test
            │               Exam.class
            │
            └──src
                └──com
                    └──udayan
                        └──test
                            Exam.java
```

A. Not possible by javac command

B. javac classes\ src\com\udayan\test\Exam.java

C. javac -d classes\ src\com\udayan\test\Exam.java

D. javac -d classes\ Exam.java

3.1.4 Suppose you have created a java file, "MyClass.java".
Which of the following commands will compile the java file?

A. javac MyClass

B. java MyClass

C. javac MyClass.class

D. javac MyClass.java

E. java MyClass.java

3.1.5 What will be the result of compiling and executing TestStudent class?

```java
//TestStudent.java
class Student {
    String name;
    int age;
    boolean result;
    double height;
}

public class TestStudent {
    public static void main(String[] args) {
        Student stud = new Student();
        System.out.println(stud.name + stud.height
                            + stud.result + stud.age);
    }
}
```

A. null0.0false0

B. null0false0

C. null0.0ffalse0

D. null0.0true0

3.1.6 Given the code:

```java
public class Pen {
    public static void main(String[] args) {
        Pen p1 = new Pen(); //Line 1
        Pen p2 = new Pen(); //Line 2
        p1 = p2; //Line 3
        p1 = null; //Line 4
    }
}
```

When is the Pen object, created at Line 1 eligible for Garbage Collection?

A. After Line 2

B. After Line 3

C. After Line 4

D. At the end of main method

3.1.7 Consider 2 files:

```java
//Counter.java
package com.udayan.oca;

public class Counter {
    public int count = 0;

    public Counter(int start) {
        count = start;
    }

    public int getCount() {
        return count;
    }

    public void increase(int val) {
        count = count + val;
    }

    public String toString() {
        return this.count + "";
```

```
        }
    }


//Test.java
package com.udayan.oca.test;

import java.util.Arrays;
import com.udayan.oca.Counter;

public class Test {
    public static void main(String[] args) {
        Counter[] arr = new Counter[] {
                new Counter(-1000), new Counter(539),
                                    new Counter(0) };

        /* INSERT */

        System.out.println(Arrays.toString(arr));
    }
}
```

Currently on executing Test class, output is: [-1000, 539, 0].

And below blocks:

1.

```
for(Counter ctr : arr) {
  ctr.count = 100;
}
```

2.

```
for (Counter ctr : arr) {
  int x = ctr.getCount();
  x = 100;
}
```

3.

```
for (Counter ctr : arr) {
  ctr.getCount() = 100;
}
```

4.

```
for(Counter ctr : arr) {
  ctr.increase(100 - ctr.count);
```

```
}
```

5.

```
for (Counter ctr : arr) {
   ctr.increase(100 - ctr.getCount());
}
```

6.

```
for(Counter ctr : arr) {
   ctr.increase(-ctr.getCount() + 100);
}
```

7.

```
for(Counter ctr : arr) {
   ctr.increase(-ctr.count + 100);
}
```

How many blocks can replace /*INSERT*/ such that output is: [100, 100, 100]?

A. Only One block

B. Only Two blocks

C. Only Three blocks

D. Only Four blocks

E. Only Five blocks

F. Only Six blocks

G. All Seven blocks

3.1.8 What will be the result of compiling and executing Test class?

```java
public class Test {
    static Boolean[] arr = new Boolean[1];
    public static void main(String[] args) {
        if(arr[0]) {
            System.out.println(true);
        } else {
            System.out.println(false);
        }
    }
}
```

A. true

B. false

C. Compilation error

D. NullPointerException is thrown at runtime

E. ArrayIndexOutOfBoundsException is thrown at runtime

3.1.9   What will be the result of compiling and executing Test class?

```java
public class Test {
    public static void main(String[] args) {
        Boolean b = new Boolean("tRUe");
        switch(b) {
            case true:
                System.out.println("ONE");
            case false:
                System.out.println("TWO");
            default:
                System.out.println("THREE");
        }
    }
}
```

A.	ONE TWO THREE	B.	TWO THREE
C.	THREE	D.	None of the other options

3.1.10 What will be the result of compiling and executing Test class?

```java
public class Test {
    public static void main(String[] args) {
        m(1);
    }

    private static void m(Object obj) {
        System.out.println("Object version");
    }

    private static void m(Number obj) {
        System.out.println("Number version");
    }

    private static void m(Double obj) {
        System.out.println("Double version");
    }
}
```

A. Compilation error
B. Object version
C. Number version
D. Double version

3.1.11 What will be the result of compiling and executing Test class?

```java
public class Test {
    public static void main(String[] args) {
        System.out.println("Hello" + 1 + 2 + 3 + 4);
    }
}
```

A. Hello10
B. Hello19
C. Hello1234
D. Hello 10

3.1.12 What will be the result of compiling and executing Bonus class?

```
public class Bonus {
    public static void main(String[] args) {
        int $ = 80000;
        String msg = ($ >= 50000) ?
                        "Good bonus" : "Average bonus";
        System.out.println(msg);
    }
}
```

A. Good bonus

B. Average bonus

C. Compilation error

3.1.13 What will be the result of compiling and executing Test class?

```
public class Test {
    public static void main(String[] args) {
        int a = 20;
        int var = --a * a++ + a-- - --a;
        System.out.println("a = " + a);
        System.out.println("var = " + var);
    }
}
```

A.	a = 25 var = 363	B.	a = 363 var = 363
C.	a = 18 var = 363	D.	Compilation error

3.1.14 What will be the output of compiling and executing the Test class?

```java
public class Test {
    public static void main(String[] args) {
        int x = 2;
        switch (x) {
            default:
                System.out.println("Still no
                                    idea what x is");
            case 1:
                System.out.println("x is equal to 1");
                break;
            case 2:
                System.out.println("x is equal to 2");
                break;
            case 3:
                System.out.println("x is equal to 3");
                break;
        }
    }
}
```

A.	x is equal to 2	B.	Compilation error
C.	Still no idea what x is x is equal to 1	D.	Produces no output

3.1.15   What will be the result of compiling and executing Test class?

```java
public class Test {
    public static void main(String[] args) {
        String fruit = new String(new char[] {'M',
                                    'a', 'n', 'g', 'o'});
        switch (fruit) {
            default:
                System.out.println("ANY FRUIT WILL DO");
            case "Apple":
                System.out.println("APPLE");
            case "Mango":
                System.out.println("MANGO");
            case "Banana":
                System.out.println("BANANA");
                break;
        }
    }
}
```

A.	ANY FRUIT WILL DO	B.	MANGO
C.	MANGO BANANA	D.	ANY FRUIT WILL DO APPLE MANGO BANANA

3.1.16 What will be the result of compiling and executing Test class?

```java
public class Test {
    public static void main(String[] args) {
        int i = 5;
        if(i++ < 6) {
            System.out.println(i++);
        }
    }
}
```

A.	5	B.	6
C.	7	D.	Program executes successfully but nothing is printed on to the console

3.1.17 What will be the result of compiling and executing Test class?

```java
public class Test {
    public static void main(String[] args) {
        String msg = "Hello";
        boolean [] flag = new boolean[1];
        if(flag[0]) {
            msg = "Welcome";
        }
        System.out.println(msg);
    }
}
```

A. Hello

B. Welcome

C. ArrayIndexOutOfBoundsException

D. NullPointerException

3.1.18 What will be the result of compiling and executing Test class?

```
public class Test {
    public static void main(String[] args) {
        int [] arr1 = {5, 10, 15};
        int [] arr2 = {'A', 'B'};
        arr1 = arr2;
        System.out.println(arr1.length + arr2.length);
    }
}
```

A. Compilation error

B. An exception is thrown at runtime

C. 0

D. 4

E. 6

F. 5

3.1.19 Which of the following is true for code below?

```
public class Test {
    public static void main(String[] args) {
        byte [] arr = new byte[0];
        System.out.println(arr[0]);
    }
}
```

A. Compilation error

B. 0

C. NullPointerException

D. ArrayIndexOutOfBoundsException

3.1.20 Given code:

```
public class Test {
    public static void main(String[] args) {
        int [] arr = {1, 2, 3, 4, 5};
        int x = 0;
        for(/*INSERT*/) {
            x += arr[n];
        }
        System.out.println(x);
    }
}
```

Which 3 options, if used to replace /*INSERT*/, on execution will print 9 on to the console?

A. `int n = 0; n < arr.length; n++`
B. `int n = 0; n < arr.length; n += 2`
C. `int n = 3; n < arr.length; n++`
D. `int n = 1; n < arr.length - 1; n++`
E. `int n = 1; n < arr.length; n += 2`

3.1.21 Which of the following statement is correct for below code?

```
package com.udayan.oca;

public class Test {
    public static void main(String[] args) {
        String [] arr = new String[1];
        System.out.println(arr[0].isEmpty());
    }
}
```

A. true
B. false
C. NullPointerException is thrown at runtime
D. ArrayIndexOutOfBoundsException is thrown at runtime

3.1.22 Which of the following statement is correct for below code?

```java
public class Test {
    public static void main(String[] args) {
        final boolean flag = false;
        while(flag) {
            System.out.println("Good Morning!");
        }
    }
}
```

A. Program compiles and executes successfully but produces no output

B. Compilation error

C. Infinite loop

D. It will print "Good Morning!" once

3.1.23 What will be the result of compiling and executing Test class?

```java
public class Test {
    public static void main(String[] args) {
        int start = 1;
        int sum = 0;
        do {
            if(start % 2 == 0) {
                continue;
            }
            sum += start;
        } while(++start <= 10);
        System.out.println(sum);
    }
}
```

A. 25

B. 55

C. Compilation error

D. 24

3.1.24 What will be the result of compiling and executing Test class?

```java
public class Test {
    public static void main(String[] args) {
        for(int i=0; i<=2; i++){}
        System.out.println(i);
    }
}
```

A. 0

B. 2

C. 3

D. Compilation error

3.1.25 What will be the result of compiling and executing Test class?

```java
public class Test {
    public static void main(String[] args) {
        for:
        for (int i = 2; i <= 100; i = i + 2) {
            for(int j = 1; j <= 10; j++) {
                System.out.print(i * j + "\t");
            }
            System.out.println();
            if(i == 10) {
                break for;
            }
        }
    }
}
```

A. Total 5 rows will be there in the output

B. Total 50 rows will be there in the output

C. Total 100 rows will be there in the output

D. Compilation error

3.1.26 **What will be the result of compiling and executing Greetings class?**

```java
public class Greetings {
    String msg = null;

    public Greetings() {
        this("Good Morning!");
    }

    public Greetings(String str) {
        msg = str;
    }

    public void display() {
        System.out.println(msg);
    }

    public static void main(String [] args) {
        Greetings g1 = new Greetings();
        Greetings g2 = new Greetings("Good Evening!");
        g1.display();
        g2.display();
    }
}
```

A.	null Good Evening!	B.	Good Morning! Good Evening!
C.	Good Morning! null	D.	null null

3.1.27 What will be the result of compiling and executing Test class?

```java
public class Test {
    public static void change(int num) {
        num++;
        System.out.println(num);
    }

    public static void main(String[] args) {
        int i1 = 1;
        Test.change(i1);
        System.out.println(i1);
    }
}
```

A.	Compilation Error	B.	2 1
C.	2 2	D.	None of the other options

3.1.28 When does a class get the default constructor?

A. If you define parameterized constructor for the class.

B. You have to define at least one constructor to get the default constructor.

C. If the class does not define any constructors explicitly.

D. All classes in Java get a default constructor.

3.1.29 For the class Apple, which option, if used to replace /*INSERT*/, will print GREEN on to the console?

```java
public class Apple {
    public String color;

    public Apple(String color) {
        /*INSERT*/
    }

    public static void main(String [] args) {
        Apple apple = new Apple("GREEN");
        System.out.println(apple.color);
    }
}
```

A. color = color;

B. this.color = color;

C. color = GREEN;

D. this.color = GREEN;

3.1.30 What will be the result of compiling and executing following program?

```java
class Rectangle {
    private int height;
    private int width;

    public Rectangle(int height, int width) {
        this.height = height;
        this.width = width;
    }

    public int getHeight() {
        return height;
    }

    public int getWidth() {
        return width;
    }
}

public class Test {
    public static void main(String[] args) {
        private int i = 100;
        private int j = 200;
        Rectangle rect = new Rectangle(i, j);
        System.out.println(rect.getHeight()
                          + ", " + rect.getWidth());
    }
}
```

A. 100, 200

B. 200, 100

C. Compilation Error

D. 0, 0

3.1.31 Which of the following statement declares a constant field in Java?

A. const int x = 10;

B. static int x = 10;

C. final static int x = 10;

D. int x = 10;

3.1.32 Consider code of Test.java file:

```
public class Test {
    public static void main(String [] args) {
        int [] arr = {0, 1, 2, 3, 4, 5, 6, 7, 8, 9};
        System.out.println(process(arr, 3, 8)); //Line 5
    }

    /*INSERT*/
}
```

Line 5 is giving compilation error as process method is not found.

Which of the following method definitions, if used to replace /*INSERT*/, will resolve the compilation error? Select 3 options.

A.	`private static int[] process(int [] arr,`
	`                        int start, int end) {`
	`    return null;`
	`}`

B.	`private static String process(int [] arr,`
	`                        int start, int end) {`
	`    return null;`
	`}`

C.	`private static int process(int [] arr,`
	`                        int start, int end) {`
	`    return null;`
	`}`

D.	`private static String[] process(int [] arr,`
	`                        int start, int end) {`
	`    return null;`
	`}`

3.1.33 **What will be the result of compiling and executing Test class?**

```java
//Test.java
package com.udayan.oca;

class Point {
    static int x;
    private int y;

    public String toString() {
        return "Point(" + x + ", " + y + ")";
    }
}

public class Test {
    public static void main(String[] args) {
        Point p1 = new Point();
        p1.x = 100;
        p1.y = 200;

        Point p2 = new Point();
        p2.x = 100;
        p2.y = 200;

        System.out.println(p1);
    }
}
```

A. Point(100, 100)

B. Point(100, 200)

C. Point(200, 200)

D. Point(0, 200)

E. Point(100, 0)

F. Point(200, 0)

G. Compilation error

3.1.34 super keyword in java is used to:

   A. refer to static variable of the class.
   B. refer to static method of the class.
   C. refer to current class object.
   D. refer to parent class object.

3.1.35 What will be the result of compiling and executing Test class?

```java
class Super {
    public Super(int i) {
        System.out.println(100);
    }
}

class Sub extends Super {
    public Sub() {
        System.out.println(200);
    }
}

public class Test {
    public static void main(String[] args) {
        new Sub();
    }
}
```

A.	200	B.	200
			100
C.	100	D.	Compilation Error
	200		

3.1.36 What will be the result of compiling and executing TestBaseDerived class?

```java
//TestBaseDerived.java
class Base {
    protected void m1() {
        System.out.println("Base: m1()");
    }
}

class Derived extends Base {
    void m1() {
        System.out.println("Derived: m1()");
    }
}

public class TestBaseDerived {
    public static void main(String[] args) {
        Base b = new Derived();
        b.m1();
    }
}
```

A.	Base: m1()	B.	Derived: m1()
C.	Base: m1() Derived: m1()	D.	None of the other options

3.1.37 What will be the result of compiling and executing Test class?

```java
class M { }
class N extends M { }
class O extends N { }
class P extends O { }

public class Test {
    public static void main(String args []) {
        M obj = new O();
        if(obj instanceof M)
            System.out.print("M");
        if(obj instanceof N)
            System.out.print("N");
        if(obj instanceof O)
            System.out.print("O");
        if(obj instanceof P)
            System.out.print("P");
    }
}
```

A.	MNO	B.	MNP
C.	NOP	D.	MOP

3.1.38 Which one of these top level classes cannot be sub-classed?

A. class Dog {}

B. abstract class Cat {}

C. final class Electronics {}

D. private class Car {}

3.1.39 For the given code:

```
interface I01 {
    void m1();
}

public class Implementer extends Object implements I01{
    protected void m1() {

    }
}
```

Which of the statement is true?

A. interface I01 causes compilation error as method m1 is not public.

B. Implementer class declaration is not correct.

C. Method m1() in Implementer class is not implemented correctly.

D. None of the other options.

3.1.40 For the below code, fill in the blank with one option.

```
class TestException extends Exception {
    public TestException() {
        super();
    }

    public TestException(String s) {
        super(s);
    }
}

public class Test {
    public void m1() throws _____ {
        throw new TestException();
    }
}
```

A. Exception

B. Object

C. RuntimeException

D. Error

3.1.41 What will be the result of compiling and executing Test class?

```
public class Test {
    private static void m1() {
        System.out.println(1/0);
    }

    public static void main(String[] args) {
        try {
            m1();
        } finally {
            System.out.println("A");
        }
    }
}
```

A. A is printed to the console and program ends normally.
B. A is printed to the console, stack trace is printed and then program ends normally.
C. A is printed to the console, stack trace is printed and then program ends abruptly.
D. Compilation error.

3.1.42 What will be the result of compiling and executing Test class?

```
class Base {
    public void m1() throws NullPointerException {
        System.out.println("Base: m1()");
    }
}

class Derived extends Base {
    public void m1() throws RuntimeException {
        System.out.println("Derived: m1()");
    }
}

public class Test {
    public static void main(String[] args) {
        Base obj = new Derived();
        obj.m1();
    }
}
```

A. Base: m1()

B. Derived: m1()

C. Compilation error in Derived class

D. Compilation error in Test class

3.1.43 What will be the result of compiling and executing Test class?

```java
//Test.java
package com.udayan.oca.test;

import java.io.FileNotFoundException;

public class Test {
    public static void main(String[] args) {
        try {
            System.out.println(1);
        } catch (NullPointerException ex) {
            System.out.println("ONE");
        } catch (FileNotFoundException ex) {
            System.out.println("TWO");
        }
        System.out.println("THREE");
    }
}
```

A.	ONE THREE	B.	TWO THREE
C.	THREE	D.	None of the System.out.println statements are executed
E.	Compilation error		

3.1.44 Consider below code:

```
public class Test {
    static Double d1;
    static int x = d1.intValue();

    public static void main(String[] args) {
        System.out.println("HELLO");
    }
}
```

On execution, does Test class print "HELLO" on to the console?

A. Yes, HELLO is printed on to the console

B. No, HELLO is not printed on to the console

3.1.45 What will be the result of compiling and executing Test class?

```
package com.udayan.oca;

public class Test {
    public static void main(String[] args) {
        Error obj = new Error();
        boolean flag1 = obj instanceof
                    RuntimeException; //Line n1
        boolean flag2 = obj instanceof
                        Exception; //Line n2
        boolean flag3 = obj instanceof
                        Error; //Line n3
        boolean flag4 = obj instanceof
                        Throwable; //Line n4
        System.out.println(flag1 + ":" +
            flag2 + ":" + flag3 + ":" + flag4);
    }
}
```

A. Compilation error

B. false:false:true:true

C. false:true:true:true

D. true:true:true:true

3.1.46 What will be the result of compiling and executing Test class?

```java
public class Test {
    public static void main(String[] args) {
        String str = "Java Rocks!";
        System.out.println(str.length() + " : "
                                + str.charAt(10));
    }
}
```

A. 11 : !

B. An exception is thrown at runtime

C. 11 : s

D. Compilation error

3.1.47 What will be the result of compiling and executing Test class?

```java
public class Test {
    public static void main(String[] args) {
        String str = "Good"; //Line 3
        change(str); //Line 4
        System.out.println(str); //Line 5
    }

    private static void change(String s) {
        s.concat("_Morning"); //Line 9
    }
}
```

A. Good

B. _Morning

C. Good_Morning

D. None of the other options

3.1.48 What will be the result of compiling and executing Test class?

```java
public class Test extends String {
    @Override
    public String toString() {
        return "TEST";
    }

    public static void main(String[] args) {
        Test obj = new Test();
        System.out.println(obj);
    }
}
```

A. TEST

B. Output string contains @ symbol

C. Exception is thrown at runtime

D. Compilation error

3.1.49 What will be the result of compiling and executing Test class?

```java
public class Test {
    public static void main(String[] args) {
        StringBuilder sb =
                new StringBuilder("SpaceStation");
        sb.delete(5, 6).insert(5, "S")
                        .toString().toUpperCase();
        System.out.println(sb);
    }
}
```

A. SPACE SATION

B. SPACE STATION

C. Space Station

D. Space Sation

3.1.50 Consider below code:

```java
//Test.java
package com.udayan.oca;

public class Test {
    public static void main(String[] args) {
        final int i1 = 1;
        final Integer i2 = 1;
        final String s1 = ":ONE";

        String str1 = i1 + s1;
        String str2 = i2 + s1;

        System.out.println(str1 == "1:ONE");
        System.out.println(str2 == "1:ONE");
    }
}
```

What will be the result of compiling and executing Test class?

A.	true true	B.	true false
C.	false false	D.	false true

3.1.51 What will be the result of compiling and executing Test class?

```java
package com.udayan.oca;

public class Test {
    public static void main(String[] args) {
        StringBuilder sb = new StringBuilder(5);
        sb.append("0123456789");
        sb.delete(8, 1000);
        System.out.println(sb);
    }
}
```

A. Compilation error

B. An exception is thrown at runtime

C. 01234567

D. 89

3.1.52 Consider below code:

```java
//Test.java
import java.time.LocalDate;

public class Test {
    public static void main(String [] args) {
        LocalDate date = LocalDate.of(2020, 9, 6);
        System.out.println(date);
    }
}
```

What will be the result of compiling and executing Test class?

A. 2020-9-6

B. 2020-09-06

C. 2020-6-9

D. 2020-06-09

3.1.53 Consider below code:

```
//Test.java
import java.time.LocalDate;

public class Test {
    public static void main(String [] args) {
        LocalDate date = LocalDate.parse("2018-06-06");
        date.minusDays(10);
        System.out.println(date);
    }
}
```

What will be the result of compiling and executing Test class?

A. 2018-05-26

B. 2018-05-27

C. 2018-06-26

D. 2018-06-25

E. 2018-06-06

3.1.54 Consider below code:

```
//Test.java
import java.time.LocalDate;

public class Test {
    public static void main(String [] args) {
        LocalDate joiningDate = LocalDate.parse("2006-03-
16");
        System.out.println(joiningDate.withDayOfYear(29));
    }
}
```

What will be the result of compiling and executing Test class?

A. 2006-03-29

B. 2006-01-01

C. 2006-01-29

D. None of the other options

3.1.55 Consider below code:

```
//Test.java
import java.time.LocalDate;
import java.time.Period;

public class Test {
    public static void main(String [] args) {
        LocalDate obj = new LocalDate(2020, 2, 14);
        System.out.println(obj.minus(Period.ofDays(10)));
    }
}
```

What will be the result of compiling and executing Test class?

A. 2020-02-04

B. 2020-02-03

C. Compilation error

D. Runtime exception

3.1.56 Consider below code:

```
//Test.java
import java.time.LocalDate;

public class Test {
    public static void main(String [] args) {
        LocalDate date = LocalDate.parse("2000-06-25");
        while(date.getDayOfMonth() >= 20) {
            System.out.println(date);
            date.plusDays(-1);
        }
    }
}
```

What will be the result of compiling and executing Test class?

A. Compilation error

B. An exception is thrown at runtime

C. System.out.println(date); is executed 6 times

D. System.out.println(date); is executed more than 6 times

3.1.57 Consider below code:

```
//Test.java
import java.time.LocalDate;
import java.time.format.DateTimeFormatter;

public class Test {
    public static void main(String [] args) {
        LocalDate date = LocalDate.of(1987, 9, 1);
        String str = date.
                format(DateTimeFormatter.ISO_DATE_TIME);
        System.out.println("Date is: " + str);
    }
}
```

What will be the result of compiling and executing Test class?

A. Date is: 1987-09-01

B. Date is: 1987-01-09

C. Date is: 01-09-1987

D. Given code executes successfully but output does not match with the given options

E. Runtime exception

3.1.58 Consider below code:

```
//Test.java
import java.time.LocalDate;
import java.time.Month;
import java.time.Period;

public class Test {
    public static void main(String [] args) {
        LocalDate date = LocalDate.of(2000, Month.JANUARY,
1);

        Period period = Period.parse("p-30000y");
        System.out.println(date.plus(period));
    }
}
```

What will be the result of compiling and executing Test class?

A. Compilation error

B. Runtime exception

C. -28000-01-01

D. 28000-01-01

E. 32000-01-01

3.1.59 Consider below code:

```java
//Test.java
package com.udayan.oca.test;

import java.util.ArrayList;
import java.util.List;

class Student {
    private String name;
    private int age;

    Student(String name, int age) {
        this.name = name;
        this.age = age;
    }

    public String toString() {
        return "Student[" + name + ", " + age + "]";
    }

    public boolean equals(Student obj) {
        if(obj instanceof Student) {
            Student stud = (Student)obj;
            if(this.name.equals(stud.name) &&
                            this.age == stud.age) {
                return true;
            }
        }
        return false;
    }
}

public class Test {
    public static void main(String[] args) {
        List<Student> students = new ArrayList<>();
        students.add(new Student("James", 25));
        students.add(new Student("James", 27));
        students.add(new Student("James", 25));
        students.add(new Student("James", 25));

        students.remove(new Student("James", 25));

        for(Student stud : students) {
            System.out.println(stud);
        }
```

```
        }
    }
```

What will be the result of compiling and executing Test class?

A.	Student[James, 27] Student[James, 25] Student[James, 25]	B.	Student[James, 25] Student[James, 27] Student[James, 25]
C.	Student[James, 27]	D.	Student[James, 25] Student[James, 27] Student[James, 25] Student[James, 25]

3.1.60 Consider below code:

```
//Test.java
import java.util.ArrayList;
import java.util.List;

public class Test {
    public static void main(String[] args) {
        List<StringBuilder> dryFruits = new ArrayList<>();
        dryFruits.add(new StringBuilder("Walnut"));
        dryFruits.add(new StringBuilder("Apricot"));
        dryFruits.add(new StringBuilder("Almond"));
        dryFruits.add(new StringBuilder("Date"));

        for(int i = 0; i < dryFruits.size(); i++)
        {
            if(i == 0) {
                dryFruits.remove(
                        new StringBuilder("Almond"));
            }
        }

        System.out.println(dryFruits);
    }
}
```

What will be the result of compiling and executing Test class?

A. [Walnut, Apricot, Almond, Date]

B. [Walnut, Date]

C. An exception is thrown at runtime

D. [Walnut, Apricot, Date]

3.1.61 Consider below code:

```java
//Test.java
import java.util.ArrayList;
import java.util.List;

public class Test {
    public static void main(String[] args) {
        List<Boolean> list = new ArrayList<>();
        list.add(true);
        list.add(new Boolean("tRue"));
        list.add(new Boolean("abc"));

        if(list.remove(1)) {
            list.remove(1);
        }

        System.out.println(list);
    }
}
```

What will be the result of compiling and executing Test class?

A. Compilation error

B. An exception is thrown at runtime

C. [true]

D. [false]

E. [true, false]

3.1.62 Consider below code:

```java
//Test.java
import java.util.ArrayList;
import java.util.List;

public class Test {
    public static void main(String[] args) {
        List<String> list = new ArrayList<>();
        list.add(0, "Array");
        list.set(0, "List");

        System.out.println(list);
    }
}
```

What will be the result of compiling and executing Test class?

A. [Array]
B. [List]
C. [Array, List]
D. [List, Array]
E. An exception is thrown at runtime

3.1.63 Consider below code:

```java
//Test.java
import java.util.ArrayList;
import java.util.List;

public class Test {
    public static void main(String[] args) {
        List<String> trafficLight = new ArrayList<>();
        trafficLight.add(1, "RED");
        trafficLight.add(2, "ORANGE");
        trafficLight.add(3, "GREEN");

        trafficLight.remove(new Integer(2));

        System.out.println(trafficLight);
    }
}
```

What will be the result of compiling and executing Test class?

A. Compilation error
B. An exception is thrown at runtime
C. [RED, GREEN]
D. [RED, ORANGE]
E. [RED, ORANGE, GREEN]

3.1.64 Consider below code snippet:

```
public static void process(/*INSERT*/ list) {
    list.add(100); //Line 2
    int x = list.get(0); //Line 3
    System.out.println(list.size() + ":" + x);
}
```

Which of the following options, if used to replace /*INSERT*/, compiles successfully?

A. List
B. List<Integer>
C. List<Object>
D. List<int>

3.1.65 Consider below code of Test.java file:

```java
import java.util.ArrayList;
import java.util.List;

interface Sellable {}
abstract class Animal {}
class Mammal extends Animal{}
class Rabbit extends Mammal implements Sellable{}

public class Test {
    {
        List<Animal> list = new ArrayList<>();
        list.add(new Rabbit());
    }
    {
        List<Animal> list = new ArrayList<>();
        list.add(new Mammal());
    }
    {
        List<Mammal> list = new ArrayList<>();
        list.add(new Rabbit());
    }
    {
        List<Sellable> list = new ArrayList<>();
        list.add(new Mammal());
    }
    {
        List<Sellable> list = new ArrayList<>();
        list.add(new Rabbit());
    }
}
```

Which of the following statement is true?

A. Only one initializer block causes compilation error.

B. Two initializer blocks cause compilation error.

C. Three initializer blocks cause compilation error.

D. Four initializer blocks cause compilation error.

E. Five initializer blocks cause compilation error.

3.1.66 **What will be the result of compiling and executing Test class?**

```java
import java.util.ArrayList;
import java.util.List;

public class Test {
    public static void main(String[] args) {
        List<String> fruits = new ArrayList<>();
        fruits.add("apple");
        fruits.add("orange");
        fruits.add("grape");
        fruits.add("mango");
        fruits.add("banana");
        fruits.add("grape");

        if(fruits.remove("grape"))
            fruits.remove("papaya");

        System.out.println(fruits);
    }
}
```

A. An exception is thrown at runtime

B. Compilation error

C. [apple, orange, mango, banana]

D. [apple, orange, mango, banana, grape]

3.1.67 What will be the result of compiling and executing Test class?

```java
import java.util.function.Predicate;

public class Test {
    public static void main(String[] args) {
        printNumbers(i -> i % 2 != 0);
    }

    private static void printNumbers(Predicate<Integer>
                                                   predicate) {
        for(int i = 1; i <= 10; i++) {
            if(predicate.test(i)) {
                System.out.print(i);
            }
        }
    }
}
```

A. 12345678910

B. 1234567891011

C. 246810

D. 13579

E. 1357911

3.1.68 What will be the result of compiling and executing Test class?

```java
import java.util.ArrayList;
import java.util.List;

public class Test {
    public static void main(String[] args) {
        List<Integer> list = new ArrayList<>();
        list.add(100);
        list.add(7);
        list.add(50);
        list.add(17);
        list.add(10);
        list.add(5);

        list.removeIf(a -> a % 10 == 0);

        System.out.println(list);
    }
}
```

A. [100, 7, 50, 17, 10, 5]

B. [100, 50, 10]

C. [7, 17, 5]

D. Compilation error

E. Runtime Exception

3.1.69 What will be the result of compiling and executing Test class?

```
import java.util.ArrayList;
import java.util.List;

public class Test {
    public static void main(String[] args) {
        List<Integer> list = new ArrayList<>();
        list.add(110);
        list.add(new Integer(110));
        list.add(110);

        list.removeIf(i -> i == 110);
        System.out.println(list);
    }
}
```

A. [110, 110, 110]

B. [110, 110]

C. [110]

D. []

3.1.70 Consider below Lambda expression:

```
Predicate<String> predicate = s -> true;
```

Which of the lambda expression can successfully replace the lambda expression in above statement?

A. s -> {true}

B. s -> {true;}

C. s -> {return true}

D. s -> {return true;}

3.2   Answers of Practice Test - 3 with Explanation

3.1.1   Answer: A

Reason:
In java, it is allowed to put multiple statements on one line. E.g. below code is legal:

```java
public class Test {
  public static void main(String [] args) {
    String symbol = "!";System.out.print("Hello
");System.out.print("World");System.out.println(symbol);
  }
}
```

Above code is similar to:

```java
public class Test {
  public static void main(String [] args) {
    String symbol = "!";
    System.out.print("Hello ");
    System.out.print("World");
    System.out.println(symbol);
  }
}
```

Empty statements (just the semicolon) are also allowed in java, therefore below code is also legal:

```java
public class Test {
  public static void main(String [] args) {
    System.out.println("Hello");
    ;
    ;
    ;
    ;
    ;
    ;
    ;
    ;
  }
}
```

```
    }

    As shown above, java statements (including empty statements) can be placed on one
    line, therefore below code is legal:
    public class Test {
       public static void main(String [] args) {
          System.out.println("Hello");;;;;;;;;;
       }
    }
```

3.1.2   Answer: C

Reason:
Following import statements are correct:
import com.masaimara.*;
import com.masaimara.Animal;
NOTE: all small case letters in import keyword.

3.1.3   Answer: C

Reason:
Use -d option with javac command. As you are typing javac command from within
Sec07 directory, hence path of java file relative to Sec07 directory needs to be given.
So, correct command is: javac -d classes\ src\com\udayan\test\Exam.java

3.1.4   Answer: D

Reason:
Command to compile a java file: javac <java_file_name>.java [.java extension is
compulsory],
Command to execute a java class: java <class_file_name> [.class extension should not
be used]

3.1.5   Answer: A

Reason:
name, height, result and age are instance variables of Student class. And instance variables are initialized to their respective default values.
name is initialized to null, age to 0, result to false and height to 0.0.
Statement System.out.println(stud.name + stud.height + stud.result + stud.age); prints null0.0false0

3.1.6   Answer: B

Reason:
At Line 3, p1 starts referring to the object referred by p2(Created at Line 2).
So, after Line 3, object created at Line 1 becomes unreachable and thus eligible for Garbage Collection.

3.1.7   Answer: E

Reason:
There are 2 ways to change the value of count variable of Counter class:
1. As access modifier of count variable is public, hence it can easily be accessed from other classes using the instance of Counter class, such as `new Counter().count` or `obj.count` (where obj is reference variable of Counter type, referring to Counter variable's instance)
2. By invoking the increase(int) method of Counter class.

Now let's check all the blocks one by one:
1.
```
for(Counter ctr : arr) {
    ctr.count = 100;
}
```
√ It will assign 100 to count variables of three instances of Counter class.

2.
```
for (Counter ctr : arr) {
    int x = ctr.getCount();
    x = 100;
```

}

✗ x is local variable and is copy of ctr.count. Hence, assigning 100 to x will not affect the value of ctr.count.

3.
```
for (Counter ctr : arr) {
    ctr.getCount() = 100;
}
```
✗ ctr.getCount() returns int value and not a variable, hence cannot be used on left side of assignment operator. It causes compilation error.

4.
```
for(Counter ctr : arr) {
    ctr.increase(100 - ctr.count);
}
```
✓ You must have noticed that value of count variable of 3 array elements are: -1000, 539, 0. How will you change all 3 values to 100 using same expression? It is by adding 100 and subtracting current value. For example,

-1000 + 100 -(-1000) = 100

or

539 + 100 - 539 = 100

or

0 + 100 - 0 = 100

And same this is done by executing `ctr.increase(100 - ctr.count);` statement.

5.
```
for (Counter ctr : arr) {
    ctr.increase(100 - ctr.getCount());
}
```
✓ Same as block no. 4. Only difference is ctr.getCount() is used instead of ctr.count.

6.
```
for(Counter ctr : arr) {
    ctr.increase(-ctr.getCount() + 100);
}
```
✓ Same as block no. 5.

7.

```
for(Counter ctr : arr) {
  ctr.increase(-ctr.count + 100);
}
```
✓ Same as block no. 4.

Hence, out of given 7 blocks, 5 will give you expected output.

3.1.8   Answer: D

Reason:
All the array elements are initialized to their default values. arr is of Boolean type (reference type), so arr[0] is initialized to null.
if expression works with Boolean type variable, so "if(arr[0])" doesn't cause compilation error but java runtime extracts the boolean value stored in arr[0] and it uses booleanValue() method. arr[0].booleanValue() means booleanValue() method is invoked on null reference and hence NullPointerException is thrown at runtime.

3.1.9   Answer: D

Reason:
switch can accept primitive types: byte, short, int, char; wrapper types: Byte, Short, Integer, Character; String and enums. switch(b) causes compilation failure as b is of Boolean type.

3.1.10 Answer: C

Reason:
There are 3 overloaded method m. Note all the numeric wrapper classes (Byte, Short, Integer, Long, Float and Double) extend from Number and Number extends from Object.

Compiler either does implicit casting or Wrapping but not both. 1 is int literal, Java compiler can't implicit cast it to double and then box it to Double rather it boxes i to Integer and as Number is the immediate super class of Integer so Number version refers to Integer object.
Number version is printed on to the console.

3.1.11 Answer: C

Reason:
As expression contains + operator only, which is left to right associative. Let us group the expression.
"Hello" + 1 + 2 + 3 + 4
= ("Hello" + 1) + 2 + 3 + 4
= (("Hello" + 1) + 2) + 3 + 4
= ((("Hello" + 1) + 2) + 3) + 4
[Let us solve it now, + operator with String behaves as concatenation operator.]
= (("Hello1" + 2) + 3) + 4
= ("Hello12" + 3) + 4
= "Hello123" + 4
= "Hello1234"

3.1.12 Answer: A

Reason:
$ is valid identifier. $ = 80000

This is an example of ternary operator. First operand ($ >= 50000) is a boolean expression which is true, as 80000 >= 50000 is true.

msg will refer to "Good bonus".

3.1.13 Answer: C

Reason:
int var = --a * a++ + a-- - --a;
int var = --a * (a++) + (a--) - --a;
int var = (--a) * (a++) + (a--) - (--a);
int var = ((--a) * (a++)) + (a--) - (--a);
int var = (((--a) * (a++)) + (a--)) - (--a);
int var = ((19 * (a++)) + (a--)) - (--a); //a = 19
int var = ((19 * 19) + (a--)) - (--a); //a = 20

int var = (361 + 20) - (--a); //a = 19
int var = 381 - (--a); //a = 19
int var = 381 - 18; //a = 18
int var = 363 // a = 18
So,
a = 18
var = 363

3.1.14 Answer: A

Reason:
Even though default block is available at the top but matching case is present. So control goes inside matching case and prints "x is equal to 2" on to the console. After that break; statement takes the control out of the switch- case block.

3.1.15 Answer: C

Reason:
fruit refers to String object "Mango". Matching case is available, MANGO is printed on to the console. No break statement inside case "Mango":, hence control enters in fall-through and executes remaining blocks until the break; is found or switch block ends. So in this case, it prints BANANA and break; statement takes control out of switch block. main method ends and program terminates successfully.

3.1.16 Answer: B

Reason:
Initially i = 5. if(i++ < 6) means if(5 < 6) and then i = 6.
5 < 6 is true, control goes inside if-block and executes System.out.println(i++); This prints current value of i to the console, which is 6 and after that increments the value of i by 1, so i becomes 7.

3.1.17   Answer: A

Reason:
Variable msg is referring to String object "Hello". There is only one element in boolean array object and it is initialized to default value of boolean, which is false. flag[0] is false, if-check fails and control doesn't enter if block.
System.out.println(msg) prints original value of msg, which is "Hello".

3.1.18   Answer: D

Reason:
I Initially arr1 refers to an int array object of 3 elements.
And arr2 refers to an int array object of 2 elements [char type is compatible with int type]
When the statement `arr1 = arr2;` executes, variable arr1 copies the content of arr2, which is the address of array object containing 2 elements. Hence, arr1 also starts referring to same array object. arr1.length = 2 and arr2.length = 2.
Therefore, output is: 4

3.1.19   Answer: D

Reason:
arr refers to an array object of size 0. That means arr stores some memory address. So we will not get NullPointerException in this case.
But index 0 is not available for an array object of size 0 and thus ArrayIndexOutOfBoundsException is thrown at runtime.

3.1.20   Answer: B,C,D

Reason:
Logic in for loop is adding array elements. You need to find out which array elements when added will result in 9. Possible options are: {1+3+5, 2+3+4, 4+5}. Based on these 3 combinations you can select 3 correct options.

3.1.21 Answer: C

Reason:
All the elements of array are initialized to respective zeros (in case of primitive type) or null (in case of reference type).
So, arr[0] refers to null.
Method 'isEmpty()' is invoked on null reference and hence NullPointerException is thrown at runtime.

3.1.22 Answer: B

Reason:
final boolean flag = false; statement makes flag a compile time constant.
Compiler knows the value of flag, which is false at compile time and hence it gives "Unreachable Code" error.

3.1.23 Answer: A

Reason:
When start is divisible by 2 [2, 4, 6, 8, 10], continue; statement takes the control to boolean expression and hence sum += start; is not executed.
Hence result is the sum of numbers 1,3,5,7,9.

3.1.24 Answer: D

Reason:
Variable i is declared inside for loop, hence it is not accessible beyond loop's body.
System.out.println(i); causes compilation error.

3.1.25   Answer: D

Reason:

for is a keyword and hence can't be used as a label. Java labels follow the identifier naming rules and one rule is that we can't use java keywords as identifier. Hence, Compilation error.

3.1.26   Answer: B

Reason:

Greetings g1 = new Greetings(); invokes no-arg constructor.
No-argument constructor calls parameterized constructor with the argument "Good Morning!"
Parameterized constructor assigns "Good Morning!" to msg variable of the object referred by g1.
Greetings g2 = new Greetings("Good Evening!"); invokes parameterized constructor, which assigns "Good Evening!" to msg variable of the object referred by g2.
g1.display(); prints Good Morning!
g2.display(); prints Good Evening!

3.1.27   Answer: B

Reason:

It is pass-by-value scheme. On method invocation, parameter variable num gets a copy and changes are made to this copy inside the method. Original value of i1 stay intact.

3.1.28   Answer: C

Reason:

Default constructor (which is no-argument constructor) is added by Java compiler, only if there are no constructors in the class.

3.1.29 Answer: B

Reason:
Instance variable color is shadowed by the parameter variable color of parameterized constructor. So, color = color will have no effect, because short hand notation within constructor body will always refer to LOCAL variable. To refer to instance variable, this reference is needed. Hence Option B is correct.

'color = GREEN;' and 'this.color = GREEN;' causes compilation error as GREEN is not within double quotes("").

NOTE: 'color = "GREEN";' will only assign 'GREEN' to local variable and not instance variable but 'this.color = "GREEN";' will assign 'GREEN' to instance variable.

3.1.30 Answer: C

Reason:
i and j cannot be declared private as i and j are local variables.
Only final modifier can be used with local variables.

3.1.31 Answer: C

Reason:
Fields declared with final are constant fields.

3.1.32 Answer: A, B, D

Reason:
It is clear from Line 5 that, method name should be process, it should be static method, it should accept 3 parameters (int[], int, int).

As process(arr, 3, 8) is passed as an argument of System.out.println method, hence process method's return type can be anything apart from void. println method is overloaded to accept all primitive types, char [], String type and Object type. int[] are String [] are of Object type.

In the given options, method specifying int as return type cannot return null as null can't be assigned to primitive type. int process(...) would cause compilation error.

3.1.33 Answer: G

Reason:
Variable y is private so it cannot be accessed outside the boundary of Point class. p1.y and p2.y used inside Test class, cause the compilation error.

3.1.34 Answer: D

Reason:
super refers to parent class object and this refers to currently executing object.

3.1.35 Answer: D

Reason:
super(); is added by the compiler as the first statement in both the constructors. Class Super extends from Object class and Object class has no-argument constructor, hence no issues with the constructor of Super class.

But no-argument constructor is not available in Super class, hence calling super(); from Sub class constructor causes compilation error.

3.1.36 Answer: D

Reason:
Derived class overrides method m1() of Base class. Access modifier of method m1() in Base class is protected, so overriding method can use protected or public.
But overriding method in this case used default modifier and hence there is compilation error.

3.1.37   Answer: A

Reason:
M

^

N

^

O [obj refers to instance of O class]

^

P

obj instanceof M -> true
obj instanceof N -> true
obj instanceof O -> true
but
obj instanceof P -> false

3.1.38   Answer: C

Reason:
class Dog {}: can be sub-classed within the same package.
abstract class Cat {}: can be sub-classed within the same package.
final class Electronics {}: a class with final modifier cannot be sub-classed.
private class Car {}: a top level class cannot be declared with private modifier.

3.1.39   Answer: C

Reason:
void m1(); in interface I01 is equivalent to public abstract void m1(); So method m1() is implicitly public and abstract.

In java, a class can extend from only one class but can implement multiple interfaces. Correct keywords are: extends and implements. So, class declaration is correct.

As method m1() is implicitly public in I01, hence overriding method in Implementer class should also be public. But it is protected and hence compiler complains.

215

3.1.40 Answer: A

Reason:
Method m1() throws an instance of TestException, which is a checked exception as it extends Exception class.
So in throws clause we must provide:
1. Checked exception.
2. Exception of TestException type or it's super types (Exception, Throwable), Object cannot be used in throws clause.

3.1.41 Answer: C

Reason:
Method m1() throws an instance of ArithmeticException and method m1() doesn't handle it, so it forwards the exception to calling method main.

Method main doesn't handle ArithmeticException so it forwards it to JVM, but just before that finally block is executed. This prints A on to the console.

After that JVM prints the stack trace and terminates the program abruptly.

3.1.42 Answer: B

Reason:
NullPointerException extends RuntimeException, but there are no overriding rules related to unchecked exceptions.

So, method m1() in Derived class correctly overrides Base class method.

Rest is simple polymorphism. obj refers to an instance of Derived class and hence obj.m1(); invokes method m1() of Derived class, which prints "Derived: m1()" to the console.

3.1.43 Answer: E

Reason:
Java doesn't allow to catch specific checked exceptions if these are not thrown by the statements inside try block. catch(FileNotFoundException ex) {} causes compilation error in this case as System.out.println(1); will never throw FileNotFoundException.

NOTE: Java allows to catch Exception type. catch(Exception ex) {} will never cause compilation error.

3.1.44 Answer: B

Reason:
To invoke the special main method, JVM loads the class in the memory. At that time, static fields of Test class are initialized. d1 is of Double type so null is assigned to it.

x is also static variable so d1.intValue(); is executed and as d1 is null hence d1.intValue() throws a NullPointerException and as a result an instance of java.lang.ExceptionInInitializerError is thrown.

3.1.45 Answer: A

Reason:
class Error extends Throwable, so `obj instanceof Error;` and `obj instanceof Throwable;` return true.
But Error class is not related to Exception and RuntimeException classes in multilevel inheritance and that is why Line n1 and Line n2 causes compilation error.

3.1.46 Answer: A

Reason:
String class has length() method, which returns number of characters in the String. So length() method returns 11. String class has charAt(int index) method, which returns character at passed index. str.charAt(10) looks for character at index 10. index starts with 0. ! sign is at index 10.
Hence output is: 11 : !

3.1.47 Answer: A

Reason:
When change(String) method is called, both variable s and str refers to same String object.
Line 9 doesn't modify the passed object instead creates a new String object "Good_Morning".
But this newly created object is not referred and hence is a candidate for GC.
When control goes back to calling method main(String[]), str still refers to "Good".
Line 5 prints "Good" on to the console.

3.1.48 Answer: D

Reason:
String is a final class so it cannot be extended.

3.1.49 Answer: C

Reason:
sb - > "SpaceStation"
sb.delete(5, 6) -> "Spacetation"
sb.insert(5, " S") -> "Space Station"
sb.toString() -> Creates a new String object "Space Station"
"Space Station".toUpperCase() -> Creates another String object "SPACE STATION" but the String object is not referred and used.

Method invocation on sb modifies the same object, so after insert(5, " S") method invocation sb refers to "Space Station" and this is printed to the Console.

3.1.50 Answer: B

Reason:
Please note that Strings computed by concatenation at compile time, will be referred by String Pool during execution. Compile time String concatenation happens when both of the operands are compile time constants, such as literal, final variable etc. Whereas, Strings computed by concatenation at run time (if the resultant expression is not constant expression) are newly created and therefore distinct.

For the statement, String str1 = i1 + s1;, i1 is a final variable of int type and s1 is a final variable of String type. Hence, `i1 + s1` is a constant expression which is computed at compile-time and results in String literal "1:ONE".
This means during compilation, Java compiler translates the statement
String str1 = i1 + s1;
to
String str1 = "1:ONE";

As "1:ONE" is a String literal, hence at runtime it will be referred by String Pool.

On the other hand, for the statement, String str2 = i2 + s1;, `i2 + s1` is not a constant expression because i2 is neither of primitive type nor of String type, hence it is computed at run-time and returns a non-pool String object "1:ONE".

As, str1 refers to String Pool object "1:ONE", hence `str1 == "1:ONE"` returns true, whereas str2 refers to non-Pool String object "1:ONE" and hence `str2 == "1:ONE"` returns false.

3.1.51 Answer: C

Reason:
`new StringBuilder(5);` creates a StringBuilder instance, whose internal char array's length is 5 but the internal char array's length is adjusted when characters are added/removed from the StringBuilder instance. `sb.append("0123456789");` successfully appends "0123456789" to the StringBuilder's instance referred by sb. delete method accepts 2 parameters: delete(int start, int end), where start is inclusive and end is exclusive.
This method throws StringIndexOutOfBoundsException for following scenarios:
A. start is negative

B. start is greater than sb.length()

C. start is greater than end

If end is greater than the length of StringBuilder object, then StringIndexOutOfBoundsException is not thrown and end is set to sb.length(). So, in this case, `sb.delete(8, 1000);` is equivalent to `sb.delete(8, sb.length());` and this deletes characters at 8th index (8) and 9th index (9). So remaining characters are: "01234567".

StringBuilder class overrides toString() method, which prints the text stored in StringBuilder instance. Hence, `System.out.println(sb);` prints 01234567 on to the console.

3.1.52   Answer: B

Reason:
In LocalDate.of(int, int, int) method, 1st parameter is year, 2nd is month and 3rd is day of the month.
toString() method of LocalDate class prints the LocalDate object in ISO-8601 format: "uuuu-MM-dd".

3.1.53   Answer: E

Reason:
date --> {2018-06-06}, date.minusDays(10); => as LocalDate is immutable, hence a new LocalDate object is created {2018-05-27} but no variable refers to it. date still refers to {2018-06-06}.
2018-06-06 is displayed on to the console.

3.1.54   Answer: C

Reason:
joiningDate --> {2006-03-16}. joiningDate.withDayOfYear(29) returns a new LocalDate object with the day of the Year altered.
A year has 365 days, so 29 means 29th day of the year, which is 29th Jan 2006.

NOTE: There are other with methods, you should know for the exam.
withDayOfMonth(int), withMonth(int) and withYear(int).

3.1.55 Answer: C

Reason:
Constructor of LocalDate is declared private so cannot be called from outside, hence
new LocalDate(2020, 2, 14); causes compilation failure.

Overloaded static methods "of" and "parse" are provided to create the instance of
LocalDate.
LocalTime, LocalDateTime, Period also specify private constructors and provide "of"
and "parse" methods to create respective instances.

3.1.56 Answer: D

Reason:
date --> {2000-06-25}. date.getDayOfMonth() = 25, 25 >= 20 is true, hence control
goes inside while loop and executes System.out.println(date); statement.

date.plusDays(-1); creates a new LocalDate object {2000-06-24} but date reference
variable still refers to {2000-06-25}. date.getDayOfMonth() again returns 25, this is an
infinite loop.

3.1.57 Answer: E

Reason:
LocalDate object doesn't contain time part but ISO_DATE_TIME looks for time portion
and throws exception at runtime.
For the OCA exam, you can check following DateTimeFormatter types:
BASIC_ISO_DATE, ISO_DATE, ISO_LOCAL_DATE, ISO_TIME, ISO_LOCAL_TIME,
ISO_DATE_TIME, ISO_LOCAL_DATE_TIME.

3.1.58 Answer: C

Reason:
There are 2 of methods available in LocalDate class: of(int, int, int) and of(int, Month, int). Month can either be passed as int value (1 to 12) or enum constants Month.JANUARY to Month.DECEMBER.

Period.parse(CharSequence) method accepts the String parameter in "PnYnMnD" format, over here P,Y,M and D can be in any case. "p-30000y" means Period of -30000 years.

The minimum supported LocalDate is: {-999999999-01-01} and maximum supported LocalDate is: {+999999999-12-31}. If period of -30000 years is added to 1st Jan 2000, then result is 1st Jan -28000.

3.1.59 Answer: D

Reason:
Before you answer this, you must know that there are 5 different Student object created in the memory (4 at the time of adding to the list and 1 at the time of removing from the list). This means these 5 Student objects will be stored at different memory addresses.

remove(Object) method removes the first occurrence of matching object and equals(Object) method decides whether 2 objects are equal or not. equals(Object) method has NOT been overridden by the Student class. In fact, equals(Student) is overloaded. But overloaded version is not invoked while equating the Student objects.

equals(Object) method defined in Object class is invoked and equals(Object) method defined in Object class uses == operator to check the equality and in this case as all the Student objects are stored at different memory location, hence not equal.

Nothing is removed from the students list, all the 4 Student objects are printed in the insertion order.

3.1.60 Answer: A

Reason:
In this example, code is trying to remove an item from the list while iterating using traditional for loop so one can think that this code would throw java.util.ConcurrentModificationException.

But note, java.util.ConcurrentModificationException will never be thrown for traditional for loop. It is thrown for for-each loop or while using Iterator/ListIterator.

In this case dryFruits.remove(new StringBuilder("Almond")); will never remove any items from the list as StringBuilder class doesn't override the equals(Object) method of Object class.

StringBuilder instances created at "dryFruits.add(new StringBuilder("Almond"));" and "dryFruits.remove(new StringBuilder("Almond"));" are at different memory locations and equals(Object) method returns false for these instances.

3.1.61 Answer: C

Reason:
list.add(true); => Auto-boxing converts boolean literal true to Boolean instance containing true. Element at index 0 represents true.

Boolean class code uses equalsIgnoreCase method to validate the passed String, so if passed String is "true" ('t', 'r', 'u' and 'e' can be in any case), then boolean value stored in Boolean object is true otherwise false.
list.add(new Boolean("tRue")); => Element at index 1 represents true.
list.add(new Boolean("abc")); => Element at index 2 represents false.
So initially list contains [true, true, false].
As generic list is used, so list.remove(1) removes the Boolean instance (true) stored at index 1 and returns it. So after this operation list contains [true, false].
For the boolean expression of if-block, Java runtime extracts the stored boolean value using booleanValue() method, which returns true. Control goes inside if-block and executes list.remove(1); This removes element at index 1 so after this operation list contains [true] and [true] is printed on to the console.

3.1.62 Answer: B

Reason:
list.add(0, "Array"); means list --> [Array],
list.set(0, "List"); means replace the current element at index 0 with the passed
element "List". So after this operation, list --> [List]. In the console, [List] is printed.

3.1.63 Answer: B

Reason:
There is no element at index 0 so call to add element at index 1, "trafficLight.add(1,
"RED");" throws an instance of java.lang.IndexOutOfBoundsException.

trafficLight.remove(new Integer(2)); matches with trafficLight.remove(Object) and
hence no compilation error.

3.1.64 Answer: B

Reason:
Generic type can only be reference type and not primitive type, hence List<int> is not
a valid syntax.

If you use raw type List or List<Object> then Line 3 will cause compilation error as
list.get(0) will return Object type. Object type cannot be converted to primitive type
int, so List and List<Object> will cause compilation failure of Line 3.
List<Integer> is the only correct option left.

3.1.65 Answer: A

Reason:
Even though code seems to be checking the knowledge of ArrayList but it actually
checks the knowledge of Polymorphism.

List<Sellable> list = new ArrayList<>(); is valid statement and list can accept any object
passing instanceof check for Sellable type.

Rabbit implements Sellable hence new Rabbit() can be added to list.

But as Mammal doesn't implement Sellable hence new Mammal() can't be added to list.
Other initializer blocks can be verified on similar lines. So there is only one initializer block, which causes compilation error.

3.1.66 Answer: D

Reason:
remove(Object) method of List interface removes the first occurrence of the specified element from the list, if it is present. If this list does not contain the element, it is unchanged. remove(Object) method returns true, if removal was successful otherwise false.

Initially list has: [apple, orange, grape, mango, banana, grape]. fruits.remove("grape") removes the first occurrence of "grape" and after the successful remove, list has: [apple, orange, mango, banana, grape]. fruits.remove("grape") returns true, control goes inside if block and executes fruits.remove("papaya");

fruits list doesn't have "papaya", so the list remain unchanged. In the console, you get: [apple, orange, mango, banana, grape].

3.1.67 Answer: D

Reason:
In the boolean expression (predicate.test(i)): i is of primitive int type but auto-boxing feature converts it to Integer wrapper type.

test(Integer) method of Predicate returns true if passed number is an odd number, so given loop prints only odd numbers. for loops works for the numbers from 1 to 10.

3.1.68 Answer: C

Reason:
removeIf(Predicate) method was added as a default method in Collection interface in JDK 8 and it removes all the elements of this collection that satisfy the given predicate.

Predicate's test method returns true for all the Integers divisible by 10.

3.1.69 Answer: D

Reason:
As list can store only wrapper objects and not primitives, hence for list.add(110); auto-boxing creates an Integer object {110}.

For list.add(new Integer(110)); as new keyword is used so another Integer object {110} is created.

For 3rd add method call, list.add(110); auto-boxing kicks in and as 110 is between -128 to 127, hence Integer object created at 1st statement is referred.

removeIf(Predicate) method was added as a default method in Collection interface in JDK 8 and it removes all the elements of this collection that satisfy the given predicate.

Boolean expression is : i == 110; in this expression i is wrapper object and 110 is int literal so java extracts int value of wrapper object, i and then equates. As all the 3 objects store 110, hence true is returned. All integer objects are removed form the list.

If list.removeIf(i -> i == new Integer(110)); was used, then all three list elements would return false as object references are equated and not contents.

3.1.70 Answer: D

Reason:
In the lambda expression's body, if used, all 3 [return, {}, ;] must be used together.

4 Practice Test - 4

4.1 70 questions covering all topics

4.1.1 For the code below, what should be the name of java file?

```java
public class HelloWorld {
    public static void main(String [] args) {
        System.out.println("Hello World!");
    }
}
```

A. Hello.java

B. World.java

C. HelloWorld.java

D. helloworld.java

4.1.2 What is the signature of special main method?

A. `public static void main(String args) {}`
B. `public static void main(String [] a) {}`
C. `public static void main() {}`
D. `private static void main(String [] args) {}`

4.1.3 Which of the following is the correct package declaration to declare Test class in com.exam.oca package?

A. `package com.exam.oca.Test;`
B. `package com.exam.oca;`
C. `package com.exam.oca.*;`
D. `Package com.exam.oca;`

4.1.4 Consider following code snippet:

```
package com.udayan.test;
public class Exam {
    public static void main(String [] args) {
        System.out.println("All the best!");
    }
}
```

Location of files:

```
D:.
└──WORK
    └──QUIZ
        └──SEC07
            ├──classes
            │   └──com
            │       └──udayan
            │           └──test
            │                   Exam.class
            │
            └──src
                └──com
                    └──udayan
                        └──test
                                Exam.java
```

You are currently at **WORK** folder.

D:\WORK>

Which of the following java command will show All the best! on to the console?

A. java Exam

B. java com.udayan.test.Exam

C. java -cp Quiz\Sec07\classes\com\udayan\test\ Exam

D. java -cp Quiz\Sec07\classes\ com.udayan.test.Exam

4.1.5   Consider below code:

```
public class Test {
    public static void main(String[] args) {
        System.out.println("ONE");
    }

    public static void main(Integer[] args) {
        System.out.println("TWO");
    }

    public static void main(byte [] args) {
        System.out.println("THREE");
    }
}
```

What will be the result if Test class is executed by below command?
java Test 10

A. TWO
B. ONE
C. THREE
D. Compilation error

4.1.6   What will be the result of compiling and executing Test class?

```
public class Test {
    public static void main(String[] args) {
        byte b1 = (byte) (127 + 21);
        System.out.println(b1);
    }
}
```

A. 148
B. Compilation error
C. -108
D. -128

4.1.7   Wrapper classes are defined in which of the following package?

A. java.util
B. java.lang
C. java.io
D. default package

4.1.8   Consider below code:

```java
public class Counter {
    int count;

    private static void increment(Counter counter) {
        counter.count++;
    }

    public static void main(String [] args) {
        Counter c1 = new Counter();
        Counter c2 = c1;
        Counter c3 = null;
        c2.count = 1000;
        increment(c2);
    }
}
```

On executing Counter class, how many Counter objects are created in the memory?

A. 1
B. 2
C. 3
D. 4

4.1.9 What will be the result of compiling and executing Test class?

```java
public class Test {
    public static void main(String[] args) {
        Boolean [] arr = new Boolean[2];
        System.out.println(arr[0] + ":" + arr[1]);
    }
}
```

A. NullPointerException is thrown at runtime

B. true:true

C. false:false

D. null:null

4.1.10 What will be the result of compiling and executing Test class?

```java
public class Test {
    public static void main(String[] args) {
        extractInt(2.7);
        extractInt(2);
    }

    private static void extractInt(Double obj) {
        System.out.println(obj.intValue());
    }
}
```

A.	2 2	B.	3 2
C.	Compilation error in main method	D.	Compilation error in extractInt method
E.	An exception is thrown at runtime		

4.1.11 What will be the result of compiling and executing Test class?

```
package com.udayan.oca;

public class Test {
    public static void main(String[] args) {
        String [] arr = {"abc", "TrUe", "false",
                                    null, "FALSE"};
        for(String s : arr) {
            System.out.print(Boolean.valueOf(s) ?
                                        "T" : "F");

        }
    }
}
```

A. FTFFF

B. FFFFF

C. TTFTT

D. TTTFT

E. NullPointerException is thrown at runtime

4.1.12 What will be the result of compiling and executing DivModTest class?

```
public class DivModTest {
    public static void main(String[] args) {
        System.out.println( 23 / 2.0 );
        System.out.println( 23 % 2.0 );
    }
}
```

A.	11 1	B.	11.5 1.0
C.	11.0 1.0	D.	11.5 0.0

4.1.13 What will be the result of compiling and executing Test class?

```
public class Test {
    public static void main(String[] args) {
        System.out.println(1 + 2 + 3 + 4 + "Hello");
    }
}
```

A. 10Hello

B. 1234Hello

C. 64Hello

D. 10 Hello

4.1.14 What will be the result of compiling and executing Test class?

```
public class Test {
    public static void main(String[] args) {
        int a = 7;
        boolean res = a++ == 7 && ++a == 9 || a++ == 9;
        System.out.println("a = " + a);
        System.out.println("res = " + res);
    }
}
```

A.	a = 10 res = true	B.	a = 9 res = true
C.	a = 10 res = false	D.	Compilation error

4.1.15 What will be the output of compiling and executing the Test class?

```
public class Test {
    public static void main(String[] args) {
        int a = 5;
        int x = 10;
        switch(x) {
            case 10:
                a *= 2;
            case 20:
                a *= 3;
            case 30:
                a *= 4;
        }
        System.out.println(a);
    }
}
```

A. 5

B. 10

C. 30

D. 120

4.1.16 For the class Test, which option, if used to replace /*INSERT*/, will print "Lucky no. 7" on to the console?

```
public class Test {
    public static void main(String[] args) {
        /*INSERT*/
        switch(var) {
            case '7':
                System.out.println("Lucky no. 7");
                break;
            default:
                System.out.println("DEFAULT");
        }
    }
}
```

A. int var = 7;

B. Integer var = 7;

C. int var = '7';

D. None of the other options

4.1.17 What will be the result of compiling and executing Test class?

```java
public class Test {
    public static void main(String [] args) {
        int a = 3;
        System.out.println(a++ == 3 || --a == 3 && --a ==
3);
    }
}
```

A. true

B. false

C. Compilation error

4.1.18 What will be the result of compiling and executing Test class?

```java
public class Test {
    public static void main(String [] args) {
        int a = 3;
        m(++a, a++);
        System.out.println(a);
    }

    private static void m(int i, int j) {
        i++;
        j--;
    }
}
```

A. 4

B. 5

C. 6

D. 3

4.1.19 What will be the result of compiling and executing Test class?

```java
public class Test {
    public static void main(String[] args) {
        char [][] arr = {
                {'A', 'B', 'C'},
                {'D', 'E', 'F'},
                {'G', 'H', 'I'}
        };

        for(int i = 0; i < arr.length; i++) {
            for(int j = 0; j < arr[i].length; j++) {
                System.out.print(arr[i][1]);
            }
            System.out.println();
        }
    }
}
```

A.	ABC DEF GHI	B.	BBB EEE HHH
C.	AAA DDD GGG	D.	CCC FFF III

4.1.20 What will be the result of compiling and executing Test class?

```java
public class Test {
    public static void main(String[] args) {
        int [] arr1 = {1, 2, 3};
        char [] arr2 = {'A', 'B'};
        //ASCII code of 'A' is 65, 'B' is 66
        arr1 = arr2;
        for(int i = 0; i < arr1.length; i++) {
            System.out.print(arr1[i] + " ");
        }
    }
}
```

A. 1 2 3

B. A B

C. 65 66

D. Compilation error

4.1.21 What will be the result of compiling and executing Test class?

```
public class Test {
    public static void main(String[] args) {
        String [] arr = {"A", "B", "C", "D"};
        arr[0] = arr[1];
        arr[1] = "E";
        for(String s : arr) {
            System.out.print(s + " ");
        }
    }
}
```

A. Compilation error

B. An exception is thrown at runtime

C. B E C D

D. E E C D

E. A E C D

4.1.22 Which of the following statement is correct for below code?

```
public class Test {
    public static void main(String[] args) {
        final boolean flag;
        flag = false;
        while(flag) {
            System.out.println("Good Morning!");
        }
    }
}
```

A. Program compiles and executes successfully but produces no output.

B. Compilation error.

C. Infinite loop.

D. It will print "Good Morning!" once.

4.1.23 Which of the following statement is correct about below code?

```java
public class Test {
    public static void main(String[] args) {
        do {
            System.out.println(100);
        } while (true);

        System.out.println("Bye");
    }
}
```

A.	Compiles successfully and prints "Bye"	B.	Compiles successfully and prints 100 in infinite loop
C.	Unreachable code compilation error	D.	100 Bye

4.1.24 What will be the result of compiling and executing Test class?

```java
public class Test {
    public static void main(String[] args) {
        int i;
        for(i=0; i<=2; i++){}
        System.out.println(i);
    }
}
```

A. 0

B. 2

C. 3

D. Compilation error

4.1.25 What will be the result of compiling and executing Test class?

```
public class Test {
    public static void main(String[] args) {
        int i;
        outer:
        do {
            i = 5;
            inner:
            while (true) {
                System.out.println(i--);
                if (i == 4) {
                    break outer;
                }
            }
        } while (true);
    }
}
```

A.	Prints 5 in an infinite loop	B.	Prints 5 once
C.	Compilation error	D.	5 3 2 1

4.1.26 Which of the following can be used as a constructor for the class given below?
```
public class Planet {

}
```

A. **public void** Planet(){}
B. **public void** Planet(**int** x){}
C. **public** Planet(String str) {}
D. None of the other options

239

4.1.27 **What will be the result of compiling and executing Greetings class?**

```java
public class Greetings {
    String msg = null;
    public Greetings() {
    }

    public Greetings(String str) {
        msg = str;
    }

    public void display() {
        System.out.println(msg);
    }

    public static void main(String [] args) {
        Greetings g1 = new Greetings();
        Greetings g2 = new Greetings("Good Evening!");
        g1.display();
        g1.display();
    }
}
```

A.	null Good Evening!	B.	null null
C.	Good Evening! null	D.	Compilation error

4.1.28 What will be the result of compiling and executing Test class?

```
public class Test {
    public static void print() {
        System.out.println("static method.");
    }

    public static void main(String[] args) {
        Test obj = null;
        obj.print();
    }
}
```

A. NullPointerException is thrown.

B. Compilation error.

C. static method.

D. None of the other options.

4.1.29 What will be the result of compiling and executing Wall class?

```
public class Wall {
    public static void main(String args[]) {
        double area = 5.7;
        String color;
        if (area < 7)
            color = "green";

        System.out.println(color);
    }
}
```

A. green

B. null

C. NullPointerException

D. Compilation error

4.1.30 What will be the result of compiling and executing Test class?

```java
public class Test {
    static String msg; //Line 2
    public static void main(String[] args) {
        String msg; //Line 4
        if(args.length > 0) {
            msg = args[0]; //Line 6
        }
        System.out.println(msg); //Line 8
    }
}
```

A. null
B. Line 2 causes compilation failure
C. Line 4 causes compilation failure
D. An exception is thrown at runtime by Line 6
E. Line 8 causes compilation failure

4.1.31 Consider below code:

```java
public class Test {

    private static void add(int i, int j) {
        System.out.println("int version");
    }

    private static void add(Integer i, Integer j) {
        System.out.println("Integer version");
    }

    public static void main(String[] args) {
        add(10, 20);
    }

}
```

Which modifications, done independently, print "Integer version" on to the console? Select 3 options.

A. Remove add(int i, int j) method declaration and definition.
B. Replace add(10, 20); by add(new Integer(10), new Integer(20));
C. Replace add(10, 20); by add(10.0, 20.0);
D. Replace add(10, 20); by add(null, null);

4.1.32 What will be the result of compiling and executing Test class?

```java
public class Test {

    private static void add(double d1, double d2) {
        System.out.println("double version: " + (d1 +
d2));
    }

    private static void add(Double d1, Double d2) {
        System.out.println("Double version: " + (d1 +
d2));
    }

    public static void main(String[] args) {
        add(10.0, new Double(10.0));
    }

}
```

A. Compilation error
B. double version: 20.0
C. Double version: 20.0
D. An exception is thrown at runtime

4.1.33 Consider the code of Test.java file:

```
package com.udayan.oca.test;

class Student {
    String name;
    int age;

    Student() {
        Student("James", 25);
    }

    Student(String name, int age) {
        this.name = name;
        this.age = age;
    }
}

public class Test {
    public static void main(String[] args) {
        Student s = new Student();
        System.out.println(s.name + ":" + s.age);
    }
}
```

There is a compilation error in the Student class.
Which modifications, done independently, print "James:25" on to the console?
Select 2 options.

A. Add below code in the Student class:
```
    void Student(String name, int age) {
        this.name = name;
        this.age = age;
    }
```
B. Replace Student("James", 25); with super("James", 25);
C. Replace Student("James", 25); with this("James", 25);
D. Replace Student("James", 25); with this.Student("James", 25);

4.1.34 What will be the result of compiling and executing Test class?

```
class A {
    A() {
        this(1);
        System.out.println("M");
    }

    A(int i) {
        System.out.println("N");
    }
}

class B extends A {

}

public class Test {
    public static void main(String[] args) {
        new B();
    }
}
```

A.	M	B.	N
C.	N M	D.	M N

4.1.35 What will be the result of compiling and executing Circus class?

```java
//Circus.java
class Animal {
    protected void jump() {
        System.out.println("Animal");
    }
}

class Cat extends Animal {
    public void jump(int a) {
        System.out.println("Cat");
    }
}

class Deer extends Animal {
    public void jump() {
        System.out.println("Deer");
    }
}

public class Circus {
    public static void main(String[] args) {
        Animal cat = new Cat();
        Animal deer = new Deer();
        cat.jump();
        deer.jump();
    }
}
```

A.	Animal Deer	B.	Cat Deer
C.	Animal Animal	D.	Cat Animal

4.1.36 Given the following definitions of the class Insect and the interface Flyable, the task is to declare a class Mosquito that inherits from the class Insect and implements the interface Flyable.

```
class Insect {}
interface Flyable {}
```

Select the correct option to accomplish this task:

A. class Mosquito implements Insect extends Flyable{}
B. class Mosquito implements Insect, Flyable{}
C. class Mosquito extends Insect implements Flyable{}
D. class Mosquito extends Insect, Flyable{}

4.1.37 Consider below code of Test.java file:

```
package com.udayan.oca;

class Document {
    int pages;
    Document(int pages) {
        this.pages = pages;
    }
}

class Word extends Document {
    String type;
    Word(String type) {
        super(20); //default pages
        /*INSERT-1*/
    }

    Word(int pages, String type) {
        /*INSERT-2*/
        super.pages = pages;
    }
}

public class Test {
    public static void main(String[] args) {
        Word obj = new Word(25, "TEXT");
```

```
        System.out.println(obj.type + "," + obj.pages);
    }
}
```

Currently above code causes compilation error.

Which of the options can successfully print TEXT,25 on to the console?

A.	Replace /*INSERT-1*/ with: `this(type);` Replace /*INSERT-2*/ with: `this.type = type;`	B.	Replace /*INSERT-1*/ with: `this.type = type;` Replace /*INSERT-2*/ with: `this(type);`
C.	Replace /*INSERT-1*/ with: `super.type = type;` Replace /*INSERT-2*/ with: `this(type);`	D.	Replace /*INSERT-1*/ with: `super.type = type;` Replace /*INSERT-2*/ with: `super(type);`
E.	None of the other options		

4.1.38 Consider codes below:

```
//A.java
package com.udayan.oca;

public class A {
    public void print() {
        System.out.println("A");
    }
}

//B.java
package com.udayan.oca;

public class B extends A {
    public void print() {
        System.out.println("B");
    }
}

//C.java
package com.udayan.oca;

public class C extends A {
    public void print() {
        System.out.println("C");
```

```
        }
    }

//Test.java
package com.udayan.oca.test;

import com.udayan.oca.*;

public class Test {
    public static void main(String[] args) {
        A obj1 = new C();
        A obj2 = new B();
        C obj3 = (C)obj1;
        C obj4 = (C)obj2;
        obj3.print();
    }
}
```

What will be the result of compiling and executing Test class?

A. A

B. B

C. C

D. Compilation error

E. ClassCastException is thrown at runtime

4.1.39 Predict Output, if the below code is run with given command?
java Test

```
public class Test {
    private static int [] arr;
    public static void main(String [] args) {
        if(arr.length > 0 && arr != null) {
            System.out.println(arr[0]);
        }
    }
}
```

A. Compilation error

B. No Output

C. NullPointerException is thrown at runtime

D. ArrayIndexOutOfBoundsException is thrown at runtime

4.1.40 What will be the result of compiling and executing Test class?

```java
import java.io.FileNotFoundException;
import java.io.IOException;

abstract class Super {
    public abstract void m1() throws IOException;
}

class Sub extends Super {
    @Override
    public void m1() throws IOException {
        throw new FileNotFoundException();
    }
}

public class Test {
    public static void main(String[] args) {
        Super s = new Sub();
        try {
            s.m1();
        } catch (FileNotFoundException e) {
            System.out.print("X");
        } catch (IOException e) {
            System.out.print("Y");
        } finally {
            System.out.print("Z");
        }
    }
}
```

A. XZ

B. YZ

C. XYZ

D. Compilation Error

4.1.41 What will be the result of compiling and executing Test class?

```java
public class Test {
    private static String s;
    public static void main(String[] args) {
        try {
            System.out.println(s.length());
        } catch (NullPointerException | RuntimeException
ex) {
            System.out.println("DONE");
        }
    }
}
```

A. DONE

B. Executes successfully but no output

C. Compilation error

D. None of the above

4.1.42 Given Code:

```java
import java.io.*;

class ReadTheFile {
    static void print() { //Line 4
        throw new IOException(); //Line 5
    }
}

public class Test {
    public static void main(String[] args) { //Line 10
        ReadTheFile.print(); //Line 11
        //Line 12
    }
}
```

Which 2 changes are necessary so that code compiles successfully?

A.	Replace Line 4 with: `static void print() throws Exception { //Line 4`
B.	Replace Line 4 with: `static void print() throws Throwable { //Line 4`

C.	```Replace Line 10 with:```
	`public static void main(String[] args) throws`
	`IOException { //Line 10`

D.	Surround Line 11 with below try-catch block:
	<pre>try {
	    ReadTheFile.print(); //Line 11
	} catch(IOException e) {
	    e.printStackTrace();
	}</pre>

E.	Surround Line 11 with below try-catch block:
	<pre>try {
	    ReadTheFile.print(); //Line 11
	} catch(IOException | Exception e) {
	    e.printStackTrace();
	}</pre>

F.	Surround Line 11 with below try-catch block:
	<pre>try {
	    ReadTheFile.print(); //Line 11
	} catch(Exception e) {
	    e.printStackTrace();
	}</pre>

4.1.43 Consider codes of 3 java files:

```
//Class1.java
package com.udayan.oca;

import java.io.FileNotFoundException;

public class Class1 {
    public void read() throws FileNotFoundException {}
}

//Class2.java
public class Class2 {
    String Class2;
    public void Class2() {}
}

//Class3.java
public class Class3 {
    private void print() {
        private String msg = "HELLO";
        System.out.println(msg);
    }
}
```

Which of the following statement is true?

A. Only Class1.java compiles successfully

B. Only Class2.java compiles successfully

C. Only Class3.java compiles successfully

D. Class1.java and Class2.java compile successfully

E. Class1.java and Class3.java compile successfully

F. Class2.java and Class3.java compile successfully

4.1.44 Consider below code:

```java
public class Test {
    static Double d1;
    int x = d1.intValue();

    public static void main(String[] args) {
        System.out.println("HELLO");
    }
}
```

On execution, does Test class print "HELLO" on to the console?

A. Yes, HELLO is printed on to the console

B. No, HELLO is not printed on to the console

4.1.45 Consider below code:

```java
package com.udayan.oca;

public class Test {
    public static void main(String[] args) {
        StringBuilder sb = new StringBuilder();
        try {
            for(;;) {
                sb.append("OCA");
            }
        } catch(Exception e) {
            System.out.println("Exception!!!");
        }
        System.out.println("Main ends!!!");
    }
}
```

What will be the result of compiling and executing Test class?

A. "Main ends!!!" is printed on to the console and program terminates successfully

B. "Exception!!!" and "Main ends!!!" are printed on to the console and program terminates successfully

C. "Exception!!!" is printed on to the console and program terminates successfully

D. "Exception!!!" is printed on to the console and program terminates abruptly

E. Program terminates abruptly

4.1.46 What will be the result of compiling and executing Test class?

```java
public class Test {
    public static void main(String[] args) {
        String fName = "James";
        String lName = "Gosling";
        System.out.println(fName = lName);
    }
}
```

A. Compilation error

B. false

C. true

D. None of the other options

4.1.47 Which of the method of String class is used to remove leading and trailing white spaces?

A. ltrim()

B. rtrim()

C. trim()

D. trimBoth()

4.1.48 What will be the result of compiling and executing Test class?

```
public class Test {
    public static void main(String[] args) {
        StringBuilder sb =
                new StringBuilder("Good"); //Line 3
        change(sb); //Line 4
        System.out.println(sb); //Line 5
    }

    private static void change(StringBuilder s) {
        s.append("_Morning"); //Line 9
    }
}
```

A. Good
B. _Morning
C. Good_Morning
D. None of the other options

4.1.49 How many String objects are there in the HEAP memory, when control is at Line 9?

```
public class Test {
    public static void main(String[] args) {
        String s1 = new String("Java"); //Line 3
        String s2 = "JaVa"; //Line 4
        String s3 = "JaVa"; //Line 5
        String s4 = "Java"; //Line 6
        String s5 = "Java"; //Line 7

        int i = 1; //Line 9

    }
}
```

A. 2
B. 3
C. 4
D. 5

4.1.50 Consider below code:

```
//Test.java
package com.udayan.oca;

public class Test {
    public static void main(String[] args) {
        String javaworld = "JavaWorld";
        String java = "Java";
        String world = "World";
        java += world;
        System.out.println(java == javaworld);
    }
}
```

What will be the result of compiling and executing Test class?

A. JavaWorld

B. Java

C. World

D. true

E. false

4.1.51 What will be the result of compiling and executing Test class?

```
package com.udayan.oca;

public class Test {
    public static void main(String[] args) {
        StringBuilder sb = new StringBuilder();
        System.out.println(sb.append("").append("")
                                    .append("").length());
    }
}
```

A. 0

B. 1

C. 2

D. 3

4.1.52 Consider below code:

```
//Test.java
import java.time.LocalDate;

public class Test {
    public static void main(String [] args) {
        LocalDate date = LocalDate.of(2068, 4, 15);
        System.out.println(date.getMonth() + ":"
                            + date.getMonthValue());
    }
}
```

What will be the result of compiling and executing Test class?

A. APRIL:3
B. APRIL:4
C. April:3
D. April:4

4.1.53 Consider below code:

```
//Test.java
import java.time.LocalDate;

public class Test {
    public static void main(String [] args) {
        LocalDate date1 = LocalDate.parse("1980-03-16");
        LocalDate date2 = LocalDate.parse("1980-03-16");
        System.out.println(date1.equals(date2)
                        + " : " + date1.isEqual(date2));
    }
}
```

What will be the result of compiling and executing Test class?

A. true : false
B. true : true
C. false : true
D. false : false

4.1.54 Consider below code:

```
//Test.java
import java.time.LocalTime;

public class Test {
    public static void main(String [] args) {
        LocalTime time = LocalTime.of(23, 60);
        System.out.println(time);
    }
}
```
What will be the result of compiling and executing Test class?

A. 23:60

B. 00:00

C. 00:01

D. Compilation error

E. An exception is thrown at runtime

4.1.55 Consider below code:

```
//Test.java
import java.time.Period;

public class Test {
    public static void main(String [] args) {
        Period period = Period.of(0, 1000, 0);
        System.out.println(period);
    }
}
```

What will be the result of compiling and executing Test class?

A. P0Y1000M0D

B. p0y1000m0d

C. P1000M

D. p1000m

4.1.56 Consider below code:

```
//Test.java
import java.time.LocalDate;

public class Test {
    public static void main(String [] args) {
        LocalDate obj = LocalDate.now();
        System.out.println(obj.getHour());
    }
}
```

Which of the following statement is correct?

A. Code fails to compile
B. Code compiles successfully but throws Runtime exception
C. It will print any int value between 0 and 23
D. It will print any int value between 1 and 24

4.1.57 Consider below code:

```
//Test.java
import java.time.LocalDate;
import java.time.format.DateTimeFormatter;

public class Test {
    public static void main(String [] args) {
        LocalDate date1 = LocalDate.parse("1947-08-15",
DateTimeFormatter.ISO_DATE);
        LocalDate date2 = LocalDate.parse("1947-08-15",
DateTimeFormatter.ISO_LOCAL_DATE);
        LocalDate date3 = LocalDate.of(1947, 8, 15);

        System.out.println(date1.equals(date2)
                    + " : " +
date2.equals(date3));
    }
}
```

What will be the result of compiling and executing Test class?

A. true : true

B. false : false

C. true : false

D. false : true

E. Runtime exception

4.1.58 DateTimeFormatter is defined inside which package?

A. java.time

B. java.util

C. java.text

D. java.time.format

4.1.59 Which of the following will give you current system time? Select 2 options.

A. `System.out.println(new LocalDate());`

B. `System.out.println(LocalDate.now());`

C. `System.out.println(new LocalTime());`

D. `System.out.println(LocalTime.now());`

E. `System.out.println(new LocalDateTime());`

F. `System.out.println(LocalDateTime.now());`

4.1.60 Consider below code:

```java
//Test.java
import java.util.ArrayList;
import java.util.List;

public class Test {
    public static void main(String[] args) {
        List<String> dryFruits = new ArrayList<>();
        dryFruits.add("Walnut");
        dryFruits.add("Apricot");
        dryFruits.add("Almond");
        dryFruits.add("Date");

        for(String dryFruit : dryFruits) {
            if(dryFruit.startsWith("A")) {
                dryFruits.remove(dryFruit);
            }
        }

        System.out.println(dryFruits);
    }
}
```

What will be the result of compiling and executing Test class?

A. [Walnut, Apricot, Almond, Date]
B. [Walnut, Date]
C. An exception is thrown at runtime
D. Compilation error

4.1.61 Consider below code:

```java
//Test.java
import java.util.ArrayList;
import java.util.List;

public class Test {
    public static void main(String[] args) {
        StringBuilder sb = new StringBuilder("Hello");
        List<StringBuilder> list = new ArrayList<>();
        list.add(sb);
        list.add(new StringBuilder("Hello"));
        list.add(sb);
        sb.append("World!");

        System.out.println(list);
    }
}
```

What will be the result of compiling and executing Test class?

A. [Hello, Hello, Hello]

B. [HelloWorld!, Hello, Hello]

C. [HelloWorld!, Hello, HelloWorld!]

D. [HelloWorld!, HelloWorld!, HelloWorld!]

4.1.62 Consider below code:

```java
//Test.java
import java.util.ArrayList;
import java.util.List;

public class Test {
    public static void main(String[] args) {
        Boolean [] arr = new Boolean[2];
        List<Boolean> list = new ArrayList<>();
        list.add(arr[0]);
        list.add(arr[1]);

        if(list.remove(0)) {
            list.remove(1);
        }

        System.out.println(list);
    }
}
```

What will be the result of compiling and executing Test class?

A. Compilation error

B. ArrayIndexOutOfBoundsException is thrown at runtime

C. NullPointerException is thrown at runtime

D. [true]

E. [false]

F. []

4.1.63 Consider below code:

```java
//Test.java
import java.util.ArrayList;
import java.util.List;

public class Test {
    public static void main(String[] args) {
        List<String> list = new ArrayList<>(4);
        list.add(0, "Array");
        list.add(2, "List");

        System.out.println(list);
    }
}
```

What will be the result of compiling and executing Test class?

A. [Array, List]

B. [Array, null, List, null]

C. An exception is thrown at runtime

D. Compilation error

4.1.64 Consider below code:

```java
import java.util.ArrayList;
import java.util.List;

public class Test {
    public static void main(String[] args) {
        List<String> days = new ArrayList<>();
        days.add("SUNDAY");
        days.add("SUNDAY");
        days.add("MONDAY");
        System.out.println(days.size());
        days.clear();
        System.out.println(days.size());
    }
}
```

What will be the result of compiling and executing Test class?

A.	3 3	B.	3 0
C.	2 0	D.	An exception is thrown at runtime

4.1.65   Consider code of Test.java file:

```java
import java.util.ArrayList;
import java.util.List;

public class Test {
    public static void main(String[] args) {
        List<Character> list = new ArrayList<>();
        list.add(0, 'V');
        list.add('T');
        list.add(1, 'E');
        list.add(3, 'O');

        if(list.contains('O')) {
            list.remove(3);
        }

        for(char ch : list) {
            System.out.print(ch);
        }
    }
}
```

What will be the result of compiling and executing Test class?

A.	Compilation error	B.	Runtime exception
C.	VET	D.	VTE
E.	VTEO	F.	VETO

4.1.66 Below is the code of Test.java file:

```java
import java.util.ArrayList;
import java.util.List;

abstract class Animal {}
class Dog extends Animal{}

public class Test {
    public static void main(String [] args) {
        List<Animal> list = new ArrayList<Dog>();
        list.add(0, new Dog());
        System.out.println(list.size() > 0);
    }
}
```

What will be the result of compiling and executing Test class?

A. true

B. false

C. Compilation error

D. Runtime exception

4.1.67 **What will be the result of compiling and executing Test class?**

```java
import java.util.ArrayList;
import java.util.List;

public class Test {
    public static void main(String[] args) {
        List<String> fruits = new ArrayList<>();
        fruits.add("apple");
        fruits.add("orange");
        fruits.add("grape");
        fruits.add("mango");
        fruits.add("banana");
        fruits.add("grape");

        if(fruits.remove("grape"))
            fruits.remove("apple");

        System.out.println(fruits);
    }
}
```

A. An exception is thrown at runtime

B. Compilation error

C. [orange, mango, banana, grape]

D. [orange, grape, mango, banana]

4.1.68 What will be the result of compiling and executing Test class?

```java
import java.util.function.Predicate;

public class Test {
    public static void main(String[] args) {
        String [] arr = {"*", "**", "***", "****",
                                            "*****",
"******"};
        Predicate<String> pr1 = s -> s.length() < 4;
        print(arr, pr1);
    }

    private static void print(String [] arr,
                            Predicate<String> predicate) {
        for(String str : arr) {
            if(predicate.test(str)) {
                System.out.println(str);
            }
        }
    }
}
```

A.	`****`
	`*****`
	`******`
		B.	`*`
			`**`
			`***`

C.	`*`
	`**`
	`***`
	`****`
		D.	`*`
			`**`
			`***`
			`****`
			`*****`
			`******`

4.1.69 Which of the following method is declared in Predicate<T> interface?

A. **boolean** `verify(T t);`
B. **boolean** `check(T t);`
C. **boolean** `test(T t);`
D. **boolean** `validate(T t);`

4.1.70 What will be the result of compiling and executing Test class?

```java
import java.util.ArrayList;
import java.util.List;

public class Test {
    public static void main(String[] args) {
        Integer i = 10;
        List<Integer> list = new ArrayList<>();
        list.add(i);
        list.add(new Integer(i));
        list.add(i);

        list.removeIf(i -> i == 10);

        System.out.println(list);
    }
}
```

A. [10, 10, 10]
B. [10, 10]
C. [10]
D. []
E. Compilation Error

4.2 Answers to Practice Test - 4 with Explanation

4.1.1 Answer: C

Reason:
Java is case sensitive language. File name should match with public class's name, which is "HelloWorld".
"helloworld" is different from "HelloWorld".

4.1.2 Answer: B

Reason:
Special main method should have public access specifier and it takes argument of String [] type. String [] argument can use any identifier name, even though in most of the cases you will see "args" is used.

4.1.3 Answer: B

Reason:
To declare Test class in com.exam.oca package, use following declaration:
package com.exam.oca;
No wildcard (*) allowed in package declaration. Don't include class name in package declaration. NOTE: all small case letters in package keyword.

4.1.4 Answer: D

Reason:
To execute Exam class from WORK folder, you should specify the classpath (Quiz\Sec07\classes\) which contains whole path of the class(com\udayan\test\Exam.class). And you should also use fully qualified name of the class, which is com.udayan.test.Exam.
Hence correct option is: java -cp Quiz\Sec07\classes\ com.udayan.test.Exam

4.1.5 Answer: B

Reason:
Like any other method, main method can also be overloaded. But main method called by JVM is always with String [] parameter. Don't get confused with 10 as it is passed as "10". Run above class with any command line arguments or 0 command line argument, output will always be ONE.

4.1.6 Answer: C

Reason:
127 + 21 = 148 = 00000000 00000000 00000000 10010100
Above binary number is +ve, as left most bit is 0.
Same binary number after type-casting to byte: 10010100, negative number as left most bit is 1.
10010100 = -108.

4.1.7 Answer: B

Reason:
All the wrapper classes are defined in java.lang package. String and StringBuilder are also defined in java.lang package and that is why import statement is not required to use these classes.

4.1.8 Answer: A

Reason:
new Counter(); is invoked only once, hence only one Counter object is created in the memory. c1, c2, c3 and counter are reference variables of Counter type and not Counter objects.

4.1.9   Answer: D

Reason:
Array elements are initialized to their default values. arr is referring to an array of Boolean type, which is reference type and hence both the array elements are initialized to null and hence in the output null:null is printed.

4.1.10 Answer: C

Reason:
extractInt method accepts argument of Double type.

extractInt(2.7); => 2.7 is double literal, so Java compiler would box it into Double type. At runtime obj.intValue() would print int portion of the Double data, which is 2.

extractInt(2); => Java compiler either does implicit casting or Wrapping but not both. 2 is int literal, Java compiler can't implicit cast it to double and then box it to Double. So this statement causes compilation failure.

4.1.11 Answer: A

Reason:
Boolean.valueOf(String s) returns true if passed String argument is not null and is equal, ignoring case, to the String "true". In all other cases it returns false.
Boolean.valueOf("abc") => false. As "abc".equalsIgnoreCase("true") is false.
Boolean.valueOf("TrUe") => true. As "TrUe".equalsIgnoreCase("true") is true.
Boolean.valueOf("false") => false. As "false".equalsIgnoreCase("true") is false.
Boolean.valueOf(null) => false. As passed argument is null.
Boolean.valueOf("FALSE") => false. As "FALSE".equalsIgnoreCase("true") is false.

4.1.12 Answer: B

Reason:
As floating point numbers are used in the expression, hence result should be in floating point number.
Correct result is:

23 / 2.0 = 11.5
23 % 2.0 = 1.0

4.1.13 Answer: A

Reason:

As expression contains + operator only, which is left to right associative. Let us group the expression.

1 + 2 + 3 + 4 + "Hello"
= (1 + 2) + 3 + 4 + "Hello"
= ((1 + 2) + 3) + 4 + "Hello"
= (((1 + 2) + 3) + 4) + "Hello"
[Let us solve it now,]
= ((3 + 3) + 4) + "Hello"
= (6 + 4) + "Hello"
= 10 + "Hello"
[+ operator with String behaves as concatenation operator.]
= 10Hello

4.1.14 Answer: B

Reason:

boolean res = a++ == 7 && ++a == 9 || a++ == 9;
= (a++) == 7 && ++a == 9 || (a++) == 9;
= (a++) == 7 && (++a) == 9 || (a++) == 9;
= ((a++) == 7) && ((++a) == 9) || ((a++) == 9);
= ((a++) == 7) && ((++a) == 9) || ((a++) == 9);
= (((a++) == 7) && ((++a) == 9)) || ((a++) == 9);
= ((7 == 7) && ((++a) == 9)) || ((a++) == 9); //a = 8
= (true && ((++a) == 9)) || ((a++) == 9); //a = 8
= (true && (9 == 9)) || ((a++) == 9); //a = 9
= (true && true) || ((a++) == 9); //a = 9
= true || ((a++) == 9); //a = 9
= true; //a = 9
So,
a = 9
res = true

4.1.15 Answer: D

Reason:
Matching case block "case 10:" is found, a *= 2; is executed, which means a = a * 2; =>
a = 5 * 2; => a = 10;
No break statement, hence it enters in fall-through.
a *= 3; is executed, which means a = a * 3; => a = 10 * 3; => a = 30;
a *= 4; is executed, which means a = a * 4; => a = 30 * 4; => a = 120;

4.1.16 Answer: C

Reason:
int var = 7; => DEFAULT,
Integer var = 7; => var is of Integer type and case contains char '7'. char '7' cannot be
compared with Integer and hence compilation error. case '7' can easily be compared
with int value but not with Integer type.
int var = '7'; => Lucky no. 7

HINT: There is no need to remember. case '7' value means you are trying to equate or
compare var (Integer value) with '7' (char). If assignment operation works then
method invocation, switch expression parameter etc. will also work. Integer var = 7; is
possible but Integer var = '7'; causes compilation error as char cannot be converted to
Integer.

4.1.17 Answer: A

Reason:
a++ == 3 || --a == 3 && --a == 3; [Given expression].
(a++) == 3 || --a == 3 && --a == 3; [Postfix has got higher precedence than other
operators].
(a++) == 3 || (--a) == 3 && (--a) == 3; [After postfix, precedence is given to prefix].
((a++) == 3) || ((--a) == 3) && ((--a) == 3); [== has higher precedence over && and ||].
((a++) == 3) || (((--a) == 3) && ((--a) == 3)); [&& has higher precedence over ||].
Let's start solving it:
((a++) == 3) || (((--a) == 3) && ((--a) == 3)); [a=3, res=false].

(3 == 3) || (((--a) == 3) && ((--a) == 3)); [a=4, res=false].
true || (((--a) == 3) && ((--a) == 3)); [a=4, res=false]. || is a short-circuit operator,
hence no need to evaluate expression on the right.
res is true and a is 4.

4.1.18   Answer: B

Reason:
This example is on pass-by-value scheme and very simple to solve. Method m will
work on copies and changes done to i and j are local to method m only.
m(++a, a++); [a=3].
m(4, a++); [a=4].
m(4, 4); [a=5].

System.out.println(a); => Prints 5 on to the console.

4.1.19   Answer: B

Reason:
NOTE: System.out.print statement is printing arr[i][1],
which means it prints 2nd array element of a particular row, for each iteration of inner
loop.
That is why output is:
BBB
EEE
HHH
To get all the array elements printed correctly, use arr[i][j] in System.out.print
statement.

4.1.20   Answer: D

Reason:
Initially arr1 refers to an int array object of 3 elements: 1, 2, 3
And arr2 refers to an char array object of 2 elements: 'A', 'B'.
Statement arr1 = arr2; causes compilation error as char [] is not compatible with int []
even though char is compatible with int.

4.1.21 Answer: C

Reason:
arr[0] -> "A" and arr[1] -> "B".
arr[0] = arr[1]; => arr[0] -> "B" and arr[1] -> "B".
arr[1] = "E"; => arr[0] -> "B" and arr[1] -> "E".
Hence output is: B E C D

4.1.22 Answer: A

Reason:
final boolean flag; flag = false; doesn't make flag a compile time constant.
Compiler doesn't know flag's value at compile-time and hence it allows this syntax.
At runtime, as boolean expression of while loop is false, loop doesn't execute even
once and hence no output.

4.1.23 Answer: C

Reason:
Boolean expression of do-while loop uses literal true (compile-time constant), hence
Java compiler knows that this loop is an infinte loop.
It also knows that once at runtime Java Control enters an infinite loop, none of the
statements after loop block will get executed.
Hence it marks all the codes after infinite loop as Unreachable Code, which results in
compilation error.
If boolean variable was used instead of boolean literal, then this program would have
compiled and executed successfully.

```java
public class DoWhileTest1 {
    public static void main(String[] args) {
        boolean flag = true;
        do {
            System.out.println(100);
        } while (flag);

        System.out.println("Bye");
```

```
    }
}
```

Above program prints 100 in infinite loop and "Bye" never gets printed.

4.1.24 Answer: C

Reason:
There is nothing inside loop body, hence loop body is blank.
This loop executes 3 times, for i = 0, i = 1 and i = 2. For i = 3, control goes out of the for loop.
Now, as i is declared outside for loop, hence it is accessible outside loop body.
System.out.println(i); prints 3 to the console.

4.1.25 Answer: B

Reason:
"outer" and "inner" are valid label names.
On execution, control enters main method and creates int variable i.
On encountering do-while loop, control goes inside and initializes variable i to 5.
Then it executes while loop and it's boolean expression is always true.
System.out.println(i--); prints 5 to the console first, and then decrements the value of i by 1. So, i becomes 4.
Boolean expression of if(i == 4) evaluates to true. break outer; statement executes and takes the control out of do-while loop.
main method ends and program terminates successfully.
So, 5 gets printed only once.

4.1.26 Answer: C

Reason:
Constructor has the same name as the class, doesn't have return type and can accept parameters.

4.1.27   Answer: B

Reason:
Greetings g1 = new Greetings(); invokes no-argument constructor. Property msg (of object referred by g1) is assigned to null.
Greetings g2 = new Greetings("Good Evening!"); invokes parameterized constructor, which assigns "Good Evening!" to msg of object referred by g2.
g1.display(); prints null
Again we have same call g1.display(); which prints null.
NOTE: We haven't called display() on object referred by g2.

4.1.28   Answer: C

Reason:
print() is static method of class Test. So correct syntax to call method print() is Test.print();
but static methods can also be invoked using reference variable: obj.print(); Warning is displayed in this case.
Even though obj has null value, we don't get NullPointerException as objects are not needed to call static methods.

4.1.29   Answer: D

Reason:
color is LOCAL variable and it must be initialized before it can be used.
As area is not compile time constant, java compiler doesn't have an idea of the value of variable area.
There is no else block available as well.

So compiler cannot be sure of whether variable color will be initialized or not. So it causes compilation error at System.out.println(color);

4.1.30 Answer: E

Reason:
Line 4 code shadows the variable at Line 2. msg variable created at Line 4 is a local variable and should be initialized before it is used.
Initialization code is inside if-block, so compiler is not sure about msg variable's initialization. Hence, Line 8 causes compilation failure.

4.1.31 Answer: A,B,D

Reason:
Method add is overloaded in Test class. Which overloaded method is invoked is decided at the compile time. add(10, 20); tags to int version as 10, 20 are int literals and direct match is available. So without any changes, above code prints "int version" on to the console.

To print "Integer version" on to the console, add(Integer, Integer); method needs to be invoked. Let's check all the options one by one:
"Remove add(int i, int j) method declaration and definition." add(10, 20); => auto-boxing will convert literal 10 and 20 to Integer instances and will call the add(Integer, Integer) method. So this option is valid.

Replace add(10, 20); by add(new Integer(10), new Integer(20)); => This statement is specifically calling add(Integer, Integer); So this option is also valid.

Replace add(10, 20); by add(10.0, 20.0); 10.0 and 20.0 are default literals and can't be mapped to int or Integer types, hence this causes compilation error. Not a valid option.

Replace add(10, 20); by add(null, null); As Integer is reference type hence add(null, null); maps to add(Integer, Integer); So this is also valid option.

4.1.32 Answer: A

Reason:
add(10.0, new Double(10.0)); is an ambiguous call as compiler can't decide whether to convert 1st argument to Double reference type or 2nd argument to double primitive type. So, add(10.0, new Double(10.0)); causes compilation error.

4.1.33 Answer: A,C

Reason:
First find out the reason for compilation error, all the options are giving hint :)

No-argument constructor of Student class calling another overloaded constructor by the name and this causes compilation error. This problem can be fixed in 2 ways:
1st one: replace Student("James", 25); with this("James", 25) OR 2nd one: add void Student(String, int) method in the Student class.

Method can have same name as the class name and constructor can call other methods.

4.1.34 Answer: C

Reason:
Default constructor added by Java compiler in B class is:
B() {
    super();
}

On executing new B(); statement, class B's default constructor is invoked, which invokes no-argument constructor of class A [super();].

No-argument constructor of class A invokes parameterized constructor of class A [this(1);].

N is printed first and after that M is printed.

4.1.35 Answer: A

Reason:
Cat class doesn't override the jump() method of Animal class, in fact jump(int) method is overloaded in Cat class.
Deer class overrides jump() method of Animal class.

Reference variable cat is of Animal type, cat.jump() syntax is fine and as Cat doesn't override jump() method hence Animal version is invoked, which prints Animal to the console.

Even though reference variable deer is of Animal type but at runtime deer.jump(); invokes overriding method of Deer class, this prints Deer to the console.

4.1.36 Answer: C

Reason:
A class in Java extends class and implements interface.

4.1.37 Answer: B

Reason:
Java compiler adds super(); as the first statement inside constructor, if call to another constructor using this(...) or super(...) is not available.
Compiler adds super(); as the first line in Word's constructor: Word(int pages, String type) { super(); } but Document class doesn't have a no-argument constructor and that is why Word's constructor `Word(int pages, String type)` causes compilation error.

Word(String) constructor is actually not setting the passed type argument. Replace /*INSERT-1*/ with: `this.type = type;` will set the value to type variable.

As the first statement inside Word(int pages, String type){} constructor, you can either have `super(pages);` or `this(type);` but not both.
Replacing /*INSERT-2*/ with `super(pages);` will be redundant as in the next statement `super.pages = pages;`, pages variable of Document class is set. Hence, replacing /*INSERT-2*/ with `this(type);` is needed to set the type variable.

4.1.38 Answer: E

Reason:
Class A, B and C are declared public and inside same package com.udayan.oca.
Method print() of class A has correctly been overridden by B and C.
print() method is public so no issues in accessing it anywhere.

Let's check the code inside main method.
A obj1 = new C(); => obj1 refers to an instance of C class, it is polymorphism.
A obj2 = new B(); => obj2 refers to an instance of B class, it is polymorphism.
C obj3 = (C)obj1; => obj1 actually refers to an instance of C class, so at runtime obj3 (C type) will refer to an instance of C class. As obj1 is of A type so explicit typecasting is necessary.
C obj4 = (C)obj2; => obj2 actually refers to an instance of B class, so at runtime obj4 (C type) will refer to an instance of B class. B and C are siblings and can't refer to each other, so this statement will throw ClassCastException at runtime.

4.1.39 Answer: C

Reason:
Variable arr is a class variable of int [] type, so by default it is initialized to null.
In if block, arr.length > 0 is checked first. Accessing length property on null reference throws NullPointerException.

Correct logical if block declaration should be:
if(arr != null && arr.length > 0)

First check for null and then access properties/methods.

4.1.40 Answer: A

Reason:
Even though method m1() declares to throw IOException but at runtime an instance of FileNotFoundException is thrown.
A catch handler for FileNotFoundException is available and hence X is printed on to the console.

After that finally block is executed, which prints Z to the console.

4.1.41 Answer: C

Reason:
NullPointerException extends RuntimeException and in multi-catch syntax we can't specify multiple Exceptions related to each other in multilevel inheritance.

4.1.42 Answer: A,F

Reason:
This question is tricky as 2 changes are related and not independent. Let's first check the reason for compilation error. Line 5 throws a checked exception, IOException but it is not declared in the throws clause. So, print method should have throws clause for IOException or the classes in top hierarchy such as Exception or Throwable.

Based on this deduction, Line 4 can be replaced with either "static void print() throws Exception {" or "static void print() throws Throwable" but we will have to select one out of these as after replacing Line 4, Line 11 will start giving error as we are not handling the checked exception at Line 11.

This part is easy, do we have other options, which mention "Throwable"? NO. Then mark the first option as "Replace Line 4 with static void print() throws Exception {".

As, print() method throws Exception, so main method should handle Exception or its super type and not it's subtype. Two options working only with IOException can be ruled out.

Multi-catch statement "catch(IOException | Exception e)" causes compilation error as IOException and Exception are related to each other in multilevel inheritance. So you are left with only one option to pair with our 1st choice:
Surround Line 11 with below try-catch block:
try {
    ReadTheFile.print();
} catch(Exception e) {
    e.printStackTrace();

```
}
```

4.1.43 Answer: D

Reason:
Method declaring checked exception in its throws clause doesn't mean that it should have code to actually throw that type of Exceptions. So even though read() method of Class1 declares to throw FileNotFoundException but its body doesn't actually throw an instance of FileNotFoundException.

Variable and method name can be same as class name, so code of Class2 is also valid. Remember: Though you don't get any compilation error but it is not recommended to use the Class name for variable and method names.

LOCAL variable can be declared with final modifier only. msg variable inside print() method of Class3 is declared private and this causes compilation error.

4.1.44 Answer: A

Reason:
To invoke the special main method, JVM loads the class in the memory. At that time, static fields of Test class are initialized. d1 is of Double type so null is assigned to it.

x is not static variable, so int x = d1.intValue(); is not executed. Class is loaded successfully in the memory and "HELLO" is printed on to the console.

NOTE: new Test() will throw NullPointerException but not ExceptionInInitializerError.

4.1.45 Answer: E

Reason:
for(;;) is an infinite loop and hence `sb.append("OCA");` causes OutOfMemoryError which is a subclass of Error class. main(String []) method throws OutOfMemoryError and program terminates abruptly.

4.1.46 Answer: D

Reason:
Both fName and lName are of reference type. fName refers to "James" and lName refers to "Gosling".
In System.out.println() statement, we have used assignment operator (=) and not equality operator (==). So result is never boolean.
fName = lName means copy the contents of lName to fName.
As lName is referring to "Gosling" and so after the assignment, fName starts referring to "Gosling" as well.
System.out.println() finally prints the String referred by fName, which is "Gosling".
This option is is not available, hence correct answer is "None of the other options".

4.1.47 Answer: C

Reason:
ltrim(), rtrim() and trimBoth() are not defined in String class. trim() method is used for removing leading and trailing white spaces.

4.1.48 Answer: C

Reason:
When change method is called, both variable s and sb refers to same StringBuilder object.
Line 9 modifies the passed object and appends "_Morning" to it. As a result s now refers to "Good_Morning" and sb also refers to "Good_Morning" so when control goes back to calling method main(String[]) Line 5 prints "Good_Morning" on to the console.

4.1.49 Answer: B

Reason:
String s1 = new String("Java"); -> Creates 2 objects: 1 String Pool and 1 non-pool. s1 refers to non-pool object.
String s2 = "JaVa"; -> Creates 1 String pool object and s2 refers to it.
String s3 = "JaVa"; -> Doesn't create a new object, s3 refers to same String pool object referred by s2.

String s4 = "Java"; -> Doesn't create a new object, s4 refers to String Pool object created at Line 3.

String s5 = "Java"; -> Doesn't create a new object, s5 also refers to String Pool object created at Line 3.

So, at Line 9, 3 String objects are available in the HEAP memory: 2 String pool and 1 non-pool.

4.1.50   Answer: E

Reason:

Please note that Strings computed by concatenation at compile time, will be referred by String Pool during execution. Compile time String concatenation happens when both of the operands are compile time constants, such as literal, final variable etc. Whereas, Strings computed by concatenation at run time (if the resultant expression is not constant expression) are newly created and therefore distinct.

`java += world;` is same as `java = java + world;` and `java + world` is not a constant expression and hence is calculated at runtime and returns a non pool String object "JavaWorld", which is referred by variable 'java'.

On the other hand, variable 'javaworld' refers to String Pool object "JavaWorld". As both the variables 'java' and 'javaworld' refer to different String objects, hence `java == javaworld` returns false.

4.1.51   Answer: A

Reason:

As "" is empty string, hence nothing is appended to the StringBuilder instance and length() method returns 0.

4.1.52   Answer: B

Reason:

date.getMonth() returns the month of the year filed, using Month enum, all the enum constant names are in upper case.

date.getMonthValue() returns the value of the month.

NOTE: month value starts with 1 and it is different from java.util.Date API, where month value starts with 0.

4.1.53 Answer: B

Reason:
Both the methods "public boolean isEqual(ChronoLocalDate)" and "public boolean equals(Object)" return true if date objects are equal otherwise false.

NOTE: LocalDate implements ChronoLocalDate.

4.1.54 Answer: E

Reason:
LocalTime.of(int hour, int minute) creates an instance of LocalTime class. Valid value for hour is: 0 to 23 and valid value for minute is 0 to 59.

java.time.DateTimeException is thrown if invalid values are passed as arguments.

NOTE: There are other overloaded of methods available:
LocalTime of(int hour, int minute, int second) and
LocalTime of(int hour, int minute, int second, int nanoOfSecond).

Valid value for second is: 0 to 59 and valid value for nano second is: 0 to 999,999,999.

4.1.55 Answer: C

Reason:
Check the toString() method of Period class. ZERO period is displayed as P0D, other than that, Period components (year, month, day) with 0 values are ignored.

toString()'s result starts with P, and for non-zero year, Y is appended; for non-zero month, M is appended; and for non-zero day, D is appended. P,Y,M and D are in upper case.

NOTE: Period.parse(CharSequence) method accepts the String parameter in "PnYnMnD" format, over here P,Y,M and D can be in any case.

4.1.56 Answer: A

Reason:
LocalDate.now(); retrieves the current date from the system clock. There is no issue with this statement.

obj is of LocalDate type and getHour() method is not defined in LocalDate class, it is defined in LocalTime and LocalDateTime class. Hence obj.getHour() causes compilation failure.

4.1.57 Answer: A

Reason:
ISO_LOCAL_DATE formatter formats the date without the offset, such as "1947-08-15".
ISO_DATE formatter formats the date with offset (if available), such as "1947-08-15" or "1947-08-15+05:30", but remember LocalDate object doesn't contain any offset information.
In this case, all the three date instances are meaningfully equal.

For the OCA exam, you can check following DateTimeFormatter types:
BASIC_ISO_DATE, ISO_DATE, ISO_LOCAL_DATE, ISO_TIME, ISO_LOCAL_TIME, ISO_DATE_TIME, ISO_LOCAL_DATE_TIME.

4.1.58 Answer: D

Reason:
DateTimeFormatter is a part of "java.time.format" package, whereas LocalDate, LocalTime, LocalDateTime and Period are defined inside "java.time" package.

4.1.59 Answer: D,F

Reason:
new LocalDate(), new LocalTime() and new LocalDateTime() cause compilation error as constructor of these classes are declared private.
System.out.println(LocalDate.now()); => Prints current date only.
System.out.println(LocalTime.now()); => Prints current time only.
System.out.println(LocalDateTime.now()); => Prints current date and time both.

4.1.60 Answer: C

Reason:
ConcurrentModificationException exception may be thrown for following condition:
1. Collection is being iterated using Iterator/ListIterator or by using for-each loop.
And
2. Execution of Iterator.next(), Iterator.remove(), ListIterator.previous(), ListIterator.set(E) & ListIterator.add(E) methods. These methods may throw java.util.ConcurrentModificationException in case Collection had been modified by means other than the iterator itself, such as Collection.add(E) or Collection.remove(Object) or List.remove(int) etc.

PLEASE NOTE: for-each loop internally implements Iterator and invokes hasNext() and next() methods.

For the given code, 'dryFruits' list is being iterated using for-each loop (internally as an Iterator).
hasNext() method of Iterator has following implementation:
public boolean hasNext() {
    return cursor != size;
}
Where cursor is the index of next element to return and initially it is 0.

1st Iteration: cursor = 0, size = 4, hasNext() returns true. iterator.next() increments the cursor by 1 and returns "Walnut".
2nd Iteration: cursor = 1, size = 4, hasNext() returns true. iterator.next() increments the cursor by 1 and returns "Apricot". As "Apricot" starts with "A", hence

dryFruits.remove(dryFruit) removes "Apricot" from the list and hence reducing the list's size by 1, size becomes 3.
3rd Iteration: cursor = 2, size = 3, hasNext() returns true. iterator.next() method throws java.util.ConcurrentModificationException.

If you want to successfully remove the items from ArrayList, while using Iterator or ListIterator, then use Iterator.remove() or ListIterator.remove() method and NOT List.remove(...) method. Using List.remove(...) method while iterating the list (using the Iterator/ListIterator or for-each) may throw java.util.ConcurrentModificationException.

4.1.61 Answer: C

Reason:
ArrayList's 1st and 3rd items are referring to same StringBuilder instance referred by sb [sb --> {Hello}] and 2nd item is referring to another instance of StringBuilder.

sb.append("World!"); means sb --> {HelloWorld!}, which means 1st and 3rd items of ArrayList now refers to StringBuilder instance containing HelloWorld!

In the output, [HelloWorld!, Hello, HelloWorld!] is printed.

4.1.62 Answer: C

Reason:
Default values are assigned to all array elements. As Boolean is of reference type, hence arr[0] = null and arr[1] = null. After addition list contains [null, null].

list.remove(0) removes and returns the Boolean object referring to null. If expression can specify Boolean type, so no compilation error over here. At this point list contains [null].

For the boolean expression of if-block, Java runtime tries to extract the stored boolean value using booleanValue() method, and this throws an instance of NullPointerException as booleanValue() method is invoked on null reference.

4.1.63 Answer: C

Reason:
ArrayList are different than arrays, though behind the scene ArrayList uses Object[] to store its elements.

There are 2 things related to ArrayList, one is capacity and another is actual elements stored in the list, returned by size() method. If you don't pass anything to the ArrayList constructor, then default capacity is 10 but this doesn't mean that an ArrayList instance will be created containing 10 elements and all will be initialized to null.

In fact, size() method will still return 0 for this list. This list still doesn't contain even a single element. You need to use add method or its overloaded counterpart to add items to the list. Even if you want to add null values, you should still invoke some methods, nothing happens automatically.

In this question, new ArrayList<>(4); creates an ArrayList instance which can initially store 4 elements but currently it doesn't store any data.

Another point you should remember for the certification exam: Addition of elements in ArrayList should be continuous. If you are using add(index, Element) method to add items to the list, then index should be continuous, you simply can't skip any index.

In this case, list.add(0, "Array"); adds "Array" to 0th index. so after this operation list --> [Array]. You can now add at 0th index (existing elements will be shifted right) or you can add at index 1 but not at index 2. list.add(2, "List"); throws an instance of java.lang.IndexOutOfBoundsException.

4.1.64 Answer: B

Reason:
ArrayList can have duplicate elements, so after addition, list is: [SUNDAY, SUNDAY, MONDAY]. days.size() returns 3 so 3 is printed on to the console.
days.clear(); removes all the elements from the days list, in fact days list will be empty after successful execution of days.clear();
So 2nd System.out.println statement prints 0 on to the console.

4.1.65   Answer: C

Reason:
list.add(0, 'V'); => char 'V' is converted to Character object and stored as the first element in the list. list --> [V].

list.add('T'); => char 'T' is auto-boxed to Character object and stored at the end of the list. list --> [V,T].

list.add(1, 'E'); => char 'E' is auto-boxed to Character object and inserted at index 1 of the list, this shifts T to the right. list --> [V,E,T].

list.add(3, 'O'); => char 'O' is auto-boxed to Character object and added at index 3 of the list. list --> [V,E,T,O].

list.contains('O') => char 'O' is auto-boxed to Character object and as Character class overrides equals(String) method this expression returns true. Control goes inside if-block and executes: list.remove(3);.

list.remove(3); => Removes last element of the list. list --> [V,E,T].

for(char ch : list) => First list item is Character object, which is auto-unboxed and assigned to ch. This means in first iteration ch = 'V'; And after this it is simple enhanced for loop. Output is VET.

4.1.66   Answer: C

Reason:
List is super type and ArrayList is sub type, hence List l = new ArrayList(); is valid syntax.

Animal is super type and Dog is sub type, hence Animal a = new Dog(); is valid syntax. Both depicts Polymorphism.

But in generics syntax, Parameterized types are not polymorphic, this means ArrayList<Animal> is not super type of ArrayList<Dog>. Remember this point. So below syntaxes are not allowed:

ArrayList<Animal> list = new ArrayList<Dog>(); OR List<Animal> list = new ArrayList<Dog>();

4.1.67 Answer: C

Reason:
remove(Object) method of List interface removes the first occurrence of the specified element from the list, if it is present. If this list does not contain the element, it is unchanged. remove(Object) method returns true, if removal was successful otherwise false.

Initially list has: [apple, orange, grape, mango, banana, grape]. fruits.remove("grape") removes the first occurrence of "grape" and after the successful remove, list has: [apple, orange, mango, banana, grape]. fruits.remove("grape") returns true, control goes inside if block and executes fruits.remove("apple");

fruits list contains "apple", so after the removal list has: [orange, mango, banana, grape].

4.1.68 Answer: B

Reason:
Lambda expression for Predicate is: s -> s.length() < 4. This means return true if passed string's length is < 4.
So first three array elements are printed.

4.1.69 Answer: C

Reason:
Single abstract method declared in Predicate<T> interface is boolean test(T t);

NOTE: If you are confused, then check other questions on Predicate and from there you will know about the method declared in Predicate interface.

4.1.70 Answer: E

Reason:
Variable "i" used in lambda expression clashes with another local variable "i" and hence causes compilation error.

5 Bonus Exam - 1

5.1 72 questions covering all topics

5.1.1 Consider below code of Test.java file:

```
package com.udayankhattry.oca;

public class Test {
    public static void main(String[] args) {
        boolean flag = false;
        do {
            if(flag = !flag) { //Line n1
                System.out.print(1); //Line n2
                continue; //Line n3
            }
            System.out.print(2); //Line n4
        } while(flag); //Line n5
    }
}
```

What will be the result of compiling and executing Test class?

A. 1

B. 2

C. 12

D. 21

E. 212

F. 121

G. 112

H. 221

I. Compilation error

5.1.2 Given code of Test.java file:

```
package com.udayankhattry.oca;

interface X1 {
    default void print() {
        System.out.println("X1");
    }
}

interface X2 extends X1 {
    void print();
}

interface X3 extends X2 {
    default void print() {
        System.out.println("X3");
    }
}

class X implements X3 {}

public class Test {
    public static void main(String[] args) {
        X1 obj = new X();
        obj.print();
    }
}
```

Which of the following statements is correct?

A. interface X1 fails to compile
B. interface X2 fails to compile
C. interface X3 fails to compile
D. class X fails to compile
E. class Test fails to compile
F. class Test compiles successfully and on execution prints X1 on to the console
G. class Test compiles successfully and on execution prints X3 on to the console

5.1.3 Given code of Test.java file:

```
package com.udayankhattry.oca;

class M {
    public void main(String[] args) { //Line n1
        System.out.println("M");
    }
}

class N extends M {
    public static void main(String[] args) { //Line n2
        new M().main(args); //Line n3
    }
}

public class Test {
    public static void main(String[] args) {
        N.main(args); //Line n4
    }
}
```

Which of the following statements is true for above code?

A. Line n1 causes compilation error

B. Line n2 causes compilation error

C. Line n3 causes compilation error

D. Line n4 causes compilation error

E. It executes successfully and prints M on to the console

5.1.4 Consider below code snippet available in the same package:

```
abstract class Traveller {
    void travel(String place){}
}

abstract class BeachTraveller extends Traveller {
    /*INSERT*/
}
```

Which of the following declarations/definitions can replace /*INSERT*/ such that there is no compilation error?
Select ALL that apply.

A. `abstract void travel();`

B. `abstract void travel(String beach);`

C. `public abstract void travel();`

D. `public void travel() throws RuntimeException {}`

E. `public void travel(String beach) throws Exception {}`

F. `void travel(String beach) throws java.io.IOException {}`

G. `public void travel(Object obj) {}`

5.1.5 Given code of Test.java file:

```
package com.udayankhattry.oca;

import java.util.ArrayList;
import java.util.List;

public class Test {
    public static void main(String[] args) {
        List<StringBuilder> list = new ArrayList<>();
        list.add(new StringBuilder("AAA")); //Line n1
        list.add(new StringBuilder("BBB")); //Line n2
        list.add(new StringBuilder("AAA")); //Line n3

        list.removeIf(sb -> sb.equals(
                new StringBuilder("AAA"))); //Line n4
        System.out.println(list);
    }
}
```

What will be the result of compiling and executing Test class?

A. [AAA, BBB, AAA]

B. [BBB, AAA]

C. [BBB]

D. []

E. None of the other options

5.1.6   Consider below code of Test.java file:

```
package com.udayankhattry.oca;

public class Test {
    public static void main(String[] args) {
        boolean flag1 = "Java" ==
                        "Java".replace('J', 'J'); //Line n1
        boolean flag2 = "Java" ==
                        "Java".replace("J", "J"); //Line n2
        System.out.println(flag1 && flag2);
    }
}
```

What will be the result of compiling and executing Test class?

A. Line n1 causes compilation error
B. Line n2 causes compilation error
C. true
D. false

5.1.7   Consider below code of Test.java file:

```
package com.udayankhattry.oca;

import java.util.ArrayList;
import java.util.List;

public class Test {
    public static void main(String[] args) {
        List<String> list = new ArrayList<>();
        list.add("P");
        list.add("O");
        list.add("T");

        List<String> subList = list.subList(1, 2); //Line n1
        subList.set(0, "E"); //Line n2
        System.out.println(list);
    }
}
```

What will be the result of compiling and executing Test class?

A. [P, E, T]
B. [P, O, T]
C. Compilation error
D. An exception is thrown by Line n2

5.1.8   Consider below codes of 3 java files:

```
//Super.java
package com.udayankhattry.oca;

public interface Super {
    String name = "SUPER";  //Line n1
}
```

```
//Sub.java
package com.udayankhattry.oca;

public interface Sub extends Super {  //Line n2

}
```

```
//Test.java
package com.udayankhattry.oca;

public class Test {
    public static void main(String[] args) {
        Sub sub = null;
        System.out.println(sub.name);  //Line n3
    }
}
```

Which of the following statements is correct?

A. Line n1 causes compilation error
B. Line n2 causes compilation error
C. Line n3 causes compilation error
D. Line n3 throws an exception at runtime
E. Test class compiles successfully and on execution prints SUPER on to the console

5.1.9   java.sql.SQLException extends java.lang.Exception
        and
        java.sql.SQLWarning extends java.sql.SQLException

Given code of Test.java file:

```
package com.udayankhattry.oca;

import java.sql.*;

interface Multiplier {
    void multiply(int... x) throws SQLException;
}

class Calculator implements Multiplier {
    public void multiply(int... x) throws /*INSERT*/ {

    }
}
public class Test {
    public static void main(String[] args) {
        try {
            Multiplier obj = new Calculator(); //Line n1
            obj.multiply(1, 2, 3);
        } catch(SQLException e) {
            System.out.println(e);
        }
    }
}
```

Which of the options can be used to replace /*INSERT*/ such that there is no compilation error?
Select ALL that apply.

A. java.io.IOException

B. SQLException

C. SQLWarning

D. Throwable

E. RuntimeException

F. Error

G. Exception

H. NullPointerException

5.1.10 **Consider below code of Test.java file:**

```
package com.udayankhattry.oca;

class Shape {
    int side = 0; //Line n1

    int getSide() { //Line n2
        return side;
    }
}

class Square extends Shape {
    private int side = 4; //Line n3

    protected int getSide() { //Line n4
        return side;
    }
}

public class Test {
    public static void main(String[] args) {
        Shape s = new Square();
        System.out.println(s.side + ":" + s.getSide());
    }
}
```

What will be the result of compiling and executing above code?

A. Compilation error at Line n3

B. Compilation error at Line n4

C. 0:0

D. 0:4

E. 4:4

F. 4:0

5.1.11 Given code of Test.java file:

```
package com.udayankhattry.oca;

import java.sql.SQLException;

public class Test {
    private static void availableSeats()
                            throws SQLException {
        throw null; //Line 7
    }

    public static void main(String[] args) {
        try {
            availableSeats(); //Line 12
        } catch(SQLException e) {
            System.out.println("SEATS NOT AVAILABLE");
        }
    }
}
```

What will be the result of compiling and executing Test class?

A. SEATS NOT AVAILABLE is printed on to the console and program terminates successfully

B. Program ends abruptly

C. Line 7 causes compilation failure

D. Line 12 causes compilation failure

5.1.12 Given code of Test.java file:

```
package com.udayankhattry.oca;

import java.io.IOException;

class Parent {
    Parent() throws IOException {
        System.out.print("HAKUNA");
    }
}

class Child extends Parent {
    Child() throws Exception {
        System.out.println("MATATA");
    }
}

public class Test {
    public static void main(String[] args) throws Exception {
        new Child();
    }
}
```

What will be the result of compiling and executing Test class?

A. Compilation error in both Parent and Child classes

B. Compilation error only in Parent class

C. Compilation error only in Child class

D. Test class executes successfully and prints HAKUNAMATATA on to the console

E. Test class executes successfully and prints MATATAHAKUNA on to the console

5.1.13 Given code of Test.java file:

```
package com.udayankhattry.oca;

class Parent {
    int var = 1000; // Line n1

    int getVar() {
        return var;
    }
}

class Child extends Parent {
    private int var = 2000; // Line n2

    int getVar() {
        return super.var; //Line n3
    }
}

public class Test {
    public static void main(String[] args) {
        Child obj = new Child(); // Line n4
        System.out.println(obj.var); // Line n5
    }
}
```

There is a compilation error in the code.
Which three modifications, done independently, print 1000 on to the console?

A. Change Line n1 to `private int var = 1000;`
B. Delete the Line n2
C. Change Line n3 to `return var;`
D. Change Line n4 to `Parent obj = new Child();`
E. Delete the method getVar() from the Child class
F. Change Line n5 to `System.out.println(obj.getVar());`

5.1.14 Consider the code of Test.java file:

```
package com.udayankhattry.oca;

public class Test {
    private static void m(int i) {
        System.out.print(1);
    }

    private static void m(int i1, int i2) {
        System.out.print(2);
    }

    private static void m(char... args) {
        System.out.print(3);
    }

    public static void main(String... args) {
        m('A');
        m('A', 'B');
        m('A', 'B', 'C');
        m('A', 'B', 'C', 'D');
    }
}
```

What will be the result of compiling and executing Test class?

A. Above code causes compilation error

B. It compiles successfully and on execution prints 3333 on to the console

C. It compiles successfully and on execution prints 1233 on to the console

D. It compiles successfully and on execution prints 1333 on to the console

5.1.15 Given code of Test.java file:

```
package com.udayankhattry.oca;

class Car {
    void speed(Byte val) { //Line n1
        System.out.println("DARK"); //Line n2
    } //Line n3

    void speed(byte... vals) {
        System.out.println("LIGHT");
    }
}

public class Test {
    public static void main(String[] args) {
        byte b = 10; //Line n4
        new Car().speed(b); //Line n5
    }
}
```

Which of the following needs to be done so that LIGHT is printed on to the console?

A. No changes are required as given code prints LIGHT on execution
B. Delete Line n1, Line n2 and Line n3
C. Replace Line n4 with `byte... b = 10;`
D. Replace Line n5 with `new Car().speed((byte...)b);`

5.1.16 Consider below code of Circle.java file:

```
package com.udayankhattry.oca;

public class Circle {
    private double radius;

    public Circle(double radius) {
        this.radius = radius;
    }

    public double getArea() {
        return Math.PI * radius * radius;
    }
}
```

User must be allowed to read and change the value of radius field. What needs to be done so that all the classes can read/change the value of radius field and Circle class is well encapsulated as well?

A.
Nothing needs to be done

B.
Change radius declaration from `private double radius;` to `double radius;`

C.
Change radius declaration from `private double radius;` to `protected double radius;`

D.
Change radius declaration from `private double radius;` to `public double radius;`

E.
Add below 2 methods in Circle class:
```
public double getRadius() {
    return radius;
}

public void setRadius(double radius) {
    this.radius = radius;
}
```

F.
Add below 2 methods in Circle class:
```
protected double getRadius() {
    return radius;
}

protected void setRadius(double radius) {
    this.radius = radius;
}
```

5.1.17 Consider below code of Test.java file:

```
package com.udayankhattry.oca;

import java.time.LocalDate;

public class Test {
    public static void main(String [] args) {
        LocalDate date = LocalDate.parse("1983-06-30");
        System.out.println(date.plusMonths(8));
    }
}
```

What is the result?

A. 1983-02-30

B. 1983-02-29

C. 1983-02-28

D. 1984-02-30

E. 1984-02-29

F. 1984-02-28

G. An exception is thrown at runtime

5.1.18 Consider below code fragment:

```
package com.udayankhattry.oca;

abstract class Food {
    protected abstract double getCalories();
}

class JunkFood extends Food {
    double getCalories() {
        return 200.0;
    }
}
```

Which 3 modifications, done independently, enable the code to compile?

A. Make the getCalories() method of Food class public

B. Remove the protected access modifier from the getCalories() method of Food class

C. Make the getCalories() method of Food class private

D. Make the getCalories() method of JunkFood class protected

E. Make the getCalories() method of JunkFood class public

F. Make the getCalories() method of JunkFood class private

5.1.19 Given code of Test.java file:

```
package com.udayankhattry.oca;

class Base {
    static void print() { //Line n1
        System.out.println("BASE");
    }
}

class Derived extends Base {
    static void print() { //Line n2
        System.out.println("DERIVED");
    }
}

public class Test {
    public static void main(String[] args) {
        Base b = null;
        Derived d = (Derived) b; //Line n3
        d.print(); //Line n4
    }
}
```

Which of the following statements is true for above code?

A. Line n2 causes compilation error

B. Line n3 causes compilation error

C. Line n4 causes compilation error

D. Code compiles successfully and on execution Line n3 throws an exception

E. Code compiles successfully and on execution prints BASE on to the console

F. Code compiles successfully and on execution prints DERIVED on to the console

5.1.20 Consider below code of Test.java file:

```java
package com.udayankhattry.oca;

public class Test {
    static int i1 = 10;
    int i2 = 20;

    int add() {
        return this.i1 + this.i2; //Line n1
    }

    public static void main(String[] args) {
        System.out.println(new Test().add()); //Line n2
    }
}
```

What will be the result of compiling and executing Test class?

A. It executes successfully and prints 30 on to the console
B. It executes successfully and prints 20 on to the console
C. It executes successfully and prints 10 on to the console
D. Line n1 causes compilation error
E. Line n2 causes compilation error

5.1.21 Consider below code of Test.java file:

```java
package com.udayankhattry.oca;

public class Test {
    public static void main(String[] args) {
        String[] arr = { "L", "I", "V", "E" }; //Line n1
        int i = -2;

        if (i++ == -1) { //Line n2
            arr[-(--i)] = "F"; //Line n3
        } else if (--i == -2) { //Line n4
            arr[-++i] = "O"; //Line n5
        }

        for(String s : arr) {
            System.out.print(s);
        }
    }
```

```
        }
    }
```

What will be the result of compiling and executing Test class?

A. Compilation error
B. An exception is thrown at runtime
C. LIVE
D. LIFE
E. LIVO
F. LOVE
G. LIOE

5.1.22 Given code of Test.java file:

```
package com.udayankhattry.oca;

import java.io.IOException;
import java.sql.SQLException;

public class Test {
    public static void main(String[] args) {
        /*INSERT*/
    }

    private static void save() throws IOException {}

    private static void log() throws SQLException {}
}
```

Which of the block of codes can be used to replace /*INSERT*/ such that there is no compilation error?

Select ALL that apply.

A.
```
try {
    save();
    log();
} catch(IOException | SQLException ex) {}
```

B.
```
try {
    save();
    log();
} catch(SQLException | IOException ex) {}
```

C.
```
try {
    save();
    log();
} catch(IOException | Exception ex) {}
```

D.
```
try {
    save();
    log();
} catch(SQLException | Exception ex) {}
```

E.
```
try {
    save();
    log();
} catch(Exception | RuntimeException ex) {}
```

F.
```
try {
    save();
    log();
} catch(Exception ex) {}
```

5.1.23 **Given code of Test.java file:**

```
public class Test {
    public static void main(String[] args) {
        try {
            try {
                System.out.println(args[1]); //Line n1
            } catch(RuntimeException e) {
                System.out.print("INHALE-"); //Line n2
                throw e; //Line n3
            } finally {
                System.out.print("EXHALE-"); //Line n4
            }
        } catch(RuntimeException e) {
            System.out.print("INHALE-"); //Line n5
        } finally {
            System.out.print("EXHALE"); //Line n6
        }
    }
}
```

And the commands:
```
javac Test.java
java Test
```

What is the result?

A. INHALE-EXHALE

B. INHALE-EXHALE-

C. INHALE-EXHALE-INHALE-

D. INHALE-EXHALE-EXHALE

E. INHALE-EXHALE-INHALE-EXHALE

5.1.24 Consider below code of Test.java file:

```
package com.udayankhattry.oca;

public class Test {
    public static void main(String[] args) {
        String [][] arr = { {"%", "$$"},
                            {"***", "@@@@", "#####"}};
        for(String [] str : arr) {
            for(String s : str) {
                System.out.println(s);
                if(s.length() == 4) //Line n1
                    break; //Line n2
            }
            break; //Line n3
        }
    }
}
```

What will be the result of compiling and executing Test class?

A.	%	B.	% $$
C.	% $$ ***	D.	% $$ *** @@@@
E.	% $$ *** @@@@ #####		

5.1.25 Consider below code snippet:

```
interface ILog {
    default void log() {
        System.out.println("ILog");
    }
}

abstract class Log {
    public static void log() {
        System.out.println("Log");
    }
}

class MyLogger extends Log implements ILog {}
```

Which of the following statements is correct?

A. There is no compilation error in the above code
B. There is a compilation error in interface ILog
C. There is a compilation error in abstract class Log
D. There is a compilation error in MyLogger class

5.1.26 Consider below code of main.java file:

```
package main;

public class main {
    static String main = "ONE";

    public main() {
        System.out.println("TWO");
    }

    public static void main(String [] args) {
        main();
    }

    public static void main() {
        System.out.println(main);
    }
}
```

Also consider below statements:

1. Code doesn't compile
2. Code compiles successfully
3. Only ONE will be printed to the console
4. Only TWO will be printed to the console
5. Both ONE and TWO will be printed to the console

How many of the above statements is/are true?

A. One statement
B. Two statements
C. Three statements

5.1.27   Consider below code of Test.java file:

```
package com.udayankhattry.oca;

public class Test {
    public static void main(String[] args) {
        P p = new R(); //Line n1
        System.out.println(p.compute("Go")); //Line n2
    }
}

class P {
    String compute(String str) {
        return str + str + str;
    }
}

class Q extends P {
    String compute(String str) {
        return super.compute(str.toLowerCase());
    }
}

class R extends Q {
    String compute(String str) {
        return super.compute(str.replace('o',
                'O')); //2nd argument is uppercase O
    }
}
```

What will be the result of compiling and executing Test class?

A. gOgOgO
B. gogogo
C. GoGoGo
D. GOGOGO
E. Go
F. GO
G. go

5.1.28   Given code of Test.java file:

```
package com.udayankhattry.oca;

public class Test {
    private static void div() {
        System.out.println(1/0);
    }

    public static void main(String[] args) {
        try {
            div();
        } finally {
            System.out.println("FINALLY");
        }
    }
}
```

What will be the result of compiling and executing Test class?

A. FINALLY is printed to the console and program ends normally
B. FINALLY is printed to the console, stack trace is printed and then program ends normally
C. FINALLY is printed to the console, stack trace is printed and then program ends abruptly
D. Compilation error

5.1.29 Consider below codes of 3 java files:

```java
//M.java
package com.udayankhattry.oca;

public class M {
    public void printName() {
        System.out.println("M");
    }
}


//N.java
package com.udayankhattry.oca;

public class N extends M {
    public void printName() {
        System.out.println("N");
    }
}


//Test.java
package com.udayankhattry.oca.test;

import com.udayankhattry.oca.*;

public class Test {
    public static void main(String[] args) {
        M obj1 = new M();
        N obj2 = (N)obj1;
        obj2.printName();
    }
}
```

What will be the result of compiling and executing Test class?

A. It executes successfully and prints M on to the console

B. It executes successfully and prints N on to the console

C. Compilation error

D. An exception is thrown at runtime

5.1.30 Consider below code of Test.java file:

```
package com.udayankhattry.oca;

public class Test {
    public static void main(String[] args) {
        StringBuilder sb = new StringBuilder("TOMATO");
        System.out.println(sb.reverse().
                               replace("O", "A")); //Line n1
    }
}
```

What will be the result of compiling and executing Test class?

A. TOMATO

B. TAMATO

C. TAMATA

D. OTAMOT

E. OTAMAT

F. ATAMAT

G. Compilation error

5.1.31 Consider below code of Test.java file:

```
package com.udayankhattry.oca;

import java.util.ArrayList;
import java.util.List;

public class Test {
    public static void main(String[] args) {
        List<Integer> list = new ArrayList<>();
        byte b = 10;
        list.add(b); //Line n1
        int mul = list.get(0) * list.get(0); //Line n2
        System.out.println(mul);
    }
}
```

What will be the result of compiling and executing Test class?

A. Line n1 causes compilation error

B. Line n2 causes compilation error

C. An exception is thrown at runtime

D. 10

E. 100

5.1.32 Consider below code of Test.java file:

```
package com.udayankhattry.oca;

public class Test {
    public static void main(String[] args) {
        String word = "REBUS";
        /* INSERT */
        System.out.println(word);
    }
}
```

Following options are available to replace /*INSERT*/:

1. `word = word.substring(2);`

2. `word = word.substring(2, 4);`

3. `word = word.substring(2, 5);`

4. `word = word.replace("RE", "");`

5. `word = word.substring(2, 6);`

6. `word = word.delete(0, 2);`

How many of the above options can be used to replace /*INSERT*/ (separately and not together) such that given command prints BUS on to the console?

A. One option only

B. Two options only

C. Three options only

D. Four options only

E. Five options only

F. All 6 options

5.1.33 Given code of Test.java file:

```
package com.udayankhattry.oca;

public class Test {
    private static void div(int i, int j) {
        try {
            System.out.println(i / j);
        } catch(ArithmeticException e) {
            Exception ex = new Exception(e);
            throw ex;
        }
    }
    public static void main(String[] args) {
        try {
            div(5, 0);
        } catch(Exception e) {
            System.out.println("END");
        }
    }
}
```

What will be the result of compiling and executing Test class?

A. Compilation error
B. END is printed and program terminates successfully
C. END is printed and program terminates abruptly
D. END is not printed and program terminates abruptly

5.1.34 Consider below codes of 3 java files:

```
//Shrinkable.java
package com.udayankhattry.oca;

public interface Shrinkable {
    public static void shrinkPercentage() {
        System.out.println("80%");
    }
}
```

```
//AntMan.java
package com.udayankhattry.oca;

public class AntMan implements Shrinkable { }
```

```
//Test.java
package com.udayankhattry.oca;

public class Test {
    public static void main(String[] args) {
        AntMan.shrinkPercentage();
    }
}
```

Which of the following statements is correct?

A. There is a compilation error in Shrinkable.java file

B. There is a compilation error in AntMan.java file

C. There is a compilation error in Test.java file

D. There is no compilation error and on execution, Test class prints 80% on to the console

5.1.35   Given code of Test.java file:

```
package com.udayankhattry.oca;

import java.sql.SQLException;

public class Test {
    private static void checkData() throws SQLException {
        try {
            throw new SQLException();
        } catch (Exception e) {
            e = null; //Line 10
            throw e; //Line 11
        }
    }

    public static void main(String[] args) {
        try {
            checkData(); //Line 17
        } catch(SQLException e) {
            System.out.println("NOT AVAILABLE");
        }
```

```
        }
}
```

What will be the result of compiling and executing Test class?

A. NOT AVAILABLE is printed on to the console and program terminates successfully
B. Program ends abruptly
C. Line 10 causes compilation failure
D. Line 11 causes compilation failure
E. Line 17 causes compilation failure

5.1.36 Consider below code of Test.java file:

```
package com.udayankhattry.oca;

public class Test {
    public static void main(String [] args) {
        int a = 3;
        int b = 5;
        int c = 7;
        int d = 9;
        boolean res = --a + --b < 1 && c++ + d++ > 1;
        System.out.printf("a = %d, b = %d, c = %d,
                d = %d, res = %b", a, b, c, d, res);
    }
}
```

What will be the result of compiling and executing Test class?

A. a = 2, b = 4, c = 7, d = 9, res = false
B. a = 2, b = 4, c = 8, d = 10, res = false
C. a = 2, b = 4, c = 7, d = 9, res = true
D. a = 2, b = 4, c = 8, d = 10, res = true
E. a = 3, b = 5, c = 8, d = 10, res = false
F. a = 3, b = 5, c = 8, d = 10, res = true

5.1.37 Consider below codes of 4 java files:

```
//Moveable.java
package com.udayankhattry.oca;

public interface Moveable {
    void move();
}
```

```
//Animal.java
package com.udayankhattry.oca;

public abstract class Animal {
    void move() {
        System.out.println("ANIMAL MOVING");
    }
}
```

```
//Dog.java
package com.udayankhattry.oca;

public class Dog extends Animal implements Moveable {}
```

```
//Test.java
package com.udayankhattry.oca;

public class Test {
    public static void main(String[] args) {
        Moveable moveable = new Dog();
        moveable.move();
    }
}
```

Which of the following statements is correct?

A. There is a compilation error in Animal.java file

B. There is a compilation error in Dog.java file

C. There is a compilation error in Test.java file

D. There is no compilation error and on execution, Test class prints ANIMAL MOVING on to the console

5.1.38   Consider below code of Test.java file:

```
package com.udayankhattry.oca;

class A {
    public String toString() {
        return null;
    }
}

public class Test {
    public static void main(String[] args) {
        String text = null;
        text = text + new A(); //Line n1
        System.out.println(text.length()); //Line n2
    }
}
```

What will be the result of compiling and executing Test class?

A. Line n1 causes compilation error

B. Line n1 causes Runtime error

C. Line n2 causes Runtime error

D. 0

E. 4

F. 8

5.1.39   Below is the code of Test.java file:

```
package com.udayankhattry.oca;

public class Test {
    /* INSERT */
}
```

Below are the definitions of main method:

```
1.
public static final void main(String... a) {
    System.out.println("Java Rocks!");
}
```

2.
```
public void main(String... args) {
    System.out.println("Java Rocks!");
}
```

3.
```
static void main(String [] args) {
    System.out.println("Java Rocks!");
}
```

4.
```
public static void main(String [] args) {
    System.out.println("Java Rocks!");
}
```

5.
```
public static void main(String args) {
    System.out.println("Java Rocks!");
}
```

How many definitions of main method can replace /* INSERT */ such that on executing Test class, "Java Rocks!" is printed on to the console?

A. Only one definition
B. Only two definitions
C. Only three definitions
D. Only four definitions
E. All 5 definitions

5.1.40 **Range of short data type is from -32768 to 32767**

Which of the following code segments, written inside main method will compile successfully?

Select ALL that apply.

A.	`short s1 = 10;`	B.	`short s2 = 32768;`
C.	`final int i3 = 10;` `short s3 = i3;`	D.	`final int i4 = 40000;` `short s4 = i4;`

E.	`final int i5 = 10;`
	`short s5 = i5 + 100;`
		F.	`final int m = 25000;`
			`final int n = 25000;`
			`short s6 = m + n;`

G.	`int i7 = 10;` `short s7 = i7;`		

5.1.41 **Consider below codes of 2 java files:**

```
//Counter.java
package com.udayankhattry.oca;

public interface Counter {
    int count = 10; //Line n1
}

//Test.java
package com.udayankhattry.oca;

public class Test {
    public static void main(String[] args) {
        Counter [] arr = new Counter[2]; //Line n2
        for(Counter ctr : arr) {
            System.out.print(ctr.count); //Line n3
        }
    }
}
```

Which of the following statements is correct?

A. Only Line n1 causes compilation error

B. Only Line n2 causes compilation error

C. Line n1 and Line n2 cause compilation error

D. Only Line n3 causes compilation error

E. Line n3 throws an exception at runtime

F. Test class compiles successfully and on execution prints 1010 on to the console

5.1.42 Consider below statements:

```
1. int x = 5____0;
2. int y = ____50;
3. int z = 50____;
4. float f = 123.76_86f;
5. double d = 1_2_3_4;
```

How many statements are legal?

A. One statement only

B. Two statements only

C. Three statements only

D. Four statements only

E. All 5 statements

5.1.43 Consider below code of Test.java file:

```
package com.udayankhattry.oca;

public class Test {
    public static void main(String[] args) {
        String [] arr = new String[7];
        System.out.println(arr);
    }
}
```

What will be the result of compiling and executing Test class?

A. An exception is thrown at runtime

B. Compilation Error

C. It prints null

D. It prints some text containing @ symbol

5.1.44 Consider below code of Test.java file:

```
package com.udayankhattry.oca;

public class Test {
    public static void main(String [] args) {
        boolean flag = false;
        System.out.println((flag = true) |
                        (flag = false) || (flag = true));
        System.out.println(flag);
    }
}
```

will be the result of compiling and executing Test class?

A.	true false	B.	false true
C.	true true	D.	false false
E.	Compilation error		

5.1.45 Given code of Test.java file:

```
package com.udayankhattry.oca;

class Lock {
    public void open() {
        System.out.println("LOCK-OPEN");
    }
}

class Padlock extends Lock {
    public void open() {
        System.out.println("PADLOCK-OPEN");
    }
}
```

```
class DigitalPadlock extends Padlock {
    public void open() {
        /*INSERT*/
    }
}

public class Test {
    public static void main(String[] args) {
        Lock lock = new DigitalPadlock();
        lock.open();
    }
}
```

Which of the following options, if used to replace /*INSERT*/, will compile successfully and on execution will print LOCK-OPEN on to the console?

A. super.open();

B. super.super.open();

C. ((Lock)super).open();

D. (Lock)super.open();

E. None of the other options

5.1.46 Given code of Test.java file:

```
package com.udayankhattry.oca;

interface ILogger {
    void log();
}

public class Test {
    public static void main(String[] args) {
        ILogger [] loggers = new ILogger[2]; //Line n1
        for(ILogger logger : loggers)
            logger.log(); //Line n2
    }
}
```

What will be the result of compiling and executing Test class?
A. Line n1 causes compilation error
B. Line n2 causes compilation error
C. An exception is thrown at runtime
D. No output is displayed but program terminates successfully

5.1.47 Consider below code of Test.java file:

```
package com.udayankhattry.oca;

class Super {
    void Super() {
        System.out.print("KEEP_");
    }
}

class Base extends Super {
    Base() {
        Super();
        System.out.print("GOING_");
    }
}

public class Test {
    public static void main(String[] args) {
        new Base();
    }
}
```

What will be the result of compiling and executing above code?

A. Compilation Error in Super class
B. Compilation Error in Base class
C. Compilation Error in Test class
D. It prints KEEP_GOING_ on to the console
E. It prints GOING_KEEP_ on to the console
F. It prints KEEP_KEEP_GOING_ on to the console
G. It prints GOING_ on to the console

5.1.48 Given code of Test.java file:

```
package com.udayankhattry.oca;

import java.io.FileNotFoundException;

public class Test {
    static String [] names = {"Williamson.pdf",
                "Finch.pdf", "Kohli.pdf", "Morgan.pdf"};
    public static void main(String[] args) {
        try {
            if (search("virat.pdf"))
                System.out.println("FOUND");

        } catch(FileNotFoundException ex) {
            System.out.println("NOT FOUND");
        }
    }

    private static boolean search(String name)
                        throws FileNotFoundException {
        for(int i = 0; i <= 4; i++) {
            if (names[i].equalsIgnoreCase(name)) {
                return true;
            }
        }
        throw new FileNotFoundException();
    }
}
```

What will be the result of compiling and executing Test class?

A. FOUND

B. NOT FOUND

C. Compilation error

D. None of the other options

5.1.49 Consider below code of Test.java file:

```
package com.udayankhattry.oca;

public class Test {
    public static void main(String[] args) {
        /*INSERT*/ x = 7, y = 200;
        System.out.println(String.valueOf(x + y).length());
    }
}
```

Which of the following options, if used to replace /*INSERT*/, will compile successfully and on execution will print 3 on to the console?

Select ALL that apply.

A. byte

B. short

C. int

D. long

E. float

F. double

5.1.50 Consider below code of TestSquare.java file:

```
package com.udayankhattry.oca;

class Square {
    int length;
    Square sq;

    Square(int length) {
        this.length = length;
    }

    void setInner(Square sq) {
        this.sq = sq;
    }

    int getLength() {
        return this.length;
    }
}

public class TestSquare {
```

```
public static void main(String[] args) {
    Square sq1 = new Square(10); //Line n1
    Square sq2 = new Square(5); //Line n2
    sq1.setInner(sq2); //Line n3
    System.out.println(sq1.sq.length); //Line n4
}
}
```

What will be the result of compiling and executing TestSquare class?

A. It prints 0 on to the console

B. It prints 5 on to the console

C. It prints 10 on to the console

D. It prints null on to the console

E. Compilation error

F. An exception is thrown at runtime

5.1.51 Consider below code of Test.java file:

```
package com.udayankhattry.oca;

interface Profitable {
    double profitPercentage = 42.0;
}

class Business implements Profitable {
    double profitPercentage = 50.0; //Line n1
}

public class Test {
    public static void main(String[] args) {
        Profitable obj = new Business(); //Line n2
        System.out.println(obj.profitPercentage); //Line n3
    }
}
```

What will be the result of compiling and executing Test class?

A. Line n1 causes compilation error

B. Line n2 causes compilation error

C. Line n3 causes compilation error

D. Test class compiles successfully and on execution prints 42.0 on to the console

E. Test class compiles successfully and on execution prints 50.0 on to the console

5.1.52 Consider below code of TestBook.java file:

```
package com.udayankhattry.oca;

class Book {
    private String name;
    private String author;

    Book() {}

    Book(String name, String author) {
        name = name;
        author = author;
    }

    String getName() {
        return name;
    }

    String getAuthor() {
        return author;
    }
}

public class TestBook {
    public static void main(String[] args) {
        private Book book =
            new Book("Head First Java", "Kathy Sierra");
        System.out.println(book.getName());
        System.out.println(book.getAuthor());
    }
}
```

What will be the result of compiling and executing above code?

A.	Compilation error in Book class		
B.	Compilation error in TestBook class		
C.	null null	D.	Head First Java Kathy Sierra

5.1.53 Consider below code of Test.java file:

```
package com.udayankhattry.oca;

public class Test {
    public static void main(String[] args) {
        int val = 25;
        if(val++ < 26) {
            System.out.println(val++);
        }
    }
}
```

What will be the result of compiling and executing Test class?

A. 25

B. 26

C. 27

D. Program executes successfully but nothing is printed on to the console

5.1.54 Consider below codes of 3 java files:

```
//Animal.java
package a;

public class Animal {
    Animal() {
        System.out.print("ANIMAL-");
    }
}
```

```
//Dog.java
package d;

import a.Animal;

public class Dog extends Animal {
    public Dog() {
        System.out.print("DOG");
    }
}
```

```
//Test.java
package com.udayankhattry.oca;

import d.Dog;

public class Test {
    public static void main(String[] args) {
        new Dog();
    }
}
```

What will be the result of compiling and executing Test class?

A. Compilation error in Animal.java file

B. Compilation error in Dog.java file

C. Compilation error in Test.java file

D. It executes successfully and prints ANIMAL-DOG on to the console

E. It executes successfully and prints DOG on to the console

F. It executes successfully but nothing is printed on to the console

5.1.55 Given code of Test.java file:

```
package com.udayankhattry.oca;

import java.sql.SQLException;

public class Test {
    private static void m() throws SQLException {
        try {
            throw new SQLException();
        } catch (Exception e) {
            throw e;
        }
    }

    public static void main(String[] args) {
        try {
            m();
        } catch(SQLException e) {
            System.out.println("CAUGHT SUCCESSFULLY");
        }
    }
}
```

What will be the result of compiling and executing Test class?

A. Method m() causes compilation error
B. Method main(String []) causes compilation error
C. CAUGHT SUCCESSFULLY is printed on to the console and program terminates successfully
D. Program ends abruptly

5.1.56 Consider below code of Test.java file:

```
public class Test {
    public static void main(String[] args) {
        System.out.println("Welcome " + args[0] +"!");
    }
}
```

And the commands:
```
javac Test.java
java Test "James Gosling" "Bill Joy"
```

What is the result?

A. Welcome James Gosling!
B. Welcome Bill Joy!
C. Welcome "James Gosling!"
D. Welcome "Bill Joy!"
E. Welcome James!
F. Welcome Gosling!
G. Welcome Bill!
H. Welcome Joy!

5.1.57 Consider below code of Test.java file:

```
package com.udayankhattry.oca;

public class Test {
    public static void main(String[] args) {
        int[][] arr = new int[x][y]; //Line n1
        arr[1][4] = 100;
        arr[6][6] = 200;
        arr[3][6] = 300;
    }
}
```

And below combination of x and y values:
1. x = 6, y = 6
2. x = 2, y = 5
3. x = 4, y = 7
4. x = 7, y = 7
5. x = 8, y = 8
6. x = 0, y = 0
7. x = -1, y = -1

How many of above x,y pair(s) can replace x and y at Line n1 such that Test.java file compiles successfully?

A. All 7 pairs

B. 6 pairs

C. 5 pairs

D. 4 pairs

E. 3 pairs

F. 2 pairs

G. 1 pair

5.1.58 Consider below code of AvoidThreats.java file:

```
package com.udayankhattry.oca;

public class AvoidThreats {
    public static void evaluate(Threat t) {  //Line n5
        t = new Threat();  //Line n6
        t.name = "PHISHING";  //Line n7
    }

    public static void main(String[] args) {
        Threat obj = new Threat();  //Line n1
        obj.print();  //Line n2
        evaluate(obj);  //Line n3
        obj.print();  //Line n4
    }
}

class Threat {
    String name = "VIRUS";

    public void print() {
        System.out.println(name);
    }
}
```

What will be the result of compiling and executing AvoidThreats class?

A.	VIRUS	B.	PHISHING
	PHISHING		PHISHING
C.	VIRUS	D.	null
	VIRUS		VIRUS
E.	null	F.	None of the other options
	null		

5.1.59 Given code of Test.java file:

```
public class Test {
    public static void main(String[] args) {
        args[1] = "Day!";
        System.out.println(args[0] + " " + args[1]);
    }
}
```

And the commands:
```
javac Test.java
java Test Good
```

What is the result?

A. Good

B. Good Day!

C. Compilation Error

D. An exception is thrown at runtime

5.1.60   Consider below codes of 3 java files:

```
//Sellable.java
package com.udayankhattry.oca;

public interface Sellable {
    double getPrice();

    default String symbol() {
        return "$";
    }
}
```

```
//Chair.java
package com.udayankhattry.oca;

public class Chair implements Sellable {
    public double getPrice() {
        return 35;
    }

    public String symbol() {
        return "£";
    }
}
```

```
//Test.java
package com.udayankhattry.oca;

public class Test {
    public static void main(String[] args) {
        Sellable obj = new Chair(); //Line n1
        System.out.println(obj.symbol() +
                    obj.getPrice()); //Line n2
    }
}
```

What will be the result of compiling and executing Test class?

A. Compilation error in Chair class

B. Compilation error in Test class

C. It compiles successfully and on execution prints $35 on to the console

D. It compiles successfully and on execution prints $35.0 on to the console

E. It compiles successfully and on execution prints $35.00 on to the console

F. It compiles successfully and on execution prints £35 on to the console

G. It compiles successfully and on execution prints £35.0 on to the console

H. It compiles successfully and on execution prints £35.00 on to the console

5.1.61 Given code of Test.java file:

```
package com.udayankhattry.oca;

class X {
    void greet() {
        System.out.println("Good Morning!");
    }
}

class Y extends X {
    void greet() {
        System.out.println("Good Afternoon!");
    }
}

class Z extends Y {
    void greet() {
        System.out.println("Good Night!");
    }
}

public class Test {
    public static void main(String[] args) {
        X x = new Z();
        x.greet(); //Line n1
        ((Y)x).greet(); //Line n2
        ((Z)x).greet(); //Line n3
    }
}
```

What will be the result of compiling and executing above code?

A.	Compilation error
B.	An exception is thrown at runtime
C.	It compiles successfully and on execution prints below: Good Night! Good Afternoon! Good Morning!
D.	It compiles successfully and on execution prints below: Good Night! Good Night! Good Night!
E.	It compiles successfully and on execution prints below: Good Morning! Good Morning! Good Morning!

5.1.62 Consider below code of Test.java file:

```
package com.udayankhattry.oca;

public class Test {
    public static void main(String[] args) {
        String str = "ALASKA";
        System.out.println(str.charAt(str.indexOf("A") + 1));
    }
}
```

What will be the result of compiling and executing Test class?

A. A

B. L

C. S

D. K

E. Runtime error

5.1.63 Consider codes of 3 java files:

```java
//Planet.java
package com.udayankhattry.galaxy;

public class Planet {
    String name;
    public Planet(String name) {
        this.name = name;
    }

    public String toString() {
        return "Planet: " + name;
    }
}



//Creator.java
package com.udayankhattry.oca;

public class Creator {
    public static Planet create() {
        return new Planet("Earth");
    }
}



//TestCreator.java
package com.udayankhattry.oca.test;

public class TestCreator {
    public static void main(String[] args) {
        System.out.println(Creator.create());
    }
}
```

And below options:

1.

Add below import statement in Creator.java file:

```java
import com.udayankhattry.galaxy.Planet;
```


2.

Add below import statement in Creator.java file:

```java
import com.udayankhattry.oca.test.TestCreator;
```

3.

Add below import statement in TestCreator.java file:

```
import com.udayankhattry.oca.Creator;
```

4.

Add below import statement in TestCreator.java file:

```
import com.udayankhattry.galaxy.Planet;
```

Which of the above options needs to be done so that on executing TestCreator class, "Planet: Earth" is printed on to the console?

Please note: Unnecessary imports are not allowed.

A. Only 1

B. Only 2

C. Only 3

D. Only 4

E. 1 & 2 only

F. 3 & 4 only

G. 1 & 3 only

H. 1, 3 & 4 only

I. 1, 2, 3 & 4 are needed

5.1.64 Consider below code of Test.java file:

```
package com.udayankhattry.oca;

public class Test {
    public static void main(String [] args) {
        boolean flag1 = true;
        boolean flag2 = false;
        boolean flag3 = true;
        boolean flag4 = false;

        System.out.println(!flag1 == flag2
                    != flag3 == !flag4); //Line n1
        System.out.println(flag1 = flag2
                    != flag3 == !flag4); //Line n2
    }
}
```

What will be the result of compiling and executing Test class?

A.	Line n1 causes compilation error		
B.	Line n2 causes compilation error		
C.	true true	D.	true false
E.	false true	F.	false false

5.1.65 Consider below code of Test.java file:

```
package com.udayankhattry.oca;

public class Test {
    public static void main(String[] args) {
        String s1 = "OCP";
        String s2 = "ocp";
        System.out.println(/*INSERT*/);
    }
}
```

Which of the following options, if used to replace /*INSERT*/, will compile successfully and on execution will print true on to the console?
Select ALL that apply.

A. s1.equals(s2)
B. s1.equals(s2.toUpper())
C. s2.equals(s1.toLower())
D. s1.length() == s2.length()
E. s1.equalsIgnoreCase(s2)
F. s1.contentEquals(s2)

5.1.66 Consider below codes of 3 java files:

```java
//Profitable1.java
package com.udayankhattry.oca;

public interface Profitable1 {
    default double profit() {
        return 12.5;
    }
}


//Profitable2.java
package com.udayankhattry.oca;

public interface Profitable2 {
    default double profit() {
        return 25.5;
    }
}


//Profit.java
package com.udayankhattry.oca;

public abstract class Profit implements Profitable1,
Profitable2 {
    /*INSERT*/
}
```

Which of the following needs to be done so that there is no compilation error?

A.	No need for any modifications, code compiles as is

B.	Replace /*INSERT*/ with below code:
	`double profit() {`
	`    return 50.0;`
	`}`

C.	Replace /*INSERT*/ with below code:
	`public default double profit() {`
	`    return 50.0;`
	`}`

D.	Replace /*INSERT*/ with below code:
	`protected double profit() {`
	`    return 50.0;`
	`}`

E.	Replace /*INSERT*/ with below code:
	`public double profit() {`
	`    return Profitable1.profit();`
	`}`

F.	Replace /*INSERT*/ with below code:
	`public double profit() {`
	`    return Profitable2.super.profit();`
	`}`

5.1.67 Consider below code snippet:

```
interface Workable {
    void work();
}

/*INSERT*/ {
public void work() {} //Line n1
}
```

And the statements:

1. `abstract class Work implements Workable`
2. `class Work implements Workable`
3. `interface Work extends Workable`
4. `abstract interface Work extends Workable`
5. `abstract class Work`

How many statements can replace /*INSERT*/ such that there is no compilation error?

A. One statement

B. Two statements

C. Three statements

D. Four statements

E. Five statements

5.1.68 Consider below code of Test.java file:

```java
package com.udayankhattry.oca;

public class Test {
    public static void main(String[] args) {
        int i = 0;
        for(System.out.print(i++); i < 2;
                                System.out.print(i++)) {
            System.out.print(i);
        }
    }
}
```

What will be the result of compiling and executing Test class?

A. 112

B. 012

C. 011

D. 12

E. 01

F. Compilation error

5.1.69 Consider below code snippet:

```
import java.util.*;

class Father {}

class Son extends Father {}

class GrandSon extends Son {}

abstract class Super {
    abstract List<Father> get();
}

class Sub extends Super {
    /*INSERT*/
}
```

And the definitions of get() method:
1. List<Father> get() {return null;}
2. ArrayList<Father> get() {return null;}
3. List<Son> get() {return null;}
4. ArrayList<Son> get() {return null;}
5. List<GrandSon> get() {return null;}
6. ArrayList<GrandSon> get() {return null;}
7. List<Object> get() {return null;}
8. ArrayList<Object> get() {return null;}

How many definitions of get() method can replace /*INSERT*/ such that there is no compilation error?

A. One definition

B. Two definitions

C. Three definitions

D. Four definitions

E. Five definitions

F. Six definitions

G. Seven definitions

H. Eight definitions

5.1.70 Consider the code of Test.java file:

```
package com.udayankhattry.oca;

class Report {
    public String generateReport() {
        return "CSV";
    }

    public Object generateReport() {
        return "XLSX";
    }
}

public class Test {
    public static void main(String[] args) {
        Report rep = new Report();
        String csv = rep.generateReport();
        Object xlsx = rep.generateReport();
        System.out.println(csv + ":" + (String)xlsx);
    }
}
```

What will be the result of compiling and executing Test class?

A. Compilation error

B. An exception is thrown at runtime

C. CSV:XLSX

D. CSV:CSV

E. XLSX:CSV

F. XLSX:XLSX

5.1.71 Given code of Test.java file:

```
package com.udayankhattry.oca;

abstract class Animal {
    abstract void jump() throws RuntimeException;
}

class Deer extends Animal {
    void jump() { //Line n1
        System.out.println("DEER JUMPS");
    }

    void jump(int i) {
        System.out.println("DEER JUMPS TO " + i + " FEET");
    }
}

public class Test {
    public static void main(String[] args) {
        Animal animal = new Deer();
        ((Deer)animal).jump(); //Line n2
        ((Deer)animal).jump(5); //Line n3
    }
}
```

What will be the result of compiling and executing Test class?

A.	Line n1 causes compilation error
B.	Line n2 causes compilation error
C.	Line n3 causes compilation error
D.	An exception is thrown at runtime
E.	Test class executes successfully and prints: DEER JUMPS DEER JUMPS TO 5 FEET

5.1.72 Consider below code of Test.java file:

```
package com.udayankhattry.oca;

public class Test {
    public static void main(String[] args) {
        int i = 1;
        int j = 5;
        int k = 0;
        A: while(true) {
            i++;
            B: while(true) {
                j--;
                C: while(true) {
                    k += i + j;
                    if(i == j)
                        break A;
                    else if (i > j)
                        continue A;
                    else
                        continue B;
                }
            }
        }
        System.out.println(k);
    }
}
```

What will be the result of compiling and executing Test class?

A. Compilation error

B. Program never terminates as above code causes infinite loop

C. 6

D. 11

E. 15

F. None of the other options

5.2   Answers to Bonus Exam - 1 with Explanation

5.1.1   Answer: C

Reason:
Body of do-while loop is executed first and then condition is checked for the next iteration.
Initially, flag = false;
1st iteration: Boolean expression of if-block `flag = !flag` = `flag = !false` = `flag = true`: it assigns true to variable 'flag' and evaluates to true as well. Line n2 is executed and 1 is printed on to the console. Line n3 takes the control to the boolean expression of Line n5.
2nd iteration: As flag is true, boolean expression at Line n5 evaluates to true and control enters the loop's body. Boolean expression of if-block `flag = !flag` = `flag = !true` = `flag = false`: it assigns false to variable 'flag' and evaluates to false as well. Line n2 and Line n3 are not executed. Line n4 is executed, which prints 2 on to the console. Control goes to the boolean expression of Line n5.
3rd iteration: As flag is false, boolean expression at Line n5 evaluates to false and control exits the loop.

Program terminates successfully after printing 12 on to the console.

5.1.2   Answer: G

Reason:
As per Java 8, default methods were added in the interface. Interface X1 defines default method print(), there is no compilation error in interface X1. Method print() is implicitly public in X1.

interface X2 extends X1 and it overrides the default method print() of X1, overriding method in X2 is implicitly abstract and public. An interface in java can override the default method of super type with abstract modifier. interface X2 compiles successfully.

interface X3 extends X2 and it implements the abstract method print() of X2, overriding method in X3 is default and implicitly public. An interface in java can implement the abstract method of super type with default modifier. interface X3 compiles successfully.

class X implements X3 and therefore it inherits the default method print() defined in interface X3.

`X1 obj = new X();` compiles successfully as X1 is of super type (X implements X3, X3 extends X2 and X2 extends X1).
`obj.print();` invokes the default method print() defined in interface X3 and hence X3 is printed on to the console.

5.1.3   Answer: B

Reason:
The static method of subclass cannot hide the instance method of superclass. static main(String []) method at Line n2 tries to hide the instance main(String []) method at Line n1 and hence Line n2 causes compilation error.

There is no issue with Line n3 as it is a valid syntax to invoke the instance main(String []) method of M class.

No issue with Line n4 as well as it correctly invokes static main(String []) method of N class.

5.1.4   Answer: A, B, C, D, G

Reason:
Both Traveller and BeachTraveller are abstract classes and BeachTraveller extends Traveller. It is possible to have abstract class without any abstract method. Code as is compiles successfully as BeachTraveller inherits travel(String) method of Traveller class.
But as per the question, /*INSERT*/ must be replaced such that there is no compilation error.

Let's check all the options one by one:
abstract void travel(); ✓ This is method overloading. BeachTraveller has 2 methods: `void travel(String){}` and `abstract void travel()`.

abstract void travel(String beach); ✓ As BeachTraveller is abstract, hence travel(String) method can be declared abstract.

public abstract void travel(); ✓ This is method overloading. BeachTraveller has 2 methods: `void travel(String){}` and `abstract void travel()`.

public void travel() throws RuntimeException {}: ✓ This is method overloading. BeachTraveller has 2 methods: `void travel(String){}` and `public void travel() throws RuntimeException {}`.

public void travel(String beach) throws Exception {}: ✗ As overridden method doesn't declare to throw any checked Exception hence overriding method is not allowed to declare to throw Exception.

void travel(String beach) throws java.io.IOException {} ✗ As overridden method doesn't declare to throw any checked Exception hence overriding method is not allowed to declare to throw java.io.IOException.

public void travel(Object obj) {} ✓ This is method overloading. BeachTraveller has 2 methods: `void travel(String){}` and `public void travel(Object){}`.

5.1.5   Answer: A

Reason:
ArrayList instance referred by 'list' stores 3 StringBuilder instances.

removeIf(Predicate<? super E> filter) method was added as a default method in Collection<E> interface in JDK 8 and it removes all the elements of this collection that satisfy the given predicate.
StringBuilder class doesn't override equals(Object) method. So Object version is invoked, which uses == operator, hence `sb.equals(new StringBuilder("AAA"))` would return false as all 4 StringBuilder instances have been created at four different memory locations.
None of the StringBuilder instances are removed from the list.

StringBuilder class overrides toString() method, which returns the containing String and that is why [AAA, BBB, AAA] will be printed on to the console.

5.1.6   Answer: D

Reason:
String class has following two overloaded replace methods:
1. public String replace(char oldChar, char newChar) {}:
Returns a string resulting from replacing all occurrences of oldChar in this string with newChar. If no replacement is done, then source String object is returned. e.g.
"Java".replace('a', 'A') --> returns new String object "JAvA".
"Java".replace('a', 'a') --> returns the source String object "Java" (no change).
"Java".replace('m', "M") --> returns the source String object "Java" (no change).

2. public String replace(CharSequence target, CharSequence replacement) {}:
Returns a new String object after replacing each substring of this string that matches the literal target sequence with the specified literal replacement sequence. e.g.
"Java".replace("a", "A") --> returns new String object "JAvA".
"Java".replace("a", "a") --> returns new String object "Java" (it replaces "a" with "a").
"Java".replace("m", "M") --> returns the source String object "Java" (no change).

For Line n1, as both oldChar and newChar are same, hence source String ("Java") is returned by `"Java".replace('J', 'J');` without any change. flag1 stores true.
For Line n2, even though target and replacement are same but as "J" is found in the source String, hence a new String object "Java" is returned by `"Java".replace("J", "J");` after replacing "J" with "J". flag2 stores false.
flag1 && flag2 evaluates to false.

5.1.7   Answer: A

Reason:
list --> [P, O, T]

sublist method is declared in List interface:
List<E> subList(int fromIndex, int toIndex)
fromIndex is inclusive and toIndex is exclusive
It returns a view of the portion of this list between the specified fromIndex and toIndex. The returned list is backed by this list, so non-structural changes in the returned list are reflected in this list and vice-versa.
If returned list (or view) is structurally modified, then modification are reflected in this list as well but if this list is structurally modified, then the semantics of the list returned by this method become undefined.

If fromIndex == toIndex, then returned list is empty.
If fromIndex < 0 OR toIndex > size of the list OR fromIndex > toIndex, then
IndexOutOfBoundsException is thrown.

list.subList(1, 2) --> [O] (fromIndex is inclusive and endIndex is exclusive, so start index
is 1 and end index is also 1). subList --> [O].
At Line n2, `subList.set(0, "E");` => sublist --> [E]. This change is also reflected in the
backed list, therefore after this statement, list --> [P, E, T]

`System.out.println(list);` prints [P, E, T] on to the console.

5.1.8   Answer: E

Reason:
Variable 'name' declared inside interface Super is implicitly public, static and final. Line
n1 compiles successfully.
In Java a class can extend from only one class but an interface can extend from
multiple interfaces. Line n2 compiles successfully.
Variable 'name' can be accessed in 2 ways: Super.name and Sub.name.
Though correct way to refer static variable is by using the type name, such as
Sub.name but it can also be invoked by using Sub reference variable. Hence, sub.name
at Line n3 correctly points to the name variable at Line n1.
For invoking static fields, object is not needed, therefore even if sub refers to null,
sub.name doesn't throw NullPoionterException.
Test class compiles successfully and on execution prints SUPER on to the console.

5.1.9   Answer: B, C, E, F, H

Reason:
At Line n1, reference variable 'obj' is of Multiplier type (supertype) and it refers to an
instance of Calculator class (subtype). This is polymorphism and allowed in Java.
multiply(int...) method declared in Multiplier interface declares to throw
SQLException, hence the catch handler for Line n1 should provide handler for
SQLException or its supertype. As catch-handler for SQLException is available,
therefore Test class compiles successfully.

According to overriding rules, if super class / interface method declares to throw a checked exception, then overriding method of sub class / implementer class has following options:

1. May not declare to throw any checked exception
2. May declare to throw the same checked exception thrown by super class / interface method: SQLException is a valid option.
3. May declare to throw the sub class of the exception thrown by super class / interface method: SQLWarning is a valid option.
4. Cannot declare to throw the super class of the exception thrown by super class / interface method: Exception, Throwable are not valid options.
5. Cannot declare to throw unrelated checked exception: java.io.IOException is not a valid option as it is not related java.sql.SQLException in multi-level inheritance.
6. May declare to throw any RuntimeException or Error: RuntimeException, NullPointerException and Error are valid options.

Therefore 5 options can successfully replace /*INSERT*/: SQLException, SQLWarning, RuntimeException, Error and NullPointerException

5.1.10   Answer: D

Reason:
Subclass overrides the methods of superclass but it hides the variables of superclass.

Line n3 hides the variable created at Line n1 and Line n4 overrides the getSide() method of Line n2. There is no compilation error for Square class as it correctly overrides getSide() method. You can use any access modifier at Line n3 as well, there are no rules for variable hiding.

's' is of Shape type, hence s.side equals to 0 and s.getSide() invokes overriding method of Square class and it returns 4. Hence output is: 0:4.

5.1.11   Answer: B

Reason:
Classes in Exception framework are normal java classes, hence null can be used wherever instances of Exception classes are used, so Line 7 compiles successfully.

No issues with Line 12 as method availableSeats() declares to throw SQLException and main(String []) method code correctly handles it.

Program compiles successfully but on execution, NullPointerException is thrown, stack trace is printed on to the console and program ends abruptly.

If you debug the code, you would find that internal routine for throwing null exception causes NullPointerException.

5.1.12 Answer: D

Reason:
It is legal for the constructors to have throws clause.
Constructors are not inherited by the Child class so there is no method overriding rules related to the constructors but as one constructor invokes other constructors implicitly or explicitly by using this(...) or super(...), hence exception handling becomes interesting.

Java compiler adds super(); as the first statement inside Child class's constructor:
```
Child() throws Exception {
    super(); //added by the compiler
    System.out.println("MATATA");
}
```

super(); invokes the constructor of Parent class (which declares to throw IOException), but as no-argument constructor of Child class declares to throw Exception (super class of IOException), hence IOException is also handled. There is no compilation error and output is: HAKUNAMATATA

5.1.13 Answer: B, D, F

Reason:
Subclass overrides the methods of superclass but it hides the variables of superclass.

Line n2 hides the variable created at Line n1, there is no rules related to hiding (type and access modifier can be changed).

Line n5 causes compilation error as obj is of Child type and 'var' is declared private in Child class. Variable 'var' of Child class cannot be accessed outside the Child class.

Let's check all the options one by one:
'Change Line n1 to private int var = 1000;' => It will not rectify the existing error of Line n5, in fact after this change, Line n3 will also cause compilation error.

'Delete the Line n2' => After deleting this line, obj.var at Line n5 will refer to variable 'var' of Parent class. Hence, output will be 1000 in this case.

'Change Line n3 to return var;' => This will have no effect to the output of the code, as getVar() method has not been invoked.

'Change Line n4 to Parent obj = new Child();' => After this modification, obj becomes Parent type, hence obj.var will refer to variable 'var' of Parent class. Hence, output will be 1000 in this case.

'Delete the method getVar() from the Child class' => This will have no effect to the output of the code, as getVar() method has not been invoked.

'Change Line n5 to System.out.println(obj.getVar());' => obj.getVar() will invoke the getVar() method of Child class and this method returns the variable value from Parent class (super.var). Hence, output will be 1000 in this case.

5.1.14 Answer: C

Reason:
If choice is between implicit casting and variable arguments, then implicit casting takes precedence because variable arguments syntax was added in Java 5 version.
m('A'); is tagged to m(int) as 'A' is char literal and implicitly casted to int.
m('A', 'B'); is tagged to m(int, int) as 'A' and 'B' are char literals and implicitly casted to int.
m('A', 'B', 'C'); is tagged to m(char...)
m('A', 'B', 'C', 'D'); is tagged to m(char...)

There is no compilation error and on execution output is: 1233

5.1.15 Answer: B

Reason:
speed method is correctly overloaded in Car class as both the methods have different signature: speed(Byte) and speed(byte...). Please note that there is no rule regarding return type for overloaded methods, return type can be same or different.

`new Car().speed(b);` tags to speed(Byte) as boxing is preferred over variable arguments. Code as is prints DARK on to the console.

Variable arguments syntax '...' can be used only for method parameters and not for variable type and type-casting. Hence the option of replacing Line n4 and Line n5 are not correct.

If you delete speed(Byte) method, i.e. Line n1, Line n2 and Line n3, then `new Car().speed(b);` would tag to speed(byte...) method and on execution would print LIGHT on to the console.

5.1.16 Answer: E

Reason:
Circle class needs to be well encapsulated, this means that instance variable radius must be declared with private access modifier and getter/setter methods must be public, so that value in radius variable can be read/changed by other classes.
Out of the given options, below option is correct:
Add below 2 methods in Circle class:
public double getRadius() {
   return radius;
}

public void setRadius(double radius) {
   this.radius = radius;
}

5.1.17 Answer: E

Reason:
plusMonths(long) method of LocalDate class returns a copy of this LocalDate with the specified number of months added.
This method adds the specified amount to the months field in three steps:
  Add the input months to the month-of-year field
  Check if the resulting date would be invalid
  Adjust the day-of-month to the last valid day if necessary

For the given code,
1983-06-30 plus 8 months would result in the invalid date 1984-02-30. Instead of returning an invalid result, the last valid day of the month, 1984-02-29, is returned. Please note, 1984 is leap year and hence last day of February is 29 and not 28.

5.1.18 Answer: B, D, E

Reason:
abstract methods cannot be declared with private modifier as abstract methods need to be overridden in child classes.
abstract methods can be declared with either public, protected and package (no access modifier) modifier and hence overriding method cannot be declared which private modifier in the child class. That is why getCalories() method in Food and JunkFood classes cannot be declared private.

Access modifier of overriding method should either be same as the access modifier of overridden method or it should be less restrictive than the access modifier of overridden method. Hence below solutions will work:
1. Remove the protected access modifier from the getCalories() method of Food class: By doing this, both the overridden and overriding methods will have same access modifier (no access modifier)
or
2. Make the getCalories() method of JunkFood class protected: By doing this, both the overridden and overriding methods will have same access modifier (protected)
or
3. Make the getCalories() method of JunkFood class public: By doing this, access modifier of overriding method (which is public) is less restrictive than the access modifier of overridden method (which is protected)

5.1.19 Answer: F

Reason:
print() method at Line n2 hides the method at Line n1. So, no compilation error at Line n2.

Reference variable 'b' is of type Base, so `(Derived) b` does not cause any compilation error. Moreover, at runtime it will not throw any ClassCastException as well because b is null. Had 'b' been referring to an instance of Base class [Base b = new Base();], `(Derived) b` would have thrown ClassCastException.

d.print(); doesn't cause any compilation error but as this syntax creates confusion, so it is not a good practice to access the static variables or static methods using reference variable, instead class name should be used. Derived.print(); is the preferred syntax.

d.print(); invokes the static print() method of Derived class and prints DERIVED on to the console.

5.1.20 Answer: A

Reason:
i1 is a static variable and i2 is an instance variable. Preferred way to access static variable i1 inside add() method is by using 'i1' or 'Test.i1'. Even though 'this.i1' is not the recommended way but it works.
And instance variable i2 can be accessed inside add() method by using 'i2' or 'this.i2'. Hence, Line n1 compiles successfully.

As add() is an instance method of Test class, so an instance of Test class is needed to invoke the add() method. `new Test().add()` correctly invokes the add() method of Test class and returns 30. Line n2 prints 30 on to the console.

5.1.21   Answer: F

Reason:
Line n1 creates a String [] object of 4 elements and arr refers to this array object.
arr[0] = "L", arr[1] = "I", arr[2] = "V" and arr[3] = "E".
i = -2.
Boolean expression of Line n2: i++ == -1
=> (i++) == -1 //As Post-increment operator ++ has higher precedence over ==
=> -2 == -1 //i = -1, value of i is used in the expression and then incremented.
=> false and hence Line n3 is not executed.
But there is no issue with Line n3 and it compiles successfully.

Boolean expression of Line n4 is evaluated next:
--i == -2 //i = -1
=> (--i) == -2 //As Pre-decrement operator -- has higher precedence over ==
=> -2 == -2 //i = -2, value of i is decremented first and then used in the expression.
=> true and hence Line n5 is executed next.

Line n5:
arr[-++i] = "O"; //i = -2
=> arr[-(++i)] = "O"; //Unary minus '-' and pre-increment '++' operators have same precedence
=> arr[-(-1)] = "O"; //i = -1, value of i is incremented first and then used in the expression.
=> arr[1] = "O"; //2nd array element is changed to "O".
Hence after Line n5, arr refers to {"L", "O", "V", "E"}

Given loop prints LOVE on to the console.

5.1.22   Answer: A, B, F

Reason:
save() method throws IOException (which is a Checked Exception) and log() method throws SQLException (which is also a Checked Exception).

Let's check all the options one by one (I am just using the catch-block as try-block of all the options are same):

catch(IOException | SQLException ex) {}: ✓ As IOException and SQLException are not related to each other in multi-level inheritance, hence this multi-catch syntax is valid.

catch(SQLException | IOException ex) {}: ✓ Same as above, order of exceptions in multi-catch syntax doesn't matter.

catch(IOException | Exception ex) {}: ✗ Causes compilation error as IOException extends Exception.

catch(SQLException | Exception ex) {}: ✗ Causes compilation error as SQLException extends Exception.

catch(Exception | RuntimeException ex) {}: ✗ Causes compilation error as RuntimeException extends Exception.

catch(Exception ex) {}: ✓ As Exception is the super class of both IOException and SQLException, hence it can handle both the exceptions.

5.1.23 Answer: E

Reason:
As command-line argument is not passed, hence Line n1 throws ArrayIndexOutOfBoundsException (subclass of RuntimeException), handler is available in inner catch block, it executes Line n1 and prints INHALE- on to the console.
throw e; re-throws the exception.

But before exception instance is forwarded to outer catch-block, inner finally-block gets executed and prints EXHALE- on to the console.
In outer try-catch block, handler for RuntimeException is available, so outer catch-block gets executed and prints INHALE- on to the console.
After that outer finally-block gets executed and prints EXHALE- on to the console.

Hence, the output is: INHALE-EXHALE-INHALE-EXHALE

5.1.24 Answer: B

Reason:
Variable 'arr' refers to a two-dimensional array. for-each loops are used to iterate the given array.
In 1st iteration of outer loop, str refers to one-dimensional String array {"%", "$$"}.
In 1st iteration of inner loop, s refers to "%" and "%" will be printed on to the console. Boolean expression of Line n1 evaluates to false so Line n2 is not executed.
In 2nd iteration of inner loop, s refers to "$$" and "$$" will be printed on to the console. Boolean expression of Line n1 evaluates to false so Line n2 is not executed.
Iteration of inner for-each loop is over and control executes Line n3. break; statement at Line n3 terminates the outer loop and program ends successfully.

So, output is:
%
$$

5.1.25 Answer: D

Reason:
As per Java 8, default and static methods were added in the interface. Interface ILog defines static method log(), there is no compilation error in interface ILog.

Abstract class Log defines the static log() method. Abstract class can have 0 or more abstract methods. Hence, no compilation error in class Log as well.

Default methods of an interface are implicitly public and are inherited by the implementer class. Class MyLogger implements ILog interface and therefore it inherits the default log() method of ILog interface.
Also, the scope of static log() method of abstract class Log is not limited to class Log only but MyLogger also gets Log.log() method in its scope.
So, MyLogger class has instance method log() [inherited from ILog interface] and static method log() [from Log class] and this causes conflict. Static and non-static methods with same signature are not allowed in one scope, therefore class Log fails to compile.

5.1.26   Answer: B

Reason:
Though given code looks strange but it is possible in java to provide same name to package, class (and constructor), variable and method.
Above code compiles successfully and on execution prints ONE on to the console.
Constructor is not invoked as 'new' keyword is not used and that is why TWO will not be printed to the console.
In real world coding, you would not see such code and that is why it is a good question for the certification exam.

5.1.27   Answer: B

Reason:
Class Q correctly overrides the compute(String) method of P class and class R correctly overrides the compute(String) method of Q class. Keyword super is used to invoke the method of parent class.

At Line n1, reference variable 'p' refers to an instance of class R, hence p.compute("Go") invokes the compute(String) method of R class.
return super.compute(str.replace('o', 'O')); => return super.compute("Go".replace('o', 'O')); => return super.compute("GO");

It invokes the compute(String) method of Parent class, which is Q.
=> return super.compute(str.toLowerCase()); => return super.compute("GO".toLowerCase()); => return super.compute("go");

It invokes the compute(String) method of Parent class, which is P.
=> return str + str + str; => return "gogogo";

Control goes back to compute(String) method of Q and to the compute(String) method of R, which returns "gogogo".
Line n2 prints gogogo on to the console.

5.1.28 Answer: C

Reason:
As method div() doesn't declare to throw any Checked Exception, hence main(String [])
method is not suppose to handle it, try-finally without catch is valid here. There is no
compilation error in the code.

Method div() throws an instance of ArithmeticException and method div() doesn't
handle it, so it forwards the exception to calling method main(String []).
Method main(String []) doesn't handle ArithmeticException so it forwards it to JVM,
but just before that, finally block is executed. This prints FINALLY on to the console.
After that JVM prints the stack trace and terminates the program abruptly.

5.1.29 Answer: D

Reason:
Class M and M are declared public and inside same package com.udayankhattry.oca.
Method printName() of class M has correctly been overridden by N.
printName() method is public so no issues in accessing it anywhere.

Let's check the code inside main method.
M obj1 = new M(); => obj1 refers to an instance of class M.
N obj2 = (N)obj1; => obj1 is of type M and it is assigned to obj2 (N type), hence explicit
casting is necessary. obj1 refers to an instance of class M, so at runtime obj2 will also
refer to an instance of class M. sub type can't refer to an instance of super type so at
runtime `N obj2 = (N)obj1;` will throw ClassCastException.

5.1.30 Answer: G

Reason:
sb --> {"TOMATO"}
sb.reverse() --> {"OTAMOT"}. reverse() method returns a StringBuilder object.
replace method of StringBuilder class accepts 3 arguments: `replace(int start, int end,
String str)`. At Line n1, replace("O", "A") method accepts 2 arguments and hence it
causes compilation error.

5.1.31 Answer: A

Reason:
list is of Integer type and variable 'b' is of byte type.
At Line n1, b is auto-boxed to Byte and not Integer and List<Integer> can't store Byte objects, therefore Line n1 causes compilation error.

list.get(0) returns Integer and `list.get(0) * list.get(0)` is evaluated to int, and variable 'mul' is of int type only. Therefore, Line n2 compiles successfully.

5.1.32 Answer: C

Reason:
substring(int beginIndex, int endIndex) method of String class extracts the substring, which begins at the specified beginIndex and extends to the character at index endIndex - 1.
This method throws IndexOutOfBoundsException if the beginIndex is negative, or endIndex is larger than the length of this String object, or beginIndex is larger than endIndex. e.g.
"freeway".substring(4, 7) returns "way"
"freeway".substring(4, 8) throws IndexOutOfBoundsException

substring(int beginIndex) method of String class extracts the substring, which begins with the character at the specified index and extends to the end of this string.
This method throws IndexOutOfBoundsException if beginIndex is negative or larger than the length of this String object. e.g.
"freeway".substring(4) returns "way"
"freeway".substring(8) throws IndexOutOfBoundsException

replace(CharSequence target, CharSequence replacement) method of String class returns a new String object after replacing each substring of this string that matches the literal target sequence with the specified literal replacement sequence. e.g.
"Java".replace("a", "A") --> returns new String object "JAvA".

Let's check all the given options:
"REBUS".substring(2); [begin = 2, end = 4 (end of the string)], returns "BUS" and hence it is a correct option.

"REBUS".substring(2, 4); [begin = 2, end = 3 (endIndex - 1)], returns "BU" and hence it is incorrect option.

"REBUS".substring(2, 5); [begin = 2, end = 4 (endIndex - 1)], returns "BUS" and hence it is a correct option.

"REBUS".replace("RE", ""); It replaces "RE" with empty string "" and returns "BUS", so it is also a correct option.

"REBUS".substring(2, 6); Length of "REBUS" = 5 and endIndex = 6, which is greater than 5, hence it will thrown IndexOutOfBoundsException at runtime. Incorrect option

"REBUS".delete(0, 2); Compilation error as delete(...) method is not available in String class, it is part of StringBuilder class. Incorrect option.

So, total 3 options will replace /*INSERT*/ to print BUS on to the console.

5.1.33 Answer: A

Reason:
throw ex; causes compilation error as div method doesn't declare to throw Exception (checked) type.

5.1.34 Answer: C

Reason:
As per Java 8, default and static methods were added in the interface. There is no issue in Shrinkable.java file.

class AntMan implements Shrinkable interface but as there is no abstract method in Shrinkable interface, hence AntMan class is not needed to implement any method. AntMan.java file compiles successfully.

static method of Shrinkable interface can only be accessed by using Shrinkable.shrinkPercentage(). `AntMan.shrinkPercentage();` causes compilation error.

5.1.35 Answer: D

Reason:
Exception is a java class, so `e = null;` is a valid statement and compiles successfully.

If you comment Line 10, and simply throw e, then code would compile successfully as compiler is certain that 'e' would refer to an instance of SQLException only.

But the moment compiler finds `e = null;`, `throw e;` (Line 11) causes compilation error as at runtime 'e' may refer to any Exception type.

NOTE: No issues with Line 17 as method checkData() declares to throw SQLException and main(String []) method code correctly handles it.

5.1.36   Answer: A

Reason:
Given expression:
--a + --b < 1 && c++ + d++ > 1;
--a + --b < 1 && (c++) + (d++) > 1; //postfix has got highest precedence
(--a) + (--b) < 1 && (c++) + (d++) > 1; //prefix comes after postfix
{(--a) + (--b)} < 1 && {(c++) + (d++)} > 1; //Then comes binary +. Though parentheses are used but I used curly brackets, just to explain.
[{(--a) + (--b)} < 1] && [{(c++) + (d++)} > 1]; //Then comes relational operator (<,>). I used square brackets instead of parentheses.
This expression is left with just one operator, && and this operator is a binary operator so works with 2 operands, left operand [{(--a) + (--b)} < 1] and right operand [{(c++) + (d++)} > 1]
Left operand of && must be evaluated first, which means [{(--a) + (--b)} < 1] must be evaluated first.

[{2 + (--b)} < 1] && [{(c++) + (d++)} > 1]; //a=2, b=5, c=7, d=9
[{2 + 4} < 1] && [{(c++) + (d++)} > 1]; //a=2, b=4, c=7, d=9
[6 < 1] && [{(c++) + (d++)} > 1];
false && [{(c++) + (d++)} > 1];

&& is short circuit operator, hence right operand is not evaluated and false is returned.

Output of the given program is: a = 2, b = 4, c = 7, d = 9, res = false

5.1.37   Answer: B

Reason:
Method move() declared in Moveable interface is implicitly public and abstract.
Abstract class Animal has non-abstract method move() and it is declared with no
modifier (package scope). Abstract class in java can have 0 or more abstract methods.
Hence Animal class compiles successfully.
class Dog extends Animal and as both the classes Animal and Dog are within the same
package 'com.udayankhattry.oca', Dog inherits the move() method defined in Animal
class.
Dog class implements Moveable interface as well, therefore it must implement public
move() method as well. But as inherited move() method from Animal class is not
public, therefore Dog class fails to compile.

5.1.38   Answer: F

Reason:
You need to keep in mind an important point related to String Concatenation:
If only one operand expression is of type String, then string conversion is performed
on the other operand to produce a string at run time.
If one of the operand is null, it is converted to the string "null".
If operand is not null, then the conversion is performed as if by an invocation of the
toString method of the referenced object with no arguments; but if the result of
invoking the toString method is null, then the string "null" is used instead.

Let's check the expression of Line n1:
text = text + new A(); --> As text is of String type, hence + operator behaves as
concatenation operator.
As text is null, so "null" is used in the Expression.
new A() represents the object of A class, so toString() method of A class is invoked, but
as toString() method of A class returns null, hence "null" is used in the given
expression.
So, given expression is written as:
text = "null" + "null";
text = "nullnull";

Hence, Line n2 prints 8 on to the console.

5.1.39 Answer: B

Reason:
Special main method (called by JVM on execution) should be static and should have public access modifier. It also takes argument of String [] type (Varargs syntax String... can also be used).

String [] or String... argument can use any identifier name, even though in most of the cases you will see "args" is used.

final modifier can be used with this special main method.

Hence, from the given five definitions of main method, below two definitions will print expected output on to the console.

```
public static final void main(String... a) {
    System.out.println("Java Rocks!");
}
```
and
```
public static void main(String [] args) {
    System.out.println("Java Rocks!");
}
```

5.1.40 Answer: A, C, E

Reason:
Let's check all the statements one by one:

short s1 = 10;
Above statement compiles successfully, even though 10 is an int literal (32 bits) and s1 is of short primitive type which can store only 16 bits of data.
Here java does some background task, if value of int literal can be easily fit to short primitive type (-32768 to 32767), then int literal is implicitly casted to short type.
So above statement is internally converted to:
short s1 = (short)10;

short s2 = 32768;
It causes compilation failure as 32768 is out of range value.

final int i3 = 10;
short s3 = i3;

Above code compiles successfully. If you are working with final variable and the value is within the range, then final variable is implicitly casted to target type, as in this case i3 is implicitly casted to short.

```
final int i4 = 40000;
short s4 = i4;
```
It causes compilation failure as 40000 is out of range value.

```
final int i5 = 10;
short s5 = i5 + 100;
```
Above code compiles successfully. If you are working with constant expression and the resultant value of the constant expression is within the range, then resultant value is implicitly casted. In this case, resultant value 110 is implicitly casted.

```
final int m = 25000;
final int n = 25000;
short s6 = m + n;
```
m + n is a constant expression but resultant value 50000 is out of range for short type, hence it causes compilation failure.

```
int i7 = 10;
short s7 = i7;
```
Compilation error as i7 is non-final variable and hence cannot be implicitly casted to short type.

5.1.41 **Answer: F**

Reason:
Variable 'count' declared inside interface Counter is implicitly public, static and final. Line n1 compiles successfully.
Line n2 creates one dimensional array of 2 elements of Counter type and both the elements are initialized to null. Line n2 compiles successfully.
Though correct way to refer static variable is by using the type name, such as Counter.count but it can also be invoked by using Counter reference variable. Hence ctr.count at Line n3 correctly points to the count variable at Line n1.
For invoking static fields, object is not needed, therefore even if 'ctr' refers to null, ctr.count doesn't throw NullPoionterException. Given loop executes twice and therefore output is: 1010

5.1.42 Answer: C

Reason:
For readability purpose underscore (_) is used to separate numeric values. This is very useful in representing big numbers such as credit card numbers (1234_7654_9876_0987). Multiple underscores are also allowed within the digits. Hence, `int x = 5____0;` compiles successfully and variable x stores 50.
`float f = 123.76_86f;` compiles successfully.
1_2_3_4 is int literal 1234 and int can easily be assigned to double, hence `double d = 1_2_3_4;` compiles successfully.

____50 is a valid variable name, and as this variable is not available hence, int y = ____50; causes compilation error.

Underscores must be available within the digits. For the statement int z = 50____; as underscores are used after the digits, hence it causes compilation error.

5.1.43 Answer: D

Reason:
Variable 'arr' refers to an array object of String of 7 elements and it contains the memory address of String array object.
'arr' is of reference type, therefore when `System.out.println(arr);` is executed, toString() method defined in Object class is invoked, which returns <fully qualified name of internal array class>@<hexadecimal representation of hashcode>. That is why some text containing @ symbol is printed on to the console.

5.1.44 Answer: A

Reason:
Given statement:
System.out.println((flag = true) | (flag = false) || (flag = true)); //flag = false
System.out.println(((flag = true) | (flag = false)) || (flag = true)); //bitwise inclusive OR | has higher precedence over logical OR ||. flag = false

|| has two operands, Left: ((flag = true) | (flag = false)) and Right: (flag = true). Left operand needs to be evaluated first.

System.out.println((true | (flag = false)) || (flag = true)); //flag = true
System.out.println((true | false) || (flag = true)); //flag = false
System.out.println(true || (flag = true)); //flag = false

|| is a short-circuit operator and as left operand evaluates to true, hence right operand is not evaluated.

Above statement prints true on to the console.

And

System.out.println(flag); prints false on to the console as flag variable is false.

5.1.45   Answer: E

Reason:
super.open(); => Using super keyword, you can access methods and variables of immediate parent class, hence if you replace /*INSERT*/ with `super.open();`, then open() method of Padlock class will be invoked.

super.super.open(); => super.super is not allowed in java, it causes compilation error.

((Lock)super).open(); => Not possible to cast super keyword in java, it causes compilation error.

(Lock)super.open(); => super.open(); will be evaluated first as dot (.) operator has higher precedence than cast. super.open(); returns void and hence it cannot be casted to Lock. It also causes compilation error.

In fact, it is not possible to directly reach to 2 levels, super keyword allows to access methods and variables of immediate parent class only (just 1 level up). Hence, correct answer is: 'None of the other options'

5.1.46   Answer: C

Reason:
Line n1 creates an array instance of ILogger containing 2 elements. null is assigned to both the array elements. Line n1 compiles successfully.

As, log() method is declared in ILogger interface, hence statement at Line n2: logger.log(); doesn't cause any compilation error. Compiler is happy to see that log() method is invoked on the reference variable of ILogger type.

1st iteration:
logger --> null, logger.log(); throws NullPointerException as method log() is invoked on null reference.

5.1.47 Answer: D

Reason:
Super class defines a method with name Super() but not any constructor. Hence compiler adds below default constructor in Super class:

```
Super() {
    super();
}
```

Class Super extends from Object class and Object class has no-argument constructor, which is called by the super(); statement in above default constructor.

Java compiler also adds `super();` as the first statement inside the no-argument constructor of Base class:

```
Base() {
    super();
    Super();
    System.out.print("GOING_");
}
```

As Base extends Super and both the classes are in the same package, hence `super();` invokes the no-argument constructor of Super class and `Super();` invokes the Super() method of Super class. Base class inherits the Super() method of Super class.

No compilation error in any of the classes.

On executing Test class, main(String[]) is invoked, which executes `new Base();` statement.
No-argument constructor of Base class is invoked, which executes `super();`, hence no-argument constructor of Super class is invoked.

Next, `Super();` is executed and this invokes the Super() method of Super class and hence KEEP_ is printed on to the console.
After that, `System.out.print("GOING_");` is executed and GOING_ is printed on to the console.

main(String []) method finishes its execution and program terminates successfully after printing KEEP_GOING_ on to the console.

5.1.48   Answer: D

Reason:
search(String) method declares to throw FileNotFoundException, which is a checked exception. It returns true if match is found otherwise it throws an instance of FileNotFoundException.

main(String[]) provides try-catch block around `search("virat.pdf")` and catch handler checks for FileNotFoundException. Given code compiles successfully.

There are 4 elements in 'names' array, so starting index is 0 and end index is 3, but given for loop goes till index number 4.
As search string is "virat.pdf" (not present in names array), hence for loop will execute for i = 0, 1, 2, 3, 4.
For i = 4, `names[i].equalsIgnoreCase(name)` throws ArrayIndexOutOfBoundsException (it is a RuntimeException). main(String []) method doesn't provide handler for ArrayIndexOutOfBoundsException and therefore stack trace is printed on to the console and program terminates abruptly.

5.1.49   Answer: B, C, D

Reason:
Compound declarations are allowed in Java for primitive type and reference type.

Range of byte data type is from -128 to 127, hence if byte is used to replace /*INSERT*/, then y = 200 would cause compilation error as 200 is out of range value for byte type. Hence, byte cannot be used to replace /*INSERT*/.

short, int, long, float & double can replace /*INSERT*/ without causing any error. x + y will evaluate to 207 for short, int and long types whereas, x + y will evaluate to 207.0 for float and double types.

String class has overloaded valueOf methods for int, char, long, float, double, boolean, char[] and Object types. valueOf method returns the corresponding String object and length() method returns number of characters in the String object.

So, `String.valueOf(x + y).length()` in case of short, int and long returns 3, on the other hand, in case of float and double it would return 5.

Hence, only 3 options (short, int and long) print expected output on to the console.

5.1.50 Answer: B

Reason:
As both the classes: Square and TestSquare are in the same file, hence variables 'length' and 'sq' can be accessed using dot operator. Given code compiles successfully.

Line n1 creates an instance of Square class and 'sq1' refers to it. sq1.length = 10 and sq1.sq = null.
Line n2 creates an instance of Square class and 'sq2' refers to it. sq2.length = 5 and sq2.sq = null.

On execution of Line n3, sq1.sq = sq2.

Line n4: System.out.println(sq1.sq.length); => System.out.println(sq2.length); => Prints 5 on to the console.

5.1.51 Answer: D

Reason:
'profitPercentage' variable of Profitable interface is implicitly public, static and final.
Line n1 defines the instance variable 'profitPercentage' of Business class. There is no error at Line n1.
Super type reference variable can refer to an instance of Sub type, therefore no issues at Line n2 as well.

Even though correct syntax for accessing interface variable is by using Interface name, such as Profitable.profitPercentage but reference variable also works. obj.profitPercentage doesn't cause any compilation error.

As, obj is of Profitable type, hence obj.profitPercentage points to the 'profitPercentage' variable of Profitable type. Given code compiles successfully and on execution prints 42.0 on to the console.

5.1.52 **Answer: B**

Reason:

Variable 'book' in main(String[]) method of TestBook class cannot be declared private as it is a local variable. Hence, there is a compilation error in TestBook class.

Only final modifier can be used with local variables.

5.1.53 **Answer: B**

Reason:

Initially val = 25.

'if(val++ < 26)' means 'if(25 < 26)', value of val (25) is used in the boolean expression and then value of val is incremented by 1, so val = 26.

25 < 26 is true, control goes inside if-block and executes System.out.println(val++);

This prints current value of val to the console, which is 26 and after that increments the value of val by 1, so val becomes 27.

5.1.54 **Answer: B**

Reason:

super(); is added by the compiler as the first statement in both the constructors:

```
Animal() {
    super();
    System.out.print("ANIMAL-");
}
```

and

```
public Dog() {
    super();
```

```
        System.out.print("DOG");
    }
```

Class Animal extends from Object class and Object class has no-argument constructor, hence no issues with the constructor of Animal class.

Animal class's constructor has package scope, which means it is accessible to all the classes declared in package 'a'. But Dog class is declared in package 'b' and hence `super();` statement inside Dog class's constructor causes compilation error as no-argument constructor of Animal class is not visible.

There is no compilation error in Test.java file as Dog class's constructor is public and therefore `new Dog();` compiles successfully.

5.1.55   Answer: C

Reason:
Even though it seems like method m() will not compile successfully, but starting with JDK 7, it is allowed to use super class reference variable in throw statement referring to sub class Exception object.

In this case, method m() throws SQLException and compiler knows that variable e (Exception type) refers to an instance of SQLException only and hence allows it.

Program executes successfully and prints CAUGHT SUCCESSFULLY on to the console.

5.1.56   Answer: A

Reason:
Please note, if passed command line arguments contain space(s) in between, then it is a common practice to enclosed within double quotes. In this case "James Gosling" is passed as one String object and "Bill Joy" is also passed as one String object.
java Test "James Gosling" "Bill Joy" passes new String [] {"James Gosling", "Bill Joy"} to args of main method. args[0] refers to "James Gosling" and args[1] refers to "Bill Joy". Hence, Welcome James Gosling! is printed on to the console. While printing the String object, enclosing quotes are not shown.

To use quotes as part of the String, you can escape those using backslash, such as:
java Test "\"James Gosling"\" "\"Bill Joy"\"
Above command will print Welcome "James Gosling"! on to the console.

5.1.57   Answer: A

Reason:
Given question expects you to solve the compilation error and not care about runtime error. For array indexes, any int values can be used, hence all the 7 pairs are allowed in this case.

If question were expecting to compile and execute the program successfully, then any combination greater than the max indexes values would have worked. For example, in the given code, as max 1st dimension value = 6 and max 2nd dimension value = 6, so any int value > 6 can be used for x and any int value > 6 can be used for y.
Out of the given seven options, only two options (x = 7, y = 7) and (x = 8, y = 8) would have worked.

5.1.58   Answer: C

Reason:
Threat class doesn't specify any constructor, hence Java compiler adds below default constructor:
```
Threat() {super();}
```

Line n1 creates an instance of Threat class and initializes instance variable 'name' to "VIRUS". Variable 'obj' refers to this instance.
Line n2 prints VIRUS on to the console.
Line n3 invokes evaluate(Threat) method, as it is a static method defined in AvoidThreats class, hence `evaluate(obj);` is the correct syntax to invoke it. Line n3 compiles successfully. On invocation parameter variable 't' copies the content of variable 'obj' (which stores the address to Threat instance created at Line n1). 't' also refers to the same instance referred by 'obj'.

On execution of Line n6, another Threat instance is created, its instance variable 'name' refers to "VIRUS" and 't' starts referring to this newly created instance of

Threat class. Variable 'obj' of main(String[]) method still refers to the Threat instance created at Line n1. So, 'obj' and 't' now refer to different Threat instances.

Line n7, assigns "PHISHING" to the 'name' variable of the instance referred by 't'. evaluate(Threat) method finishes its execution and control goes back to main(String[]) method.

Line n4 is executed next, print() method is invoked on the 'obj' reference and as obj.msg still refers to "VIRUS", so this statement prints VIRUS on to the console.

Hence in the output, you get:
VIRUS
VIRUS

5.1.59 Answer: D

Reason:
public static void main(String[] args) method is invoked by JVM.
Variable args is initialized and assigned with Program arguments. For example,
java Test: args refers to String [] of size 0.
java Test Hello: args refers to String [] of size 1 and 1st array element refers to "Hello"
java Test 1 2 3: args refers to String [] of size 3 and 1st array element refers to "1", 2nd array element refers to "2" and 3rd array element refers to "3".

Command used in this question: java Test Good, so args refers to String[] of size 1 and element at 0th index is "Good".
args[1] = "Day!"; is trying to access 2nd array element at index 1, which is not available and hence an exception is thrown at runtime.

5.1.60 Answer: G

Reason:
default methods were added in Java 8. Class Chair correctly implements Sellable interface and it also overrides the default symbol() method of Sellable interface.

At Line n1, 'obj' refers to an instance of Chair class, so obj.symbol() and obj.getPrice() invoke the overriding methods of Chair class only.

obj.symbol() returns "£" and obj.getPrice() returns 35.0

At Line n2, '+' operator behaves as concatenation operator and Line n2 prints £35.0 on to the console.

5.1.61   Answer: D

Reason:
Variable x is of X type (superclass) and refers to an instance of Z type (subclass).
At Line n1, compiler checks whether greet() method is available in class X or not. As greet() method is available in class X, hence no compilation error for Line n1.
At Line n2, x is casted to Y and compiler checks whether greet() method is available in class Y or not. As greet() method is available in class Y, hence no compilation error for Line n2.
At Line n3, x is casted to Z and compiler checks whether greet() method is available in class Z or not. As greet() method is available in class Z, hence no compilation error for Line n3.

There is no compilation error in the given code it compiles successfully.

Variable x refers to an instance of Z class and at Line n1, n2 and n3 same instance is being used. Which overriding method to invoke, is decided at runtime based on the instance.
At runtime, all three statements, at Line n1, Line n2 and Line n3 would invoke the greet() method of Z class, which would print Good Night! three times on to the console.

5.1.62   Answer: B

Reason:
`int indexOf(String str)` method of String class returns the index within this string of the first occurrence of the specified substring. e.g. "Java".indexOf("a") returns 1.

`char charAt(int index)` method of String class returns the char value at the specified index. e.g. "Java".charAt(2) returns 'v'.

Let's check the given expression:

```
str.charAt(str.indexOf("A") + 1)
= "ALASKA".charAt("ALASKA".indexOf("A") + 1)
= "ALASKA".charAt(0 + 1)  //"ALASKA".indexOf("A") returns 0.
= "ALASKA".charAt(1)
= 'L'
```

Hence, L is printed on to the console.

5.1.63 Answer: G

Reason:
Planet is defined in 'com.udayankhattry.galaxy' package, Creator is defined in 'com.udayankhattry.oca' package and TestCreator is defined in 'com.udayankhattry.oca.test' package.
Planet class doesn't mention 'Creator' or 'TestCreator' and hence no import statements are needed in Planet class.
Creator class uses the name 'Planet' in its code and hence Creator class needs to import Planet class using 'import com.udayankhattry.galaxy.Planet;' statement or 'import com.udayankhattry.galaxy.*;' statement.
TestCreator class uses the name 'Creator' in its code and hence TestCreator class needs to import Creator class using 'import com.udayankhattry.oca.Creator;' statement or 'import com.udayankhattry.oca.*;' statement.

Please note, even though in TestCreator class, `Creator.create()` returns an instance of Planet class but as name 'Planet' is not used, hence Planet class is not needed to be imported.

Planet class correctly overrides toString() method, hence when an instance of Planet class is passed to println(...) method, as in the below statement:
System.out.println(Creator.create());
toString() method defined in the Planet class is invoked, which print "Planet: Earth" on to the console.

5.1.64 Answer: E

Reason:
Let's solve the expression at Line n1:

!flag1 == flag2 != flag3 == !flag4
(!flag1) == flag2 != flag3 == (!flag4) //Logical NOT has got highest precedence among given operators
((!flag1) == flag2) != flag3 == (!flag4) //== and != have same precedence and left to right associative, grouping == first
(((!flag1) == flag2) != flag3) == (!flag4) //grouping != next
Above expression is left with single operator ==, whose left side is: (((!flag1) == flag2) != flag3) and right side is: (!flag4). As == is a binary operator, so left side is evaluated first.
((false == flag2) != flag3) == (!flag4) //!flag1 is false
((false == false) != flag3) == (!flag4) //flag2 is false
(true != flag3) == (!flag4) //(false == false) evaluates to true
(true != true) == (!flag4) //flag3 is true
false == (!flag4) //(true != true) evaluates to false
false == true //!flag4 is true
false //(false == true) evaluates to false
Hence, false is printed on to the console.

Let's solve the expression at Line n2:
flag1 = flag2 != flag3 == !flag4
flag1 = flag2 != flag3 == (!flag4) //Logical NOT has got highest precedence among given operators
flag1 = (flag2 != flag3) == (!flag4) //== and != have same precedence and left to right associative, grouping == first
flag1 = ((flag2 != flag3) == (!flag4)) //grouping == next
Above expression is left with single assignment operator =, whose right side needs to be evaluated first
flag1 = ((false != flag3) == (!flag4)) //flag2 is false
flag1 = ((false != true) == (!flag4)) //flag3 is true
flag1 = (true == (!flag4)) //(false != true) evaluates to true
flag1 = (true == true) //!flag4 is true
flag1 = true //(true == true) evaluates to true
true is assigned to flag1 and true is also printed on to the console

One suggestion: In the real exam, if you find a question containing multiple expressions, then first check if there is any compilation error or not. If there is no compilation error in all the expressions, then only solve the expressions.

5.1.65 Answer: D, E

Reason:
Let's check all the statements one by one:

s1.equals(s2): equals(String) method of String class matches two String objects and it takes character's case into account while matching. Alphabet A in upper case and alphabet a in lower case are not equal according to this method. As String objects referred by s1 and s2 have different cases, hence output is false.

s1.equals(s2.toUpper()): Compilation error as there is no toUpper() method available in String class. Correct method name is: toUpperCase().

s2.equals(s1.toLower()): Compilation error as there is no toLower() method available in String class. Correct method name is: toLowerCase().

s1.length() == s2.length(): length() method returns the number of characters in the String object. s1.length() returns 3 and s2.length() also returns 3, hence output is true.

s1.equalsIgnoreCase(s2): Compares s1 and s2, ignoring case consideration and hence returns true.

s1.contentEquals(s2): String class contains two methods: contentEquals(StringBuffer) and contentEquals(CharSequence). Please note that String, StringBuilder and StringBuffer classes implement CharSequence interface, hence contentEquals(CharSequence) method defined in String class can be invoked with the argument of either String or StringBuilder or StringBuffer. In this case, it is invoked with String argument and hence it is comparing the contents of two String objects. This method also takes character's case into account while matching. As String objects referred by s1 and s2 have different cases, hence output is false.

5.1.66 Answer: F

Reason:
Profit class causes compilation error as it complains about duplicate default methods: Profitable1.profit() and Profitable2.profit(). To rectify this error abstract class Profit must override the profit() method.

default keyword for method is allowed only inside the interface and default methods are implicitly public. So overriding method should use public modifier and shouldn't use default keyword.

If you want to invoke the default method implementation from the overriding method, then the correct syntax is: [Interface_name].super.[default_method_name]. Hence, `Profitable1.super.profit();` will invoke the default method of Profitable1 interface and `Profitable2.super.profit();` will invoke the default method of Profitable2 interface.

Based on above points, let's check all the options one by one:

No need for any modifications, code compiles as is: X

Replace /*INSERT*/ with below code:
```
double profit() {
    return 50.0;
```
}: X
profit() method must be declared with public access modifier.

Replace /*INSERT*/ with below code:
```
public default double profit() {
    return 50.0;
```
}: X
default keyword for method is allowed only inside the interface.

Replace /*INSERT*/ with below code:
```
protected double profit() {
    return 50.0;
```
}: X
profit() method must be declared with public access modifier.

Replace /*INSERT*/ with below code:
```
public double profit() {
    return Profitable1.profit();
```
}: X
Profitable1.profit(); causes compilation error as correct syntax is:
Profitable1.super.profit();

Replace /*INSERT*/ with below code:
```
public double profit() {
```

```
    return Profitable2.super.profit();
}: ✓
```
It compiles successfully.

5.1.67 Answer: C

Reason:
/*INSERT*/ cannot be replaced with interface as work() method at Line n1 is neither abstract nor default. Hence, statements 3 and 4 will not work.
Let's check other statements:
1. abstract class Work implements Workable: abstract class in java can have 0 or more abstract methods. It compiles successfully.
2. class Work implements Workable: It correctly implements the work() method of Workable interface, hence it compiles successfully.
5. abstract class Work: abstract class in java can have 0 or more abstract methods. It compiles successfully.

Hence, out of 5 statements, 3 will compile successfully.

5.1.68 Answer: C

Reason:
Basic/Regular for loop has following form:
for ([ForInit] ; [Expression] ; [ForUpdate]) {...}
[ForInit] can be local variable initialization or the following expressions:
Assignment
PreIncrementExpression
PreDecrementExpression
PostIncrementExpression
PostDecrementExpression
MethodInvocation
ClassInstanceCreationExpression

[ForUpdate] can be following expressions:
Assignment
PreIncrementExpression
PreDecrementExpression

PostIncrementExpression
PostDecrementExpression
MethodInvocation
ClassInstanceCreationExpression

The [Expression] must have type boolean or Boolean, or a compile-time error occurs. If [Expression] is left blank, it evaluates to true.

All the expressions can be left blank; for(;;) is a valid for loop and it is an infinite loop as [Expression] is blank and evaluates to true.

In the given code, for [ForInit] and [ForUpdate], `System.out.print(i++);` is used, which is a method invocation statement and hence a valid statement. Given code compiles fine.

Let's check the iterations:
1st iteration: [ForInit] expression is executed, 0 is printed on to the console. i = 1. i < 2 evaluates to true, control goes inside the loop's body and execute `System.out.print(i);` statement. 1 is printed on to the console.
2nd iteration: [ForUpdate] expression is executed, 1 is printed on to the console. i = 2. 2 < 2 evaluates to false, control goes out of the for loop. main method ends and program terminates successfully after printing 011 on to the console.

5.1.69   Answer: B

Reason:
There are 2 rules related to return types of overriding method:
1. If return type of overridden method is of primitive type, then overriding method should use same primitive type.
2. If return type of overridden method is of reference type, then overriding method can use same reference type or its sub-type (also known as covariant return type).

ArrayList is a subtype of List, hence overriding method can use List<Father> or ArrayList<Father> as return type. Definitions 1 and 2 are valid.

Please note: even though Son is a subtype of Father, List<Son> is not subtype of List<Father>. Hence definitions 3 and 4 are NOT valid.

On similar lines, even though GrandSon is a subtype of Father, List<GrandSon> is not subtype of List<Father>. Hence definitions 5 and 6 are also NOT valid.

List<Object> is not subtype of List<Father>, definition 7 is NOT valid.

ArrayList<Object> is not subtype of List<Father>, definition 8 is also NOT valid.

5.1.70 Answer: A

Reason:
Both the methods of Report class have same signature(name and parameters match). Having just different return types don't overload the methods and therefore Java compiler complains about duplicate generateReport() methods in Report class.

5.1.71 Answer: E

Reason:
Method jump() in Animal class declares to throw RuntimeException.
Overriding method may or may not throw any RuntimeException. Only thing to remember is that if overridden method throws any unchecked exception or Error, then overriding method must not throw any checked exceptions. Line n1 compiles successfully as it correctly overrides the jump() method of Animal class.
Class Deer also provides overloaded jump(int) method.

Inside main(String []) method, reference variable 'animal' is of Animal class (supertype) and it refers to an instance of Deer class (subtype), this is polymorphism and allowed in Java.

As instance is of Deer class, hence 'animal' reference can easily be casted to Deer type. Line n2 and Line n3 compiles successfully and on execution prints below on to the console:
DEER JUMPS
DEER JUMPS TO 5 FEET

5.1.72   Answer: E

Reason:
No syntax error in the given code.
Initially, i = 1, j = 5 and k = 0.
1st iteration of A: i = 2.
   1st iteration of B: j = 4.
      1st iteration of C: k = k + i + j = 0 + 2 + 4 = 6. `i == j` evaluates to false and `i > j`
also evaluates to false, hence else block gets executed. `continue B` takes the control
to the loop B.
   2nd iteration of B: j = 3.
      1st iteration of C: k = k + i + j = 6 + 2 + 3 = 11. `i == j` evaluates to false and `i > j`
also evaluates to false, hence else block gets executed. `continue B` takes the control
to the loop B.
   3rd iteration of B: j = 2.
      1st iteration of C: k = k + i + j = 11 + 2 + 2 = 15. `i == j` evaluates to true, control
breaks out of the loop A.

`System.out.println(k);` prints 15 on to the console.

6 Bonus Exam - 2

6.1 72 questions covering all topics

6.1.1 Given code of Test.java file:

```
package com.udayankhattry.oca;

public class Test {
    static String str = "KEEP IT ";  //Line n1
    public static void main(String[] args) {
        String str = str + "SIMPLE";  //Line n2
        System.out.println(str);
    }
}
```

What will be the result of compiling and executing Test class?

A. KEEP IT
B. KEEP IT SIMPLE
C. SIMPLE
D. Compilation error

6.1.2 Given code of Test.java file:

```
package com.udayankhattry.oca;

interface Document {
    default String getType() {
        return "TEXT";
    }
}

interface WordDocument extends Document {
    String getType();
}

class Word implements WordDocument {}
```

```
public class Test {
    public static void main(String[] args) {
        Document doc = new Word(); //Line n1
        System.out.println(doc.getType()); //Line n2
    }
}
```

Which of the following statements is correct?

A. Interface Document causes compilation error

B. Interface WordDocument causes compilation error

C. Class Word causes compilation error

D. Test class compiles successfully and on execution prints TEXT on to the console

6.1.3   Given code of Test.java file:

```
package com.udayankhattry.oca;

class Parent {
    String quote = "MONEY DOESN'T GROW ON TREES";
}

class Child extends Parent {
    String quote = "LIVE LIFE KING SIZE";
}

class GrandChild extends Child {
    String quote = "PLAY PLAY PLAY";
}

public class Test {
    public static void main(String[] args) {
        GrandChild gc = new GrandChild();
        System.out.println(/*INSERT*/);
    }
}
```

Which of the following options, if used to replace /*INSERT*/, will compile successfully and on execution will print MONEY DOESN'T GROW ON TREES on to the console?

Select ALL that apply.

A. `gc.quote`
B. `(Parent)gc.quote`
C. `((Parent)gc).quote`
D. `((Parent)(Child)gc).quote`
E. `(Parent)(Child)gc.quote`

6.1.4   Given code of Test.java file:

```java
package com.udayankhattry.oca;

import java.io.FileNotFoundException;
import java.io.IOException;

class Base {
    Base() throws IOException {
        System.out.print(1);
    }
}

class Derived extends Base {
    Derived() throws FileNotFoundException {
        System.out.print(2);
    }
}

public class Test {
    public static void main(String[] args) throws Exception {
        new Derived();
    }
}
```

What will be the result of compiling and executing Test class?

A. Compilation error in both Base and Derived classes
B. Compilation error only in Base class
C. Compilation error only in Derived class
D. Test class executes successfully and prints 12 on to the console
E. Test class executes successfully and prints 21 on to the console

6.1.5   Consider below code of Test.java file:

```
package com.udayankhattry.oca;

import java.time.LocalDate;

public class Test {
    public static void main(String [] args) {
        LocalDate date = LocalDate.parse("2020-08-31");
        System.out.println(date.plusMonths(-6));
    }
}
```

What is the result?

A. 2020-02-31

B. 2020-02-30

C. 2020-02-29

D. 2020-02-28

E. An exception is thrown at runtime

F. Compilation error

6.1.6   Consider below code fragment:

```
String place = "MISSS";
System.out.println(place.replace("SS", "T"));
```

What is the output?

A. MIST

B. MITS

C. MISSS

D. MIT

6.1.7 Below is the code of Test.java file:

```
package com.udayankhattry.oca;

import java.util.ArrayList;
import java.util.List;

public class Test {
    public static void main(String[] args) {
        List<String> places = new ArrayList<>();
        places.add("Austin");
        places.add("Okinawa");
        places.add("Giza");
        places.add("Manila");
        places.add("Batam");
        places.add("Giza");

        if(places.remove("Giza"))
            places.remove("Austin");

        System.out.println(places);
    }
}
```

What will be the result of compiling and executing Test class?

A. An exception is thrown at runtime

B. Compilation error

C. [Okinawa, Manila, Batam]

D. [Austin, Okinawa, Giza, Manila, Batam, Giza]

E. [Austin, Okinawa, Manila, Batam, Giza]

F. [Austin, Okinawa, Manila, Batam]

G. [Okinawa, Manila, Batam, Giza]

H. [Okinawa, Giza, Manila, Batam]

6.1.8 Consider below codes of 4 java files:

```
//I1.java
package com.udayankhattry.oca;

public interface I1 {
    int i = 10;
}
```

```
//I2.java
package com.udayankhattry.oca;

public interface I2 {
    int i = 20;
}


//I3.java
package com.udayankhattry.oca;

public interface I3 extends I1, I2 { //Line n1

}


//Test.java
package com.udayankhattry.oca;

public class Test {
    public static void main(String[] args) {
        System.out.println(I1.i); //Line n2
        System.out.println(I2.i); //Line n3
        System.out.println(I3.i); //Line n4
    }
}
```

Which of the following statements is correct?

A. Line n1 causes compilation error
B. Line n2 causes compilation error
C. Line n3 causes compilation error
D. Line n4 causes compilation error
E. There is no compilation error

6.1.9   Given code of Test.java file:

```
package com.udayankhattry.oca;

interface Blogger {
    default void blog() throws Exception {
        System.out.println("GENERIC");
    }
}

class TravelBlogger implements Blogger {
    public void blog() {
        System.out.println("TRAVEL");
    }
}

public class Test {
    public static void main(String[] args) {
        Blogger blogger = new TravelBlogger(); //Line n1
        ((TravelBlogger)blogger).blog(); //Line n2
    }
}
```

What will be the result of compiling and executing Test class?

A. Compilation error in TravelBlogger class

B. Compilation error in Test class

C. GENERIC is printed on to the console and program terminates successfully

D. TRAVEL is printed on to the console and program terminates successfully

E. An exception is thrown at runtime

6.1.10 Consider below code of Test.java file:

```
package com.udayankhattry.oca;

class Super {
    public String num = "10"; //Line n1
}

class Sub extends Super {
    protected int num = 20; //Line n2
}

public class Test {
    public static void main(String[] args) {
        Super obj = new Sub();
        System.out.println(obj.num += 2); //Line n3
    }
}
```

What will be the result of compiling and executing above code?

A. Compilation error at Line n2

B. Compilation error at Line n3

C. It executes successfully and prints 12 on to the console

D. It executes successfully and prints 22 on to the console

E. It executes successfully and prints 102 on to the console

F. It executes successfully and prints 202 on to the console

6.1.11 Given code of Test.java file:

```
package com.udayankhattry.oca;

class Base {
    public void log() throws NullPointerException {
        System.out.println("Base: log()");
    }
}

class Derived extends Base {
    public void log() throws RuntimeException {
        System.out.println("Derived: log()");
    }
}

public class Test {
    public static void main(String[] args) {
        Base obj = new Derived();
        obj.log();
    }
}
```

What will be the result of compiling and executing Test class?

A. Base: log()
B. Derived: log()
C. Compilation error in Derived class
D. Compilation error in Test class

6.1.12 Given code of Test.java file:

```
package com.udayankhattry.oca;

import java.io.IOException;

class Super {
    Super() throws RuntimeException {
        System.out.print("CARPE ");
    }
}

class Sub extends Super {
    Sub() throws IOException {
        System.out.print("DIEM ");
    }
}

public class Test {
    public static void main(String[] args) throws Exception {
        new Sub();
    }
}
```

What will be the result of compiling and executing Test class?

A. Compilation error in both Super and Sub classes

B. Compilation error only in Super class

C. Compilation error only in Sub class

D. Test class executes successfully and prints CARPE DIEM on to the console

E. Test class executes successfully and prints DIEM CARPE on to the console

6.1.13 Given code of Test.java file:

```
package com.udayankhattry.oca;

class Base {
    String msg = "INHALE"; //Line n1
}

class Derived extends Base {
    Object msg = "EXHALE"; //Line n2
}

public class Test {
    public static void main(String[] args) {
        Base obj1 = new Base(); //Line n3
        Base obj2 = new Derived(); //Line n4
        Derived obj3 = (Derived) obj2; //Line n5
        String text = obj1.msg + "-" +
                obj2.msg + "-" + obj3.msg; //Line n6
        System.out.println(text); //Line n7
    }
}
```

What will be the result of compiling and executing above code?

A. Line n2 causes compilation error

B. Line n5 throws Exception at runtime

C. Line n6 causes compilation error

D. It executes successfully and prints INHALE-EXHALE-EXHALE

E. It executes successfully and prints INHALE-INHALE-EXHALE

F. It executes successfully and prints INHALE-INHALE-INHALE

G. None of the other options

6.1.14 _____ modifier is most restrictive and _____ modifier is least restrictive.

Which of the following options (in below specified order) can be filled in above blank spaces?

A. public, private
B. private, public
C. default (with no access modifier specified), public
D. protected, public
E. default (with no access modifier specified), protected

6.1.15 Consider below code of TestMessage.java file:

```
package com.udayankhattry.oca;

class Message {
    String msg = "LET IT GO!";

    public void print() {
        System.out.println(msg);
    }
}

public class TestMessage {
    public static void change(Message m) { //Line n5
        m.msg = "NEVER LOOK BACK!"; //Line n6
    }

    public static void main(String[] args) {
        Message obj = new Message(); //Line n1
        obj.print(); //Line n2
        change(obj); //Line n3
        obj.print(); //Line n4
    }
}
```

What will be the result of compiling and executing TestMessage class?

A.	null NEVER LOOK BACK!	B.	NEVER LOOK BACK! NEVER LOOK BACK!
C.	null null	D.	LET IT GO! NEVER LOOK BACK!
E.	LET IT GO! LET IT GO!	F.	Compilation error

6.1.16   Consider below code of Test.java file:

```java
package com.udayankhattry.oca;

class Super {
    Super() {
        System.out.print("Reach");
    }
}

class Sub extends Super {
    Sub() {
        Super();
        System.out.print("Out");
    }
}

public class Test {
    public static void main(String[] args) {
        new Sub();
    }
}
```

What will be the result of compiling and executing above code?

A. Compilation Error in Super class

B. Compilation Error in Sub class

C. Compilation Error in Test class

D. It prints ReachOut on to the console

E. It prints OutReach on to the console

410

6.1.17 Consider below code of Test.java file:

```
package com.udayankhattry.oca;

public class Test {
    public static void main(String[] args) {
        String arr1 [], arr2, arr3 = null; //Line n1
        arr1 = new String[2];
        arr1[0] = "A";
        arr1[1] = "B";
        arr2 = arr3 = arr1;  //Line n2
        log(arr2);  //Line n3
    }

    private static void log(String... vals) {
        for(String s : vals)
            System.out.print(s);
    }
}
```

What will be the result of compiling and executing Test class?

A. Line n1 causes compilation error
B. Line n2 causes compilation error
C. Line n3 causes compilation error
D. It executes successfully and prints AB on to the console
E. It executes successfully and prints BA on to the console
F. It executes successfully and prints A on to the console
G. It executes successfully and prints B on to the console

6.1.18 Consider below code fragment:

```
package com.udayankhattry.oca;

abstract class Log {
    abstract long count(); //Line n1
    abstract Object get(); //Line n2
}
```

```
class CommunicationLog extends Log {
    int count() { //Line n3
        return 100;
    }

    String get() { //Line n4
        return "COM-LOG";
    }
}

public class Test {
    public static void main(String[] args) {
        Log log = new CommunicationLog(); //Line n5
        System.out.print(log.count());
        System.out.print(log.get());
    }
}
```

Which of the following statement is correct?

A. Line n3 causes compilation error

B. Line n4 causes compilation error

C. Line n5 causes compilation error

D. Given code compiles successfully and on execution prints 100COM-LOG on to the console

6.1.19 Given code of Test.java file:

```
package com.udayankhattry.oca;

class Paper {
    static String getType() { //Line n1
        return "GENERIC";
    }
}

class RuledPaper extends Paper {
    String getType() { //Line n2
        return "RULED";
    }
}
```

```
public class Test {
    public static void main(String[] args) {
        Paper paper = new RuledPaper(); //Line n3
        System.out.println(paper.getType()); //Line n4
    }
}
```

Which of the following statements is true for above code?

A. Compilation error in RuledPaper class

B. Compilation error in Test class

C. Code compiles successfully and on execution prints GENERIC on to the console

D. Code compiles successfully and on execution prints RULED on to the console

6.1.20 Consider below code of Test.java file:

```
package com.udayankhattry.oca;

class Counter {
    static int ctr = 0;
    int count = 0;
}

public class Test {
    public static void main(String[] args) {
        Counter ctr1 = new Counter();
        Counter ctr2 = new Counter();
        Counter ctr3 = new Counter();

        for(int i = 1; i <= 5; i++ ) {
            ctr1.ctr++;
            ctr1.count++;
            ctr2.ctr++;
            ctr2.count++;
            ctr3.ctr++;
            ctr3.count++;
        }

        System.out.println(ctr3.ctr + ":" + ctr3.count);
    }
}
```

What will be the result of compiling and executing Test class?

A. Compilation error

B. 5:5 is printed on to the console

C. 15:15 is printed on to the console

D. 15:5 is printed on to the console

6.1.21 Consider below code of Test.java file:

```
package com.udayankhattry.oca;

public class Test {
    public static void main(String[] args) {
        int var = 3;
        String [][] arr = new String[--var][var++]; //Line n1
        arr[1][1] = "X"; //Line n2
        arr[1][2] = "Y"; //Line n3
        for(String [] arr1 : arr) {
            for(String s : arr1) {
                if(s != null)
                    System.out.print(s);
            }
        }
    }
}
```

What will be the result of compiling and executing Test class?

A. It causes compilation error at single statement

B. It causes compilation error at multiple statements

C. It throws an exception at runtime

D. It prints XY on to the console and program terminates successfully

E. It prints XY on to the console and program terminates abruptly

6.1.22 Given code of Test.java file:

```
package com.udayankhattry.oca;

public class Test {
    public static void main(String[] args) {
        try { //outer
            try { //inner
                System.out.println(1/0);
            } catch(ArithmeticException e) {
                System.out.println("INNER");
            } finally {
                System.out.println("FINALLY 1");
            }
        } catch(ArithmeticException e) {
            System.out.println("OUTER");
        } finally {
            System.out.println("FINALLY 2");
        }
    }
}
```

What will be the result of compiling and executing Test class?

A.	INNER FINALLY 1	B.	OUTER FINALLY 2
C.	INNER FINALLY 2	D.	INNER FINALLY 1 FINALLY 2

A.
```
try {
    save();
    log();
} catch(IOException | SQLException ex) {}
```

B.
```
try {
    save();
    log();
} catch(SQLException | IOException ex) {}
```

C.
```
try {
    save();
    log();
} catch(IOException | Exception ex) {}
```

D.
```
try {
    save();
    log();
} catch(SQLException | Exception ex) {}
```

E.
```
try {
    save();
    log();
} catch(Exception | RuntimeException ex) {}
```

F.
```
try {
    save();
    log();
} catch(Exception ex) {}
```

6.1.23 Given code of Test.java file:

```java
package com.udayankhattry.oca;

public class Test {
    public static void convert(String s)
        throws IllegalArgumentException,
                            RuntimeException, Exception {
        if(s.length() == 0) {
            throw new RuntimeException("
                    LENGTH SHOULD BE GREATER THAN 0");
        }
    }

    public static void main(String [] args) {
        try {
            convert("");
        }
        catch(IllegalArgumentException |
                RuntimeException | Exception e) { //Line 14
            System.out.println(e.getMessage()); //Line 15
        } //Line 16
        catch(Exception e) {
            e.printStackTrace();
        }
    }
}
```

Line 14 causes compilation error. Which of the following changes enables to code to print LENGTH SHOULD BE GREATER THAN 0?

A. Replace Line 14 with 'catch(RuntimeException | Exception e) {'

B. Replace Line 14 with 'catch(IllegalArgumentException | Exception e) {'

C. Replace Line 14 with 'catch(IllegalArgumentException | RuntimeException e) {'

D. Replace Line 14 with 'catch(RuntimeException e) {'

E. Comment out Line 14, Line 15 and Line 16

6.1.24 Consider below code of Test.java file:

```
package com.udayankhattry.oca;

public class Test {
    public static void main(String[] args) {
        int ctr = 100;
        one: for (int i = 0; i < 10; i++) {
            two: for (int j = 0; j < 7; j++) {
                three: while (true) {
                    ctr++;
                    if (i > j) {
                        break one;
                    } else if (i == j) {
                        break two;
                    } else {
                        break three;
                    }
                }
            }
        }
        System.out.println(ctr);
    }
}
```

What will be the result of compiling and executing Test class?

A. Compilation error
B. 100
C. 101
D. 102
E. 103
F. 104
G. 105
H. 106

6.1.25 **Given code of Test.java file:**

```
package com.udayankhattry.oca;

interface Rideable {
    void ride(String name);
}

class Animal {}

class Horse extends Animal implements Rideable {
    public void ride(String name) {
        System.out.println(name.toUpperCase() +
                            " IS RIDING THE HORSE");
    }
}

public class Test {
    public static void main(String[] args) {
        Animal horse = new Horse();
        /*INSERT*/
    }
}
```

Which of the following options, if used to replace /*INSERT*/, will compile successfully and on execution will print EMMA IS RIDING THE HORSE on to the console?
Select ALL that apply.

A. `horse.ride("EMMA");`

B. `(Horse)horse.ride("EMMA");`

C. `((Horse)horse).ride("Emma");`

D. `(Rideable)horse.ride("emma");`

E. `((Rideable)horse).ride("emma");`

F. `(Rideable)(Horse)horse.ride("EMMA");`

G. `(Horse)(Rideable)horse.ride("EMMA");`

H. `((Rideable)(Horse)horse).ride("EMMA");`

I. `((Horse)(Rideable)horse).ride("emma");`

6.1.26 Consider incomplete code of M.java file

```
class M {
}

_____ class N {
}
```

Following options are available to fill the above blank:

1. public
2. private
3. protected
4. final
5. abstract

How many above options can be used to fill above blank (separately and not together) such that there is no compilation error?

A. Only one option
B. Only two options
C. Only three options
D. Only four options
E. All five options

6.1.27 **Given code of Test.java file:**

```
package com.udayankhattry.oca;

class X {
    void A() {
        System.out.print("A");
    }
}

class Y extends X {
    void A() {
        System.out.print("A-");
    }

    void B() {
        System.out.print("B-");
    }

    void C() {
        System.out.print("C-");
    }
}

public class Test {
    public static void main(String[] args) {
        X obj = new Y(); //Line n1
        obj.A(); //Line n2
        obj.B(); //Line n3
        obj.C(); //Line n4
    }
}
```

What will be the result of compiling and executing above code?

A. A-B-C-

B. AB-C-

C. Compilation error in class Y

D. Compilation error in class Test

6.1.28 Given code of Test.java file:

```
package com.udayankhattry.oca;

public class Test {
    private static void test() throws Exception {
        throw new Exception();
    }

    public static void main(String [] args) {
        try {
            test();
        } finally {
            System.out.println("GAME ON");
        }
    }
}
```

What will be the result of compiling and executing Test class?

A. GAME ON is printed to the console and program ends normally
B. GAME ON is printed to the console, stack trace is printed and then program ends normally
C. GAME ON is printed to the console, stack trace is printed and then program ends abruptly
D. Compilation error

6.1.29 Consider below code of Test.java file:

```
package com.udayankhattry.oca;
class Currency {
    String notation = "-"; //Line n1

    String getNotation() { //Line n2
        return notation;
    }
}

class USDollar extends Currency {
    String notation = "$"; //Line n3

    String getNotation() { //Line n4
        return notation;
    }
}
```

```
class Euro extends Currency {
    protected String notation = "€";  //Line n5

    protected String getNotation() {  //Line n6
        return notation;
    }
}

public class Test {
    public static void main(String[] args) {
        Currency c1 = new USDollar();
        System.out.println(c1.notation + ":" +
                                    c1.getNotation());

        Currency c2 = new Euro();
        System.out.println(c2.notation + ":" +
                                    c2.getNotation());
    }
}
```

What will be the result of compiling and executing above code?

A.	Compilation error in USDollar class		
B.	Compilation error in Euro class		
C.	-:$ -:€	D.	-:- -:-
E.	$:$ €:€		

6.1.30 Consider below code of Test.java file:

```
package com.udayankhattry.oca;

public class Test {
    public static void main(String[] args) {
        StringBuilder sb = new StringBuilder("B"); //Line n1
        sb.append(sb.append("A")); //Line n2
        System.out.println(sb); //Line n3
    }
}
```

What will be the result of compiling and executing Test class?

A. B

B. BA

C. AB

D. BAB

E. ABA

F. ABAB

G. BABA

H. ABBA

I. Compilation error at Line n2

6.1.31 Consider below code of Test.java file:

```
package com.udayankhattry.oca;
import java.util.*;

public class Test {
    public static void main(String[] args) {
        List<String> list;
        list = new ArrayList<>(); //Line n1
        list.add("A");
        list.add("E");
        list.add("I");
        list.add("O");
        list.add("U");
        list.addAll(list.subList(0, 4)); //Line n2
        System.out.println(list);
    }
}
```

What will be the result of compiling and executing Test class?

A. Line n1 causes compilation error

B. Line n2 causes compilation error

C. An exception is thrown at runtime by Line n2

D. [A, E, I, O, U]

E. [A, E, I, O, U, A, E, I, O, U]

F. [A, E, I, O, U, A, E, I, O]

6.1.32 Consider below code of Test.java file:

```
package com.udayankhattry.oca;

public class Test {
    public static void main(String[] args) {
        String str = "Game on"; //Line n1
        StringBuilder sb = new StringBuilder(str); //Line n2

        System.out.println(str.contentEquals(sb)); //Line n3
        System.out.println(sb.contentEquals(str)); //Line n4
        System.out.println(sb.equals(str)); //Line n5
        System.out.println(str.equals(sb)); //Line n6
    }
}
```

Which of the following statements is correct?

A. Only one statement causes compilation error

B. Two statements cause compilation error

C. Three statements cause compilation error

D. Four statements cause compilation error

E. No compilation error

6.1.33 Given code of Test.java file:

```
package com.udayankhattry.oca;

public class Test {
    private static void div(int i, int j) {
        try {
            System.out.println(i / j);
        } catch(ArithmeticException e) {
            throw (RuntimeException)e;
        }
    }

    public static void main(String[] args) {
        try {
            div(5, 0);
        } catch(ArithmeticException e) {
            System.out.println("AE");
        } catch(RuntimeException e) {
            System.out.println("RE");
        }
    }
}
```

What will be the result of compiling and executing Test class?

A. Compilation error

B. Program ends abruptly

C. AE is printed on to the console and program terminates successfully

D. RE is printed on to the console and program terminates successfully

6.1.34 Consider below codes of 3 java files:

```
//Buyable.java
package com.udayankhattry.oca;

public interface Buyable {
    int salePercentage = 85;

    public static String salePercentage() {
        return salePercentage + "%";
    }
}
```

```java
//Book.java
package com.udayankhattry.oca;

public class Book implements Buyable {}


//Test.java
package com.udayankhattry.oca;

public class Test {
    public static void main(String[] args) {
        Buyable [] arr = new Buyable[2];
        for(Buyable b : arr) {
            System.out.println(b.salePercentage); //Line n1
            System.out.println(b.salePercentage()); //Line n2
        }

        Book [] books = new Book[2];
        for(Book b : books) {
            System.out.println(b.salePercentage); //Line n3
            System.out.println(b.salePercentage()); //Line n4
        }
    }
}
```

Which of the following statements are correct?
Select ALL that apply.

A. There is a compilation error in Buyable.java file

B. There is a compilation error in Book.java file

C. There is a compilation error at Line n1

D. There is a compilation error at Line n2

E. There is a compilation error at Line n3

F. There is a compilation error at Line n4

6.1.35 Given code of Test.java file:

```
package com.udayankhattry.oca;

import java.sql.SQLException;

public class Test {
    private static void getReport() throws SQLException {
        try {
            throw new SQLException();
        } catch (Exception e) {
            throw null; //Line 10
        }
    }

    public static void main(String[] args) {
        try {
            getReport(); //Line 16
        } catch(SQLException e) {
            System.out.println("REPORT ERROR");
        }
    }
}
```

What will be the result of compiling and executing Test class?

A. REPORT ERROR is printed on to the console and program terminates successfully
B. Program ends abruptly
C. Line 10 causes compilation failure
D. Line 16 causes compilation failure

6.1.36 Consider below code snippet:

```
int i = 10;
System.out.println(i > 3 != false);
```

What is the result?

A. Compilation error
B. true
C. false
D. null

6.1.37 Given code of Test.java file:

```
package com.udayankhattry.oca;

interface M {
    public static void log() {
        System.out.println("M");
    }
}

abstract class A {
    public static void log() {
        System.out.println("N");
    }
}

class MyClass extends A implements M {}

public class Test {
    public static void main(String[] args) {
        M obj1 = new MyClass();
        obj1.log(); //Line n1

        A obj2 = new MyClass();
        obj2.log(); //Line n2

        MyClass obj3 = new MyClass();
        obj3.log(); //Line n3
    }
}
```

Which of the following statements is correct?

A. There is a compilation error in interface M

B. There is a compilation error in class A

C. Line n1 causes compilation error

D. Line n2 causes compilation error

E. Line n3 causes compilation error

F. Given code compiles successfully

6.1.38 Consider below code of Test.java file:

```java
package com.udayankhattry.oca;

public class Test {
    public static void main(String [] args) {
        String text = "RISE ";
        text = text + (text = "ABOVE ");
        System.out.println(text);
    }
}
```

What will be the result of compiling and executing Test class?

A. RISE RISE ABOVE

B. RISE ABOVE

C. ABOVE ABOVE

D. RISE ABOVE RISE

6.1.39 Given code of Thought.java file:

```java
public class Thought {
    /*INSERT*/ {
        System.out.println("All is well");
    }
}
```

Which 3 options, if used to replace /*INSERT*/, will compile successfully and on execution will print "All is well" on to the console?

A. `public void static main(String [] args)`

B. `protected static void main(String [] args)`

C. `public void main(String... args)`

D. `static public void Main(String [] args)`

E. `static public void main(String [] args)`

F. `public static void main(String [] a)`

G. `public static Void main(String [] args)`

H. `public static void main(String... a)`

6.1.40 Consider below code of Test.java file:

```
package com.udayankhattry.oca;

public class Test {
    public static void main(String[] args) {
        boolean b1 = 0;
        boolean b2 = 1;
        System.out.println(b1 + b2);
    }
}
```

What is the result of compiling and executing Test class?

A. 0

B. 1

C. true

D. false

E. Compilation error

6.1.41 Consider below codes of 2 java files:

```
//GetSetGo.java
package com.udayankhattry.oca;

public interface GetSetGo {
    int count = 1; //Line n1
}

//Test.java
package com.udayankhattry.oca;

public class Test {
    public static void main(String[] args) {
        GetSetGo [] arr = new GetSetGo[5]; //Line n2
        for(GetSetGo obj : arr) {
            obj.count++; //Line n3
        }
        System.out.println(GetSetGo.count); //Line n4
    }
}
```

Which of the following statements is correct?

A. Line n1 causes compilation error

B. Line n2 causes compilation error

C. Line n3 causes compilation error

D. Line n4 causes compilation error

E. Test class compiles successfully and on execution prints 5 on to the console

F. Test class compiles successfully and on execution prints 6 on to the console

6.1.42 Given code of Test.java file:

```
package com.udayankhattry.oca;

public class Test {
    public static void main(String[] args) {
        byte b1 = 10; //Line n1
        int i1 = b1; //Line n2
        byte b2 = i1; //Line n3
        System.out.println(b1 + i1 + b2);
    }
}
```

What is the result of compiling and executing Test class?

A. Line n1 causes compilation error

B. Line n2 causes compilation error

C. Line n3 causes compilation error

D. 30 is printed on to the console

6.1.43 Consider below code of Test.java file:

```
package com.udayankhattry.oca;

public class Test {
    public static void main(String[] args) {
        int [] arr = {10, 20, 30}; //Line n1
        int i = 0;
        arr[i++] = arr[++i] = 40; //Line n2
        for(int x : arr)
            System.out.println(x);
    }
}
```

What will be the result of compiling and executing Test class?

A.	Compilation error at Line n2		
B.	An exception is thrown by Line n2		
C.	10 20 30	D.	10 40 30
E.	40 40 30	F.	10 40 40
G.	40 20 40		

6.1.44   Consider below code of Test.java file:

```
package com.udayankhattry.oca;

public class Test {
    public static void main(String [] args) {
        boolean status = true;
        System.out.println(status = false ||
                        status = true | status = false);
        System.out.println(status);
    }
}
```

What will be the result of compiling and executing Test class?

A.	true false	B.	false true
C.	true true	D.	false false
E.	Compilation error		

6.1.45 Given code of Test.java file:

```
package com.udayankhattry.oca;

class Super {
    final int NUM = -1;  //Line n1
}

class Sub extends Super {
    /*INSERT*/
}

public class Test {
    public static void main(String[] args) {
        Sub obj = new Sub();
        obj.NUM = 200;  //Line n2
        System.out.println(obj.NUM);  //Line n3
    }
}
```

Above code causes compilation error, which modifications, done independently, enable the code to compile and on execution print 200 on to the console?

Select ALL that apply.

A. Remove final modifier from Line n1
B. Replace /*INSERT*/ with byte NUM;
C. Replace /*INSERT*/ with short NUM;
D. Replace /*INSERT*/ with int NUM;
E. Replace /*INSERT*/ with float NUM;
F. Replace /*INSERT*/ with double NUM;
G. Replace /*INSERT*/ with boolean NUM;
H. Replace /*INSERT*/ with Object NUM;

6.1.46 Given code of Test.java file:

```
package com.udayankhattry.oca;

import java.io.FileNotFoundException;

public class Test {
    public static void main(String[] args) {
        try {
            System.out.println(args[1].length());
        } catch (RuntimeException ex) {
            System.out.println("ONE");
        } catch (FileNotFoundException ex) {
            System.out.println("TWO");
        }
        System.out.println("THREE");
    }
}
```

What will be the result of compiling and executing Test class?

A.	ONE THREE	B.	TWO THREE
C.	THREE		
D.	None of the System.out.println statements is executed		
E.	Compilation error		

6.1.47 Consider below code of Test.java file:

```java
package com.udayankhattry.oca;

class MyClass {
    MyClass() {
        System.out.println(101);
    }
}

class MySubClass extends MyClass {
    final MySubClass() {
        System.out.println(202);
    }
}

public class Test {
    public static void main(String[] args) {
        System.out.println(new MySubClass());
    }
}
```

What will be the result of compiling and executing Test class?

A.	Compilation error
B.	101 202 <Some text containing @ symbol>
C.	202 <Some text containing @ symbol>
D.	202 101 <Some text containing @ symbol>
E.	101 <Some text containing @ symbol>

6.1.48 Given code of Test.java file:

```
package com.udayankhattry.oca;

public class Test {
    public static void main(String[] args) {
        try {
            play();
            return;
        } catch(Exception ex) {
            System.out.println(ex.getMessage());
            return;
        } finally {
            System.out.println("MATCH ABANDONED");
        }
        System.out.println("DONE");
    }

    static void play() throws Exception {
        throw new Exception("INJURED");
    }
}
```

What will be the result of compiling and executing Test class?

A.	INJURED MATCH ABANDONED	B.	INJURED MATCH ABANDONED DONE
C.	MATCH ABANDONED	D.	INJURED
E.	INJURED DONE	F.	MATCH ABANDONED DONE
G.	Compilation error		

6.1.49   Consider below code of Test.java file:

```
package com.udayankhattry.oca;

public class Test {
    public static void main(String[] args) {
        String str = "PANIC";
        StringBuilder sb = new StringBuilder("THET");
        System.out.println(str.replace("N", sb)); //Line n1
    }
}
```

What will be the result of compiling and executing Test class?

A. PANIC
B. PATHETIC
C. Line n1 causes compilation error
D. Line n1 throws error at runtime

6.1.50   Consider below code fragment:

```
private void emp() {}
```

And the statements:
1. Given code compiles successfully if it is used inside the class named 'emp'
2. Given code compiles successfully if it is used inside the class named 'Emp'
3. Given code compiles successfully if it is used inside the class named 'employee'
4. Given code compiles successfully if it is used inside the class named 'Employee'
5. Given code compiles successfully if it is used inside the class named 'Student'
6. Given code compiles successfully if it is used inside the class named '_emp_'

How many statements are true?

A. Only one statement
B. Two statements
C. Three statements
D. Four statements
E. Five statements
F. All six statements

6.1.51 Consider below code of Test.java file:

```
package com.udayankhattry.oca;

interface I1 {
    public static void print(String str) {
        System.out.println("I1:" + str.toUpperCase());
    }
}

class C1 implements I1 {
    void print(String str) {
        System.out.println("C1:" + str.toLowerCase());
    }
}

public class Test {
    public static void main(String[] args) {
        I1 obj = new C1();
        obj.print("Java");
    }
}
```

Which of the following statements is correct?

A. Class C1 causes compilation error

B. Class Test causes compilation error

C. Interface I1 causes compilation error

D. Given code compiles successfully and on execution prints I1:JAVA on to the console

E. Given code compiles successfully and on execution prints C1:java on to the console

6.1.52 Consider below code snippet:

```
package com.udayankhattry.oca;

public class Test {
    String testNo;
    String desc;
    /*
    Other codes...
    */
}
```

Which of the options are correct so that instance variables 'testNo' and 'desc' are accessible only within 'com.udayankhattry.oca' package?

A.	No changes are necessary

B.	Change the instance variable declarations to:
	`private String testNo;`
	`private String desc;`

C.	Change the instance variable declarations to:
	`protected String testNo;`
	`protected String desc;`

D.	Change the instance variable declarations to:
	`public String testNo;`
	`public String desc;`

6.1.53 Consider below code of Test.java file:

```java
package com.udayankhattry.oca;

public class Test {
    public static void main(String[] args) {
        int score = 30; // Line n1
        char grade = 'F'; // Line n2
        if (50 <= score < 60) // Line n3
            grade = 'D';
        else if (60 <= score < 70) // Line n4
            grade = 'C';
        else if (70 <= score < 80) // Line n5
            grade = 'B';
        else if (score >= 80)
            grade = 'A';
        System.out.println(grade);
    }
}
```

What will be the result of compiling and executing Test class?

A. Compilation error

B. A

C. B

D. C

E. D

F. F

6.1.54 Consider below code of Test.java file:

```java
package com.udayankhattry.oca;

public class Test {
    public static void main(String[] args) {
        int x = 10; //Line n1
        if (false)
            System.out.println(x); //Line n2
        System.out.println("HELLO"); //Line n3
    }
}
```

What is the result of compiling and executing Test class?

A.	Compilation error at Line n1		
B.	Compilation error at Line n2		
C.	Compilation error at Line n3		
D.	HELLO	E.	10 HELLO

6.1.55 Given code of Test.java file:

```
package com.udayankhattry.oca;

import java.sql.SQLException;

public class Test {
    private static void getData() throws SQLException {
        try {
            throw new SQLException();
        } catch (Exception e) {
            e = new SQLException();
            throw e;
        }
    }

    public static void main(String[] args) {
        try {
            getData();
        } catch(SQLException e) {
            System.out.println("SQL");
        }
    }
}
```

What will be the result of compiling and executing Test class?

A. Method getData() causes compilation error

B. Method main(String []) causes compilation error

C. SQL is printed on to the console and program terminates successfully

D. Program ends abruptly

6.1.56 Consider below code of Test.java file:

```java
public class Test {
    public static void main(String [] args) {
        System.out.println("String");
    }

    public static void main(Integer [] args) {
        System.out.println("Integer");
    }

    public static void main(byte [] args) {
        System.out.println("byte");
    }
}
```

And the commands:
```
javac Test.java
java Test 10
```

What is the result?

A. Integer
B. String
C. byte
D. Compilation error
E. An Exception is thrown at runtime

6.1.57   Consider below code of Test.java file:

```
package com.udayankhattry.oca;

public class Test {
    public static void main(String[] args) {
        int elements = 0;
        Object [] arr = {"A", "E", "I",
                    new Object(), "O", "U"}; //Line n1
        for(Object obj : arr) { //Line n2
            if(obj instanceof String) {
                continue;
            } else {
                break;
            }
            elements++; //Line n3
        }
        System.out.println(elements); //Line n4
    }
}
```

What will be the result of compiling and executing Test class?

A. 0

B. 1

C. 3

D. 5

E. 6

F. Compilation error at Line n1

G. Compilation error at Line n2

H. Compilation error at Line n3

I. Compilation error at Line n4

6.1.58 Consider below code of Test.java file:

```java
package com.udayankhattry.oca;

public class Test {
    int i1 = 10;
    static int i2 = 20;

    private void change1(int val) {
        i1 = ++val; //Line n1
        i2 = val++; //Line n2
    }

    private static void change2(int val) {
        i1 = --val; //Line n3
        i2 = val--; //Line n4
    }

    public static void main(String[] args) {
        change1(5); //Line n5
        change2(5); //Line n6
        System.out.println(i1 + i2); //Line n7
    }
}
```

Which of the following statements are correct regarding above code?
Select ALL that apply.

A. Line n1 causes compilation error

B. Line n2 causes compilation error

C. Line n3 causes compilation error

D. Line n4 causes compilation error

E. Line n5 causes compilation error

F. Line n6 causes compilation error

G. Line n7 causes compilation error

H. Above code compiles successfully

I. Above code prints 8 on execution

J. Above code prints 30 on execution

6.1.59 Given code of Test.java file:

```
class A {
    public static void main(String [] args) {
        System.out.println("A");
    }
}

class B {
    public static void main(String [] args) {
        System.out.println("B");
    }
}

class C {
    public static void main(String [] args) {
        System.out.println("C");
    }
}

class D {
    public static void main(String [] args) {
        System.out.println("D");
    }
}
```

Which of the following options is correct?

A.	To print C on to the console, execute below commands:
	`javac Test.java`
	`java Test`

B.	To print C on to the console, execute below commands:
	`javac C.java`
	`java C`

C.	To print C on to the console, execute below commands:
	`javac Test.java`
	`java C`

D.	Test.java file is not a valid java file as it doesn't contain code for class Test
E.	Test.java file will compile successfully but expected output is not possible

6.1.60 Consider below codes of 2 java files:

```java
//Flyable.java
package com.udayankhattry.oca;

public interface Flyable {
    static int horizontalDegree() { //Line n1
        return 20;
    }

    default void fly() {
        System.out.println("Flying at " +
            horizontalDegree() + " degrees."); //Line n2
    }

    void land();
}
```

```java
//Aeroplane.java
package com.udayankhattry.oca;

public class Aeroplane implements Flyable {
    public void land() {
        System.out.println("Landing at " +
            -Flyable.horizontalDegree() +
                                " degrees."); //Line n3
    }

    public static void main(String[] args) {
        new Aeroplane().fly();
        new Aeroplane().land();
    }
}
```

What will be the result of compiling and executing Aeroplane class?

A.	Compilation error at Line n1
B.	Compilation error at Line n2
C.	Compilation error at Line n3
D.	Given code compiles successfully and on execution prints below in the output: Flying at 20 degrees. Landing at -20 degrees.

6.1.61 Given code of Test.java file:

```
package com.udayankhattry.oca;

class Base {
    int id = 1000; //Line n1

    Base() {
        Base(); //Line n2
    }

    void Base() { //Line n3
        System.out.println(++id); //Line n4
    }
}

class Derived extends Base {
    int id = 2000; //Line n5

    Derived() {} //Line n6

    void Base() { //Line n7
        System.out.println(--id); //Line n8
    }
}

public class Test {
    public static void main(String[] args) {
        Base base = new Derived(); //Line n9
    }
}
```

What will be the result of compiling and executing above code?

A. 1000

B. 1001

C. 999

D. 2000

E. 1999

F. 2001

G. 0

H. -1

I. Compilation error

J. An exception is thrown

6.1.62 Consider below code of Test.java file:

```
package com.udayankhattry.oca;

public class Test {
    public static void main(String[] args) {
        String [] arr = {"1st", "2nd", "3rd",
                                    "4th", "5th"};
        String place = "faraway";
        System.out.println(
                arr[place.indexOf("a", 3)]); //Line n1
    }
}
```

What will be the result of compiling and executing Test class?

A. 1st

B. 3rd

C. 5th

D. 2nd

E. 4th

F. An exception is raised by Line n1

6.1.63 Consider below code of Test.java file:

```
package com.udayankhattry.oca;

public class Test {
    public static void main(String[] args) {
        char c1 = 'a'; //ASCII code of 'a' is 97
        int i1 = c1; //Line n1
        System.out.println(i1); //Line n2
    }
}
```

What is the result of compiling and executing Test class?

A. a

B. 97

C. Line n1 causes compilation failure

D. Line n1 causes runtime error

6.1.64 Consider below code of Test.java file:

```
package com.udayankhattry.oca;

public class Test {
    public static void main(String [] args) {
        int num = 10;
        if(num++ == num++) {
            System.out.println("EQUAL " + num);
        } else {
            System.out.println("NOT EQUAL " + num);
        }
    }
}
```

What will be the result of compiling and executing Test class?

A. EQUAL 12

B. EQUAL 11

C. NOT EQUAL 12

D. NOT EQUAL 11

6.1.65 Consider below code of Test.java file:

```
package com.udayankhattry.oca;

public class Test {
    public static void main(String [] args) {
        String text = "ONE ";
        System.out.println(
                text.concat(text.concat("ELEVEN ")).trim());
    }
}
```

What will be the result of compiling and executing Test class?

A. ONE ELEVEN

B. ONE ONE ELEVEN

C. ONE ELEVEN ONE ELEVEN

D. ONE ELEVEN ONE

6.1.66 Consider below code of Test.java file:

```
package com.udayankhattry.oca;

interface Perishable1 {
    default int maxDays() {
        return 1;
    }
}

interface Perishable2 extends Perishable1 {
    default int maxDays() {
        return 2;
    }
}

class Milk implements Perishable2, Perishable1 {}

public class Test {
    public static void main(String[] args) {
        Perishable1 obj = new Milk();
        System.out.println(obj.maxDays());
    }
}
```

Which of the following statements is correct?

A. Interface Perishable2 causes compilation error

B. Class Milk causes compilation error

C. Class Test causes compilation error

D. Given code compiles successfully and on execution Test class prints 1 on to the console

E. Given code compiles successfully and on execution Test class prints 2 on to the console

A.	No need for any modifications, code compiles as is

B.	Replace /*INSERT*/ with below code:
	``
	double profit() {
	    return 50.0;
	}
	``

C.	Replace /*INSERT*/ with below code:
	``
	public default double profit() {
	    return 50.0;
	}
	``

D.	Replace /*INSERT*/ with below code:
	``
	protected double profit() {
	    return 50.0;
	}
	``

E.	Replace /*INSERT*/ with below code:
	``
	public double profit() {
	    return Profitable1.profit();
	}
	``

F.	Replace /*INSERT*/ with below code:
	``
	public double profit() {
	    return Profitable2.super.profit();
	}
	``

6.1.67 Given code of Test.java file:

```
package com.udayankhattry.oca;

public class Test {
    public static void main(String[] args) {
        System.out.println(new RuntimeException()); //Line n1
        System.out.println(new
                    RuntimeException("HELLO")); //Line n2
        System.out.println(new RuntimeException(new
                    RuntimeException("HELLO"))); //Line n3
    }
}
```

Does above code compile successfully?

A. Yes

B. No

6.1.68 Consider below code of Test.java file:

```
package com.udayankhattry.oca;

public class Test {
    public static void main(String[] args) {
        for(int x = 10, y = 11, z = 12;
                    y > x && z > y; y++, z -= 2) {
            System.out.println(x + y + z);
        }
    }
}
```

What will be the result of compiling and executing Test class?

A.	32	B.	33
C.	34	D.	33 32
E.	Compilation error		

6.1.69 Given code of Test.java file:

```
package com.udayankhattry.oca;

import java.util.ArrayList;
import java.util.List;
import java.util.function.Predicate;

public class Test {
    public static void main(String[] args) {
        List<String> words = new ArrayList<>();
        words.add("A");
        words.add("an");
        words.add("the");
        words.add("when");
        words.add("what");
        words.add("Where");
        words.add("whether");

        processStringArray(words, /*INSERT*/);
    }
```

```
private static void processStringArray(List<String>
                    list, Predicate<String> predicate) {
    for(String str : list) {
        if(predicate.test(str)) {
            System.out.println(str);
        }
    }
}
}
```

Which of the following options can replace /*INSERT*/ such that on executing Test class all the list elements are displayed in the output?
Select ALL that apply.

A. p -> true

B. p -> !!!!true

C. p -> !!false

D. p -> p.length() >= 1

E. p -> p.length() < 7

F. (String p) -> p.length() < 100

G. String p -> p.length() > 0

6.1.70 Given code of Test.java file:

```
package com.udayankhattry.oca;

class Calculator {
    int calculate(int i1, int i2) {
        return i1 + i2;
    }

    double calculate(byte b1, byte b2) {
        return b1 % b2;
    }
}

public class Test {
    public static void main(String[] args) {
        byte b = 100;
        int i = 20;
        System.out.println(new Calculator().calculate(b, i));
    }
}
```

What will be the result of compiling and executing Test class?

A. Compilation error

B. An exception is thrown at runtime

C. 120

D. 120.0

E. 5

F. 5.0

6.1.71 Consider below code fragment:

```
import java.util.*;

class A{}
class B extends A{}

abstract class Super {
    abstract List<A> get() throws IndexOutOfBoundsException;
}

abstract class Sub extends Super {
    /*INSERT*/
}
```

Which of the following options replaces /*INSERT*/ such that there is no compilation error?

A. `abstract List<A> get() throws ArrayIndexOutOfBoundsException;`

B. `abstract List<B> get();`

C. `abstract ArrayList<A> get() throws Exception;`

D. `abstract ArrayList<B> get();`

6.1.72 Consider below code of Test.java file:

```
package com.udayankhattry.oca;

public class Test {
    public static void main(String[] args) {
        outer: for(int i = 0; i < 3;
                                System.out.print(i)) {
            i++;
            inner: for(int j = 0; j < 3;
                                System.out.print(j)) {
                if(i > ++j) {
                    break outer;
                }
            }
        }
    }
}
```

What will be the result of compiling and executing Test class?

A. Compilation error

B. Program terminates successfully but nothing is printed on to the console

C. Program terminates successfully after printing 1 on to the console

D. Program terminates successfully after printing 12 on to the console

E. Program terminates successfully after printing 123 on to the console

F. Program terminates successfully after printing 1231 on to the console

G. Program terminates successfully after printing 121 on to the console

H. Program terminates successfully after printing 0120 on to the console

6.2 Answers to Bonus Exam - 2 with Explanation

6.1.1 Answer: D

Reason:
At Line n2, local variable 'str' shadows the static variable 'str' created at Line n1. Hence, for the expression `str + "SIMPLE"`, Java compiler complains as local variable 'str' is not initialized.

6.1.2 Answer: C

Reason:
As per Java 8, default methods were added in the interface. Interface Document defines default method getType(), there is no compilation error in interface Document. Method getType() is implicitly public in Document.

interface WordDocument extends Document and it overrides the default method getType() of Document, overriding method in WordDocument is implicitly abstract and public. An interface in java can override the default method of super type with abstract modifier. interface WordDocument compiles successfully.

class Word implements WordDocument and as WordDocument interface has abstract method getType(), and as class Word doesn't implement the getType() method hence it causes compilation failure.

6.1.3 Answer: C, D

Reason:
As instance variables are hidden by subclasses and not overridden, therefore instance variable can be accessed by using explicit casting.
Let's check all the options one by one:
gc.quote => It refers to "PLAY PLAY PLAY" as gc is of GrandChild class.

(Parent)gc.quote => gc.quote will be evaluated first as dot (.) operator has higher precedence than cast. gc.quote refers to String, hence it cannot be casted to Parent type. This would cause compilation error.

((Parent)gc).quote => Variable 'gc' is casted to Parent type, so this expression refers to "MONEY DOESN'T GROW ON TREES". It is one of the correct options.

((Parent)(Child)gc).quote => 'gc' is of GrandChild type, it is first casted to Child and then to Parent type and finally quote variable is accessed, so this expression refers to "MONEY DOESN'T GROW ON TREES". It is also one of the correct options.

(Parent)(Child)gc.quote => gc.quote will be evaluated first as dot (.) operator has higher precedence than cast. gc.quote refers to String, hence it cannot be casted to Child type. This would cause compilation error.

6.1.4   Answer: C

Reason:
It is legal for the constructors to have throws clause.
Constructors are not inherited by the Derived class so there is no method overriding rules related to the constructors but as one constructor invokes other constructors implicitly or explicitly by using this(...) or super(...), hence exception handling becomes interesting.

Java compiler adds super(); as the first statement inside Derived class's constructor:
```
Derived() throws FileNotFoundException {
    super(); //added by the compiler
    System.out.print(2);
}
```

As super(); invokes the constructor of Base class (which declares to throw IOException), compiler complains as Derived class no-argument constructor doesn't declare to throw IOException. It declares to throw FileNotFoundException (subclass of IOException), which is not enough for the instances of IOException.

6.1.5   Answer: C

Reason:

plusMonths(long) method of LocalDate class returns a copy of this LocalDate with the specified number of months added. Negative argument will subtract the passed month(s), hence date.plusMonths(-6) doesn't cause any compilation error.

This method adds the specified amount to the months field in three steps:

Add the input months to the month-of-year field

Check if the resulting date would be invalid

Adjust the day-of-month to the last valid day if necessary

For the given code,

2020-08-31 plus -6 months would subtract 6 months from the given date and would result in the invalid date 2020-02-31. Instead of returning an invalid result, the last valid day of the month, 2020-02-29, is returned.

Please note, 2020 is leap year and hence last day of February is 29 and not 28.

6.1.6 Answer: B

Reason:
According to Javadoc, replace(CharSequence target, CharSequence replacement) method of String class returns a new String object after replacing each substring of this string that matches the literal target sequence with the specified literal replacement sequence. The replacement proceeds from the beginning of the string to the end, for example, replacing "aa" with "b" in the string "aaa" will result in "ba" rather than "ab".

"MISSS".replace("SS", "T"); returns "MITS".

6.1.7 Answer: G

Reason:
remove(Object) method of List interface removes the first occurrence of the specified element from the list, if it is present. If this list does not contain the element, it is unchanged. remove(Object) method returns true, if removal was successful otherwise false.

Initially list has: [Austin, Okinawa, Giza, Manila, Batam, Giza]. places.remove("Giza") removes the first occurrence of "Giza" and after the successful removal, list has: [Austin, Okinawa, Manila, Batam, Giza]. places.remove("Giza") returns true, control goes inside if block and executes places.remove("Austin");

places list contains "Austin", so after the removal list has: [Okinawa, Manila, Batam, Giza].

6.1.8   Answer: D

Reason:
Variable 'i' declared inside interface I1 is implicitly public, static and final and similarly variable i declared inside interface I2 is implicitly public, static and final as well.
In Java a class can extend from only one class but an interface can extend from multiple interfaces. static variables are not inherited and hence there is no issue with Line n1.

I1.i points to variable 'i' of interface I1.
I2.i points to variable 'i' of interface I2.
I3.i is an ambiguous call as compiler is not sure whether to point to I1.i or I2.i and therefore, Line n4 causes compilation error.

6.1.9   Answer: D

Reason:
According to overriding rules, if super class / interface method declares to throw a checked exception, then overriding method of sub class / implementer class has following options:
1. May not declare to throw any checked exception.
2. May declare to throw the same checked exception thrown by super class / interface method.
3. May declare to throw the sub class of the exception thrown by super class / interface method.
4. Cannot declare to throw the super class of the exception thrown by super class / interface method.
5. Cannot declare to throw unrelated checked exception.
6. May declare to throw any RuntimeException or Error.

default methods were added in Java 8 and TravelBlogger class correctly overrides the default method blog() of Blogger interface. Blogger interface compiles successfully.

At Line n1, 'blogger' is of Blogger type (supertype) and it refers to an instance of TravelBlogger class (subtype), this is polymorphism and allowed in Java. Line n1 compiles successfully.

At Line n2, blog() method is being invoked on typecasting 'blogger' to TravelBlogger and as TravelBlogger class doesn't declare to throw any checked exception, hence Line n2 compiles successfully.

As instance is of TravelBlogger type, therefore on execution, Line n2 invokes blog() method of TravelBlogger instance, which prints TRAVEL on to the console.

6.1.10 Answer: E

Reason:
Subclass overrides the methods of superclass but it hides the variables of superclass.

Line n2 hides the variable created at Line n1, there is no rules related to hiding (type and access modifier can be changed).

'obj' is of Super type, hence obj.num refers to num variable at Line n1, which is of String type.
Expression at Line n3:
obj.num += 2
=> obj.num = obj.num + 2
=> obj.num = "10" + 2
=> obj.num = "102"

obj.num refers to "102" and same is printed on to the console.

6.1.11 Answer: B

Reason:
NullPointerException extends RuntimeException. Overriding method may or may not throw any RuntimeException. Only thing to remember is that if overridden method throws any unchecked exception or Error, then overriding method must not throw any checked exceptions.

So, method log() in Derived class correctly overrides Base class's method.

Rest is simple polymorphism. 'obj' refers to an instance of Derived class and hence obj.log(); invokes method log() of Derived class, which prints "Derived: log()" on to the console.

6.1.12   Answer: D

Reason:
It is legal for the constructors to have throws clause.
Constructors are not inherited by the Sub class so there is no method overriding rules related to the constructors but as one constructor invokes other constructors implicitly or explicitly by using this(...) or super(...), hence exception handling becomes interesting.

Java compiler adds super(); as the first statement inside Sub class's constructor:
```
Sub() throws IOException {
    super(); //added by the compiler
    System.out.println("DIEM");
}
```

super(); invokes the constructor of Super class (which declares to throw RuntimeException), as RuntimeException is unchecked exception, therefore no handling is necessary in the constructor of Sub class.
Sub class's constructor declares to throw IOException but main(String []) method handles it.

There is no compilation error and output is: CARPE DIEM

6.1.13   Answer: E

Reason:
Subclass overrides the methods of superclass but it hides the variables of superclass.

Line n2 hides the variable created at Line n1, there is no rules related to hiding (type and access modifier can be changed).

At Line n3, obj1 is of Base type and refers to an instance of Base class.

At Line n4, obj2 is of Base type and refers to an instance of Derived class.

At Line n5, as obj2 refers to an instance of Derived class, hence typecasting it to Derived type doesn't cause any Exception. obj3 is of Derived type and refers to an instance of Derived class.

Let's check the expression of Line n6:

obj1.msg + "-" + obj2.msg + "-" + obj3.msg;

=> (obj1.msg + "-") + obj2.msg + "-" + obj3.msg; //+ operator is left to right associative and behaves as concatenation operator as one of the operand is of String type.

=> ((obj1.msg + "-") + obj2.msg) + "-" + obj3.msg;

=> (((obj1.msg + "-") + obj2.msg) + "-") + obj3.msg;

Let's solve the expression now:

=> ((("INHALE" + "-") + obj2.msg) + "-") + obj3.msg; //obj1 is of Base type, hence obj1.msg refers to "INHALE"

=> (("INHALE-" + obj2.msg) + "-") + obj3.msg;

=> (("INHALE-" + "INHALE") + "-") + obj3.msg; //obj2 is of Base type, hence obj2.msg refers to "INHALE"

=> ("INHALE-INHALE" + "-") + obj3.msg;

=> "INHALE-INHALE-" + obj3.msg;

In above expression, left operand is of String type and right operand is of Object type, so toString() method is invoked. So, given expression is evaluated as:

=> "INHALE-INHALE-" + obj3.msg.toString();

=> "INHALE-INHALE-" + "EXHALE"; //As obj3.msg is of Object type and refers to an instance of String type, hence toString() method on "EXHALE" instance is invoked and this returns "EXHALE".

=> "INHALE-INHALE-EXHALE";

Line n7 prints INHALE-INHALE-EXHALE on to the console.

6.1.14 Answer: B

Reason:

'private' is most restrictive, then comes 'default (with no access modifier specified)', after that 'protected' and finally 'public' is least restrictive.

6.1.15   Answer: D

Reason:
Message class doesn't specify any constructor, hence Java compiler adds below default constructor:
```
Message() {super();}
```

Line n1 creates an instance of Message class and initializes instance variable 'msg' to "LET IT GO!". Variable 'obj' refers to this instance.
Line n2 prints LET IT GO! on to the console.
Line n3 invokes change(Message) method, as it is a static method defined in TestMessage class, hence `change(obj);` is the correct syntax to invoke it. Line n3 compiles successfully. On invocation parameter variable 'm' copies the content of variable 'obj' (which stores the address to Message instance created at Line n1). 'm' also refers to the same instance referred by 'obj'.

Line n6, assigns "NEVER LOOK BACK!" to the 'msg' variable of the instance referred by 'm'. As 'obj' and 'm' refer to the same instance, hence obj.msg also refers to "NEVER LOOK BACK!". change(Message) method finishes its execution and control goes back to main(String[]) method.

Line n4 is executed next, print() method is invoked on the 'obj' reference and as obj.msg refers to "NEVER LOOK BACK!", so this statement prints NEVER LOOK BACK! on to the console.

Hence in the output, you get:
LET IT GO!
NEVER LOOK BACK!

6.1.16   Answer: B

Reason:
Parent (Super) class constructor is invoked by `super();` (all letters in lowercase) from within the constructor of subclass.
First statement inside no-argument constructor of Sub class is: `Super();` (Letter 'S' is in uppercase) and hence it causes compilation error.

6.1.17   Answer: B

Reason:
arr1 is of String[] type, where as arr2 and arr3 are of String type. As all three arr1, arr2 and arr3 are of reference type, hence null can be assigned to all these variables. Line n1 compiles successfully.

Statement at Line n2: arr2 = arr3 = arr1;
=> arr2 = (arr3 = arr1); //assignment operator is right to left associative.
arr3 is of String type and arr1 is of String [] type, hence (arr3 = arr1) causes compilation error.

Though you had to select one correct option, hence no need to look further but I am providing explanation for Line n3 as well.
log(String...) method can be called using a String [] or a String instance or mutliple String instances:
log(new String[] {"A", "B"});
log("A");
log("A", "B");

As arr2 is of String type, hence `log(arr2);` (Line n3) compiles successfully.

6.1.18   Answer: A

Reason:
CommunicationLog class overrides count() and get() methods of Log class.
There are 2 rules related to return types:
1. If return type of overridden method is of primitive type, then overriding method should use same primitive type.
2. If return type of overridden method is of reference type, then overriding method can use same reference type or its sub-type (also known as covariant return type).

count() method at Line n1 returns long but overriding method at Line n3 returns int and that is why Line n3 causes compilation error.
get() method at Line n2 returns Object but overriding method at Line n4 returns String. String is a subclass of Object, so it is a case of covariant return type and hence allowed. Line n4 compiles successfully.

6.1.19 Answer: A

Reason:
Instance method of subclass cannot override the static method of superclass.

Instance method at Line n2 tries to override the static method at Line n1 and hence Line n2 causes compilation error.

There is no issue with Line n3 as reference variable of superclass can refer to an instance of subclass.

At Line n4, paper.getType() doesn't cause compilation error but as this syntax creates confusion, so it is not a good practice to access the static variables or static methods using reference variable, instead class name should be used. Paper.getType() is the preferred syntax.

6.1.20 Answer: D

Reason:
Each instance of the class contains separate copies of instance variable and share one copy of static variable.
There are 3 instances of Counter class created by main method and these are referred by ctr1, ctr2 and ctr3.
As 'ctr' is a static variable of Counter class, hence ctr1.ctr, ctr2.ctr and ctr3.ctr refer to the same variable. In fact, 'Counter.ctr' is the preferred way to refer the static variable 'ctr' but ctr1.ctr, ctr2.ctr and ctr3.ctr are also allowed.

As 'count' is an instance variable, so there are 3 separate copies: ctr1.count, ctr2.count, ctr3.count.

On the completion of for loop: ctr1.count = 5, ctr2.count = 5 and ctr3.count = 5 and Counter.ctr = 15.

15:5 is printed on to the console.

6.1.21 Answer: C

Reason:
Line n1:
String [][] arr = new String[--var][var++]; //var = 3
Access array element operator [] is left to right associative.
=> String [][] arr = new String[2][var++]; //var = 2, var is decremented first and then used in the expression.
=> String [][] arr = new String[2][2]; //var = 3, value of var is used first and then it is incremented by 1

Hence, arr refers to 2-dimensional String array object {{null, null}, {null, null}}.

At Line n2, arr[1][1] = "X"; assigns "X" to element at index [1][1], therefore arr --> {{null, null}, {null, "X"}}

At Line n3, arr[1][2] = "Y"; causes ArrayIndexOutOfBoundsException as 2nd index 2 is out of range.

As Line n3 throws Exception at runtime, hence for loop will not be executed.

6.1.22 Answer: D

Reason:
`System.out.println(1/0);` throws ArithmeticException, handler is available in inner catch-block, it executes and prints "INNER" to the console.

Once an exception is handled, no other catch block will get executed unless the exception is re-thrown.

Inner finally-block gets executed and prints "FINALLY 1" to the console.

Rule is finally-block always gets executed, so outer finally-block gets executed and prints "FINALLY 2" to the console.

6.1.23   Answer: D

Reason:
Throwable is the root class of the exception hierarchy and it contains some useful constructors:

1. public Throwable() {...} : No-argument constructor
2. public Throwable(String message) {...} : Pass the detail message
3. public Throwable(String message, Throwable cause) {...} : Pass the detail message and the cause
4. public Throwable(Throwable cause) {...} : Pass the cause

Exception and RuntimeException classes also provide similar constructors.

Throwable class also contains methods, which are inherited by all the subclasses (Exception, RuntimeException etc.)
1. public String getMessage() {...} : Returns the detail message (E.g. detail message set by 2nd and 3rd constructor)
2. public String toString() {} :
Returns a short description of this throwable. The result is the concatenation of:
the name of the class of this object
": " (a colon and a space)
the result of invoking this object's getLocalizedMessage() method

If getLocalizedMessage() returns null, then just the class name is returned.

In multi-catch statement, classes with multi-level hierarchical relationship can't be used.
RuntimeException is subclass of Exception, IllegalArgumentException is indirect subclass of Exception and IllegalArgumentException is subclass of RuntimeException, hence these pairs can't be used in multi-catch statement.

Only one option is left to replace Line 14 with 'catch(RuntimeException e) {'.

Commenting out Line 14, Line 15 and Line 16 will resolve the compilation error but it will print the whole stack trace rather than just printing the message.

6.1.24 Answer: D

Reason:
For the 1st loop variable 'i' infers to int type, so no issues for 1st loop and for the 2nd loop variable 'j' infers to int type, so no issues for 2nd loop as well.
Let's check the iteration:
1st iteration of loop one: i = 0
   1st iteration of loop two: j = 0
      1st iteration of loop three: ctr = 101. As `i == j` evaluates to true, hence `break two;` gets executed, which takes the control out of loop two and hence to the increment expression (i++) of loop one.
2nd iteration of loop one; i = 1
   1st iteration of loop two: j = 0
      1st iteration of loop three; ctr = 102. As `i > j` evaluates to true, hence `break one;` gets executed, which takes the control out of the loop one.

`System.out.println(ctr);` prints 102 on to the console.

6.1.25 Answer: C, E, H, I

Reason:
Let's check all the options one by one:
`horse.ride("EMMA");` ✗ Variable 'horse' is of Animal type and ride(String) method is not defined in Animal class, therefore it causes compilation error.

`(Horse)horse.ride("EMMA");` ✗ horse.ride("EMMA") will be evaluated first as dot (.) operator has higher precedence than cast. horse.ride("EMMA") returns void, hence it cannot be casted to Horse type. This would cause compilation error.

`((Horse)horse).ride("Emma");` ✓ Variable 'horse' refers to an instance of Horse type and variable 'horse' is casted to Horse type. Horse class has ride(String) method, hence no compilation error. ride(String) method of Horse class will get invoked at runtime and will print the expected output. As, name.toUpperCase() method is invoked, hence it doesn't matter in what case you pass the name, in the output name will always be displayed in the upper case.

`(Rideable)horse.ride("emma");` ✗ horse.ride("EMMA") will be evaluated first as dot (.) operator has higher precedence than cast. horse.ride("EMMA") returns void, hence it cannot be casted to Rideable type. This would cause compilation error.

`((Rideable)horse).ride("emma");` ✓ Variable 'horse' refers to an instance of Horse type and variable 'horse' is casted to Rideable type (super type of Horse). Rideable interface has ride(String) method, hence no compilation error. ride(String) method of Horse class will get invoked at runtime and will print the expected output.

`(Rideable)(Horse)horse.ride("EMMA");` ✗ horse.ride("EMMA") will be evaluated first as dot (.) operator has higher precedence than cast. horse.ride("EMMA") returns void, hence it cannot be casted to Horse type. This would cause compilation error.

`(Horse)(Rideable)horse.ride("EMMA");` ✗ horse.ride("EMMA") will be evaluated first as dot (.) operator has higher precedence than cast. horse.ride("EMMA") returns void, hence it cannot be casted to Rideable type. This would cause compilation error.

`((Rideable)(Horse)horse).ride("EMMA");` ✓ Variable 'horse' refers to an instance of Horse type, it is first casted to Horse type and then casted to Rideable type. Rideable interface has ride(String) method, hence no compilation error. ride(String) method of Horse class will get invoked at runtime and will print the expected output.

`((Horse)(Rideable)horse).ride("emma");` ✓ Variable 'horse' refers to an instance of Horse type, it is first casted to Rideable type and then casted to Horse type. Horse class has ride(String) method, hence no compilation error. ride(String) method of Horse class will get invoked at runtime and will print the expected output.

6.1.26 Answer: B

Reason:
Top-level class can use only two access modifiers [public and default(don't specify anything)]. private and protected cannot be used.
As file name is M.java, hence class N cannot be public.
Top-level class can be final, hence it is a correct option.

Top-level class can be abstract and hence it is also a correct option.

6.1.27 Answer: D

Reason:
Class Y correctly extends class X and it overrides method A() and provides two new methods B() and C().
At Line n1, obj is of X type and therefore obj.B(); and obj.C(); cause compilation error as these methods are not defined in class X.

6.1.28 Answer: D

Reason:
Method test() throws Exception (checked) and it declares to throw it, so no issues with method test().
But main(String []) method neither provides catch handler nor throws clause and hence main(String []) method causes compilation error.
Handle or Declare rule should be followed for checked exception if you are not re-throwing it.

6.1.29 Answer: C

Reason:
Subclass overrides the methods of superclass but it hides the variables of superclass.

Line n3 hides the variable created at Line n1 and Line n4 overrides the getNotation() method of Line n2. There is no compilation error for USDollar class as it correctly overrides getNotation() method.
Similarly, Line n5 hides the variable created at Line n1 and Line n6 overrides the getNotation() method of Line n2. There is no compilation error for Euro class as it correctly overrides getNotation() method as well.

'c1' is of Currency type, hence c1.notation refers to "-" and c1.getNotation() invokes overriding method of USDollar class and it returns "$".
Similarly, c2.notation refers to "-" and c2.getNotation() invokes overriding method of Euro class and it returns "€".

6.1.30 Answer: G

Reason:
At Line n1:
sb --> {"B"}

append(...) method in StringBuilder class is overloaded to accept various arguments and 2 such arguments are String and CharSequence. It's return type is StringBuilder and as StringBuilder class implements CharSequence interface, hence 'sb.append("A")' can easily be passed as and argument to sb.append(...) method. Line n2 compiles successfully.
At Line n2:
sb.append(sb.append("A")); //sb --> {"B"}
sb.append({"BA"}); //sb --> {"BA"}
{"BABA"}

Hence, Line n3 prints BABA

6.1.31 Answer: F

Reason:
Starting with JDK 7, Java allows to not specify type while initializing the ArrayList. As variable list is of List<String> type, therefore type of ArrayList is considered as String. Line n1 compiles successfully.

sublist method is declared in List interface:
List<E> subList(int fromIndex, int toIndex)
fromIndex is inclusive and toIndex is exclusive
It returns a view of the portion of this list between the specified fromIndex and toIndex. The returned list is backed by this list, so non-structural changes in the returned list are reflected in this list and vice-versa.
If returned list (or view) is structurally modified, then modification are reflected in this list as well but if this list is structurally modified, then the semantics of the list returned by this method become undefined.
If fromIndex == toIndex, then returned list is empty.

If fromIndex < 0 OR toIndex > size of the list OR fromIndex > toIndex, then IndexOutOfBoundsException is thrown.

At Line n2, list.subList(0, 4) --> [A, E, I, O] (toIndex is Exclusive, therefore start index is 0 and end index is 3].

list.addAll(list.subList(0, 4)); is almost equal to list.addAll(5, [A, E, I, O]); => Inserts A at index 5, E takes index 6, I takes index 7 and O is placed at index 8. list --> [A, E, I, O, U, A, E, I, O]

Last statement inside main(String []) method prints [A, E, I, O, U, A, E, I, O] on to the console.

6.1.32   Answer: A

Reason:
There are no issues with Line n1 and Line n2, both the statements compile successfully.

String class contains contentEquals(CharSequence) method. Please note that String, StringBuilder and StringBuffer classes implement CharSequence interface, hence contentEquals(CharSequence) method defined in String class cab be invoked with the argument of either String or StringBuilder or StringBuffer.
At Line n3, `str.contentEquals(sb)` is invoked with StringBuilder argument and hence it compiles fine. On execution it would compare the contents of String object and the passed StringBuilder object. As both the String object and StringBuilder object contains same content "Game on", hence on execution, Line n3 will print true.

contentEquals method is not available in StringBuilder class and hence Line n4 causes compilation error.

equals method declared in Object class has the declaration: `public boolean equals(Object)`. Generally, equals method is used to compare different instances of same class but if you pass any other object, there is no compilation error. Parameter type is Object so it can accept any Java object.

`str.equals(sb)` => It compiles fine, String class overrides equals(Object) method but as 'sb' is of StringBuilder type so `str.equals(sb)` would return false at runtime.

`sb.equals(str)` => It also compiles fine, StringBuilder class doesn't override equals(Object) method. So Object version is invoked which uses == operator, hence `sb.equals(str)` would return false as well at runtime.

6.1.33 Answer: C

Reason:
Any RuntimeException can be thrown without any need it to be declared in throws clause of surrounding method.

`throw (RuntimeException)e;` doesn't cause any compilation error.

Even though variable 'e' is type casted to RuntimeException but exception object is still of ArithmeticException, which is caught in main method and 'AE' is printed to the console.

6.1.34 Answer: D, F

Reason:
Variable 'salePercentage' declared inside interface Buyable is implicitly public, static and final. As per Java 8, default and static methods were added in the interface. There is no compilation error in Buyable.java file.
class Book implements Buyable interface but as there is no abstract method in Buyable interface, hence Book class is not needed to implement any method.
Book.java file compiles successfully.

`Buyable [] arr = new Buyable[2];` creates one dimensional array of 2 elements of Buyable type and both the elements are initialized to null.

There are some difference in which static variables and static methods of the interface are accessed.
Correct and only way to access static method of an Interface is by using the name of the interface, such as Buyable.salePercentage(). Line n2 and Line n4 cause compilation error.

As far as public static final variable of interface is concerned, even through the correct way to access static variable is by using the name of the interface, such as Buyable.salePercentage but it can also be accessed by using following:
Reference variable of the interface: Buyable obj1 = null;
System.out.println(obj1.salePercentage);
Name of the implementer class: System.out.println(Book.salePercentage);
Reference variable of the implementer class: Book obj2 = null;
System.out.println(obj2.salePercentage);
Hence, Line n1 and Line n3 compile successfully.

6.1.35 Answer: B

Reason:
Classes in Exception framework are normal java classes, hence null can be used wherever instances of Exception classes are used, so Line 10 compiles successfully. No issues with Line 16 as method getReport() declares to throw SQLException and main(String []) method code correctly handles it.

Program compiles successfully but on execution, NullPointerException is thrown, stack trace is printed on to the console and program ends abruptly.

If you debug the code, you would find that internal routine for throwing null exception causes NullPointerException.

6.1.36 Answer: B

Reason:
Given Expression:
i > 3 != false
It has 2 operators > and !=. > has higher precedence over !=, hence given expression can be written as:
(i > 3) != false
Let's solve above expression:
true != false
true

Hence true is printed on to the console.

6.1.37 Answer: C

Reason:
As per Java 8, default and static methods were added in the interface. Interface M defines static method log(), there is no compilation error in interface M.
Also the scope of static log() method of M is limited to interface M and it can be invoked by using Interface name only, M.log().

Abstract class A also defines the static log() method. Abstract class can have 0 or more abstract methods. Hence, no compilation error in class A as well.

Super type reference variable can refer to an instance of Sub type, therefore the statement `M obj1 = new MyClass();` compiles successfully.
obj1 is of M type, hence `obj1.log();` tries to tag the static method of M but static log() method of M can only be invoked by using M.log();.
Therefore, Line n1 causes compilation error.

Scope of static log() method of A is not limited to class A only but MyClass also gets A.log() method in its scope.
There are different ways in which static method of an abstract class can be accessed:
1. By using the name of the abstract class: M.log(); //Preferred way
2. By using the reference variable of abstract class: A o1 = null; o1.log();
3. By using the name of the subclass: MyClass.log();
4. By using the reference variable of the subclass: MyClass o2 = null; o2.log();
Hence, Line n2 and Line n3 compile successfully.

6.1.38 Answer: B

Reason:
Initially text refers to "RISE ".
Given statement:
text = text + (text = "ABOVE ");
text = "RISE " + (text = "ABOVE "); //Left operand of + operator is evaluated first, text --> "RISE "
text = "RISE " + "ABOVE "; //Right operand of + operator is evaluated next, text --> "ABOVE "

text = "RISE ABOVE "; //text --> "RISE ABOVE "

Hence `System.out.println(text);` prints 'RISE ABOVE ' on to the console.

6.1.39 Answer: E, F, H

Reason:
As System.out.println needs to be executed on executing the Test class, this means special main method should replace /*INSERT*/.
Special main method's name should be "main" (all characters in lower case), should be static, should have public access specifier and it accepts argument of String [] type (Varargs syntax String... can also be used). String [] argument can use any identifier name, even though in most of the cases you will see "args" is used. Position of static and public can be changed but return type 'void' must come just before the method name.

Let's check all the given options one by one:
public void static main(String [] args): Compilation error as return type 'void' must come just before the method name 'main'.
protected static void main(String [] args): Compiles successfully but as this method is not public, hence an Error regarding missing main method is thrown on execution.
public void main(String... args): Compiles successfully but as this method is not static, hence an Error regarding non-static main method is thrown on execution.
static public void Main(String [] args): Compiles successfully but as 'M' is capital in method 'Main', hence it is not special main method. An Error regarding missing main method is thrown on execution.
static public void main(String [] args): Valid definition, it compiles successfully and on execution prints "All is well" on to the console.
public static void main(String [] a): Valid definition, it compiles successfully and on execution prints "All is well" on to the console.
public static Void main(String [] args): Compilation error as Void is a final class in Java and in this case compiler expects main method to return a value of Void type. If you add `return null;` to the main method code will compile successfully but on execution an Error will be thrown mentioning that return type must be 'void' ('v' in lower-case).
public static void main(String... a): Valid definition, it compiles successfully and on execution prints "All is well" on to the console.

6.1.40 Answer: E

Reason:

In Java language, boolean type can store only two values: true and false and these values are not compatible with int type.

Also + operator is not defined for boolean types. Hence, all the 3 statements inside main method causes compilation error.

6.1.41 Answer: C

Reason:

Variable 'count' declared inside interface GetSetGo is implicitly public, static and final. Line n1 compiles successfully.

Line n2 creates one dimensional array of 5 elements of GetSetGo type and all 5 elements are initialized to null. Line n2 compiles successfully.

Though correct way to refer static variable is by using the type name, such as GetSetGo.count but it can also be invoked by using GetSetGo reference variable. Hence, obj.count at Line n3 correctly points to the count variable at Line n1. But as variable 'count' is implicitly final, therefore obj.count++ causes compilation error. Line n3 fails to compile.

Line n4 compiles successfully as variable 'count' is implicitly static and GetSetGo.count is the correct syntax to point to 'count' variable of interface GetSetGo.

6.1.42 Answer: C

Reason:

Let us first check Line n1: byte b1 = 10;

Above statement compiles successfully, even though 10 is an int literal (32 bits) and b1 is of byte primitive type which can store only 8 bits of data.

Here java does some background task, if value of int literal can be easily fit to byte primitive type (-128 to 127), then int literal is implicitly casted to byte type.

So above statement is internally converted to:

byte b1 = (byte)10;

But if you specify any out of range value then it would not be allowed, e.g.

byte b = 128; // It would cause compilation failure as 128 is out of range value for byte type.

There is no issue with Line n2 as byte type (8 bits) can be easily assigned to int type (32 bits).

For line n3, `byte b2 = i1;`, expression on right hand side (i1) is neither a withing range literal value nor constant expression, hence it causes compilation failure.
To compile successfully, this expression needs to be explicitly casted, such as: `byte b2 = (byte)i1;`

6.1.43 Answer: G

Reason:
At Line n1, an int [] object of three elements is created and 'arr' refers to this array object.
arr[0] = 10, arr[1] = 20 and arr[2] = 30;

Given expression at Line n2:
arr[i++] = arr[++i] = 40;
Multiple assignment operators are available, so let's group it first.
=> arr[i++] = (arr[++i] = 40); //Assignment operator is right to left associative
Above expression is valid, hence Line n2 compiles successfully.
Let's solve the expression now. Left operand is 'arr[i++]' and right operand is '(arr[++i] = 40)'. Left operand is evaluated first.
=> arr[0] = (arr[++i] = 40); //i = 1
Right hand operand is evaluated next.
=> arr[0] = (arr[2] = 40); //i = 2
=> arr[0] = 40; //i = 2, arr[2] = 40.
Hence after Line n2, arr refers to int [] object {40, 20, 40}.

Given loop prints below on to the console:
40
20
40

6.1.44 Answer: E

Reason:

Given statement:

System.out.println(status = false || status = true | status = false);

As it contains multiple operators, hence let's group the operators first.

System.out.println(status = false || status = (true | status) = false); //Bitwise inclusive OR | has highest precedence over logical or || and assignment =

For assignment operator to work, left operand must be variable but in above case, `(true | status) = false` causes compilation failure as left operand (true | status) evaluates to a boolean value and not boolean variable.

6.1.45 Answer: A, C, D, H

Reason:

Variable NUM is declared in Super class and class Sub extends Super, hence NUM can be accessed by using obj.NUM.

But as NUM Is final, hence it cannot be reassigned, therefore Line n2 causes compilation error. Let's check all the options one by one:

Remove final modifier from Line n1 => ✓ Valid option and in this case output is 200.

Replace /*INSERT*/ with byte NUM; => X In this case, class Sub hides the variable NUM of Super class but Line n2 will still not compile as byte range is from -128 to 127 and 200 is out of range value.

Replace /*INSERT*/ with short NUM; => ✓ In this case, class Sub hides the variable NUM of Super class and 200 can be easily assigned to short type. In this case output is 200.

Replace /*INSERT*/ with int NUM; => In this case, class Sub hides the variable NUM of Super class and 200 can be easily assigned to int type. In this case output is 200.

Replace /*INSERT*/ with float NUM; => X In this case, class Sub hides the variable NUM of Super class and 200 can be easily assigned to float type. But output in this case will be 200.0 and not 200.

Replace /*INSERT*/ with double NUM; => X In this case, class Sub hides the variable NUM of Super class and 200 can be easily assigned to double type. But output in this case will be 200.0 and not 200.

Replace /*INSERT*/ with boolean NUM; => ✗ In this case, class Sub hides the variable NUM of Super class but Line n2 will still not compile as boolean type in java allows 2 values true and false. 200 is not compatible with boolean type.

Replace /*INSERT*/ with Object NUM; => ✓ In this case, class Sub hides the variable NUM of Super class and at Line n2, value 200 is boxed to Integer, which is then assigned to obj.NUM. So, obj.NUM refers to an instance of Integer class. Line n3 invokes toString() method of Integer class and hence 200 is printed on to the console.

6.1.46 Answer: E

Reason:

java.io.FileNotFoundException exception is a checked exception.

Java doesn't allow to catch specific checked exceptions if these are not thrown by the statements inside try block. catch(FileNotFoundException ex) {} causes compilation error in this case as System.out.println(1); will never throw FileNotFoundException.

NOTE: Java allows to catch Exception type. catch(Exception ex) {} will never cause compilation error.

6.1.47 Answer: A

Reason:

Constructors cannot use final, abstract or static modifiers. As no-argument constructor of MySubClass uses final modifier, therefore it causes compilation error.

6.1.48 Answer: G

Reason:

Both try and catch blocks have return; statement, which means either of the return statements will definitely get executed. Hence, compiler tags `System.out.println("DONE");` as unreachable and this causes compilation error.

6.1.49 Answer: B

Reason:
String class has following two overloaded replace methods:
1. public String replace(char oldChar, char newChar) {}:
Returns a string resulting from replacing all occurrences of oldChar in this string with newChar. If no replacement is done, then source String object is returned. e.g.
"Java".replace('a', 'A') --> returns new String object "JAvA".
"Java".replace('a', 'a') --> returns the source String object "Java" (no change).
"Java".replace('m', "M") --> returns the source String object "Java" (no change).

2. public String replace(CharSequence target, CharSequence replacement) {}:
Returns a new String object after replacing each substring of this string that matches the literal target sequence with the specified literal replacement sequence. e.g.
"Java".replace("a", "A") --> returns new String object "JAvA".
"Java".replace("a", "a") --> returns new String object "Java" (it replaces "a" with "a").
"Java".replace("m", "M") --> returns the source String object "Java" (no change).

As String, StringBuilder and StringBuffer all implement CharSequence, hence instances of these classes can be passed to replace method. Line n1 compiles successfully and on execution replaces "N" with "THET", and hence Line n1 prints PATHETIC on to the console.

6.1.50 Answer: F

Reason:
`private void emp() {}` is a valid method declaration.
Class name and method name can be same and that is why given method can be declared in any of the given classes: 'emp', 'Emp', 'employee', 'Employee', 'Student' and '_emp_'.
'_emp_' is also a valid Java identifier.

6.1.51 Answer: B

Reason:
As per Java 8, default and static methods were added in the interface. Interface I1 defines static method print(String), there is no compilation error in interface I1.

Also the scope of print(String) method of I1 is limited to interface I1 and it can be invoked by using Interface name only, I1.print("").

class C1 implements I1 and it also defines print(String) instance method. Even though class C1 implements I1, it doesn't have static print(String) method in its scope, therefore class C1 compiles successfully.

Super type reference variable can refer to an instance of Sub type, therefore the statement `I1 obj = new C1();` compiles successfully.
obj is of I1 type, hence `obj.print("Java");` tries to tag the static method of I1 but static print(String) method of I1 can only be invoked by using I1.print("Java");.
Therefore, `obj.print("Java");` causes compilation error.

6.1.52 Answer: A

Reason:
As member variables 'testNo' and 'desc' are declared with no explicit access specifier, this means these variables have package scope, hence these variables are accessible only to classes within the same package. Hence, no changes are necessary.
If you use private, then instance variables will not be accessible to any other classes, even within the same package.
If you use protected, then instance variables will be accessible to the subclasses outside 'com.udayankhattry.oca' package.
If you use public, then instance variables will be accessible to all the classes.

6.1.53 Answer: A

Reason:
Line n1 and Line n2 compile successfully.

Let's check the boolean expression of Line n3:
50 <= score < 60
As multiple operators are available, so let's group the operators first on the basis of precedence and associativity.
Relational operators (<, >, <= and >=) are at same level and left to right associative, hence given expression can be grouped as:
(50 <= score) < 60

< is a binary operator with two operands: (50 <= score) on the left is of boolean type and 60 on the right is of int type. But < operator is not defined for boolean, int type and hence Line n3 causes compilation error. Line n4 and Line n5 cause compilation error for the same reason.

6.1.54   Answer: D

Reason:
Even though compiler is aware that Line n2 will never execute, but it doesn't tag it as unreachable code. Reason for this odd behavior is explained in the Java Language specification:
https://docs.oracle.com/javase/specs/jls/se8/html/jls-14.html#jls-14.21
Following statement results in a compile-time error:
while (false) { x=3; }
because the statement x=3; is not reachable; but the superficially similar case:
if (false) { x=3; }
does not result in a compile-time error. An optimizing compiler may realize that the statement x=3; will never be executed and may choose to omit the code for that statement from the generated class file, but the statement x=3; is not regarded as "unreachable" in the technical sense specified here.

The rationale for this differing treatment is to allow programmers to define "flag" variables such as:

static final boolean DEBUG = false;
and then write code such as:

if (DEBUG) { x=3; }
The idea is that it should be possible to change the value of DEBUG from false to true or from true to false and then compile the code correctly with no other changes to the program text.

Line n2 is not executed but Line n3 executes successfully and prints HELLO on to the console.

6.1.55 Answer: A

Reason:
If you don't initialize variable e inside catch block using `e = new SQLException();` and simply throw e, then code would compile successfully as compiler is certain that 'e' would refer to an instance of SQLException only.

But the moment compiler finds `e = new SQLException();`, `throw e;` causes compilation error as at runtime 'e' may refer to any Exception type.

6.1.56 Answer: B

Reason:
Like any other method, main method can also be overloaded. But main method called by JVM is always with String [] parameter. Don't get confused with 10 as it is passed as "10".
Execute above class with any command line arguments or 0 command line argument, output will always be "String".

6.1.57 Answer: H

Reason:
Line n1 and Line n2 don't cause any compilation error.

if-else block uses break; and continue; statements. break; will exit the loop and will take the control to Line n4 on the other hand continue; will take the control to Line n2. In both the cases Line n3 will never be executed.
As Compiler knows about it, hence it tags Line n3 as unreachable, which causes compilation error.

6.1.58 Answer: C, E, G

Reason:
i1 is an instance variable and i2 is a static variable.
Instance method can access both instance and static members. Hence, Line n1 and Line n2 compile successfully.

Static method can access only static members. Hence, Line n3 [accessing instance variable i1], Line n5 [accessing instance method change1(int)] and Line n7 [accessing instance variable i1] cause compilation error.

6.1.59 Answer: C

Reason:
Test.java is a valid java file. As none of the classes in Test.java file are public, hence file name can use any valid Java identifier.
As file name is Test.java, hence to compile the code below command is used:
javac Test.java

Execution of above command creates 4 class files: A.class, B.class, C.class & D.class.
To print C on to the console, class C must be executed. To execute C class, command is:
java C

6.1.60 Answer: D

Reason:
As per Java 8, default and static methods were added in the interface and default methods can invoke static method as well. Hence, there is no issue with the Flyable interface.

class Aeroplane implements Flyable interface, hence it inherits the default method fly() and static method horizontalDegree() can be accessed using Flyable.horizontalDegree(). It also provides the implementation of land() method. There is no issue with Aeroplane class as well.

On execution below text is printed on to the console:
Flying at 20 degrees.
Landing at -20 degrees.

Reason:
Method can have same name as that of the Class. Hence, void Base() is a valid method declaration in Base class.

Line n2 invokes the Base() method and not the constructor.

Subclass overrides the methods of superclass but it hides the variables of superclass.

Line n5 hides the variable created at Line n1, there is no rules related to hiding (type and access modifier can be changed).

Line n7 correctly overrides the Base() method of class Base.

Compiler adds super(); as the 1st statement inside the no-argument constructor of Base class and Derived class.

There is no compilation error, so let's check the execution.

new Derived() at Line n9 invokes the constructor of Base class, at this point instance variable id is declared and 0 is assigned to it. In fact, instance variable id of Base class is also declared and 0 is assigned to it. Compiler added super(); as the first statement inside this constructor, hence control goes to the no-argument constructor of Base class.

Compiler added super(); as the first statement inside this constructor as well, hence it invokes the no-argument constructor of the Object class. No-argument constructor of Object class finishes its execution and control goes back to the constructor of Base class. Before it starts executing remaining statements inside the constructor, instance variable assignment statement (if available) are executed. This means 1000 is assigned to variable id of Base class.

Line n2 is executed next, Base() method defined in Derived class is executed. Which overriding method to invoke, is decided at runtime based on the instance. Instance is of Derived class (because of Line n9), hence control starts executing Base() method of Derived class.

Line n8 is executed next, Derived class hides the id variable of Base class and that is why at Line n8, id points to variable created at Line n5. This id variable still stores the value 0 as Base class's constructor has not finishes its execution.

value of id is decremented by 1, so id becomes -1 and -1 is printed on to the console. Base() method finishes its execution and control goes back to Line n2. No-argument constructor of Base class finishes its execution and control goes back to the constructor of Derived class. Before it starts executing remaining statements inside the constructor, instance variable assignment statement (if available) are executed. This means 2000 is assigned to variable id of Base class.

No-argument constructor of Derived class finishes its execution and control goes back to Line n9. main(String []) method finishes its execution and program terminates successfully.

Hence, output is -1.

6.1.62 Answer: E

Reason:
`int indexOf(String str, int fromIndex)` method of String class returns the index within this string of the first occurrence of the specified substring, starting at the specified index. e.g.
"alaska".indexOf("a", 1) returns 2
"alaska".indexOf("a", 2) returns 2
"alaska".indexOf("a", 3) returns 5

In the given question, 'arr' refers to a String array of size 5. Element at index 0 refers to "1st", element at index 1 refers to "2nd" and so on.

Let's solve the given expression of Line n1:
arr[place.indexOf("a", 3)]
= arr["faraway".indexOf("a", 3)] //Starts looking for "a" from index 3 of the given String "faraway" and "a" is found at index 3.
= arr[3]
= "4th" //Array element at index 3 refers to "4th".

Hence, 4th is printed on to the console.

6.1.63 Answer: B

Reason:
Range of char data type is from 0 to 65535 and hence it can be easily assigned to int type. println() method is overloaded to accept char type and int type both. If char type value is passed, it prints char value and if int type value is passed, it prints int value. As i1 is of int type, hence corresponding int value, which is 97, is printed on to the console.

6.1.64 Answer: C

Reason:
Given boolean expression:
(num++ == num++) //num=10
(10 == num++) //Left side operand is evaluated first, value 10 is used in the expression and variable num is incremented by 1, so num=11
(10 == 11) //Right side operand is evaluated next, value 11 is used in the expression and variable num is incremented by 1, so num = 12
Above expression evaluates to false, hence else block is executed and NOT EQUAL 12 is printed on to the console.

6.1.65 Answer: B

Reason:
Given statement:
System.out.println(text.concat(text.concat("ELEVEN ")).trim()); //'text' refers to "ONE "
System.out.println(text.concat("ONE ELEVEN ").trim()); //As String is immutable, hence there is no change in the String object referred by 'text', 'text' still refers to "ONE "
System.out.println(("ONE ONE ELEVEN ").trim()); //'text' still refers to "ONE "
System.out.println("ONE ONE ELEVEN"); //trim() method removes the trailing space in this case
ONE ONE ELEVEN is printed on to the console.

6.1.66 Answer: E

Reason:
As per Java 8, default methods were added in the interface. Interface Perishable1 defines default method maxDays(), there is no compilation error in interface Perishable1. Method maxDays() is implicitly public in Perishable1.

interface Perishable2 extends Perishable1 and it overrides the default method maxDays() of Document, overriding method in Perishable2 is implicitly public. Interface Perishable2 compiles successfully.

Class Milk implements Perishable2 and Perishable1. Although it is redundant for Milk class to implement Preishable1 as Perishable2 already extends Perishable1. There is no conflict in Milk class as it inherits the default method maxDays() of Perishable2 interface. Milk class compiles successfully.

`Perishable1 obj = new Milk();` It compiles fine as Perishable1 is supertype and Milk is subtype.
`obj.maxDays()` executes the default maxDays() method of Perishable2 interface and it returns 2. `System.out.println(obj.maxDays());` prints 2 on to the console.

6.1.67 Answer: A

Reason:
Throwable is the root class of the exception hierarchy and it contains some useful constructors:

1. public Throwable() {...} : No-argument constructor
2. public Throwable(String message) {...} : Pass the detail message
3. public Throwable(String message, Throwable cause) {...} : Pass the detail message and the cause
4. public Throwable(Throwable cause) {...} : Pass the cause

Exception and RuntimeException classes also provide similar constructors.

Hence all 3 statements Line n1, Line n2 and Line n3 compile successfully.

Throwable class also contains methods, which are inherited by all the subclasses (Exception, RuntimeException etc.)
1. public String getMessage() {...} : Returns the detail message (E.g. detail message set by 2nd and 3rd constructor)
2. public String toString() {} :
Returns a short description of this throwable. The result is the concatenation of:
the name of the class of this object
": " (a colon and a space)
the result of invoking this object's getLocalizedMessage() method

If getLocalizedMessage returns null, then just the class name is returned.

Because of the toString() method,
Line n1 prints "java.lang.RuntimeException".
Line n2 prints "java.lang.RuntimeException: HELLO"
Line n3 prints "java.lang.Exception: java.lang.RuntimeException: HELLO"

6.1.68   Answer: B

Reason:
Basic/Regular for loop has following form:
for ([ForInit] ; [Expression] ; [ForUpdate]) {...}
[ForInit] can be local variable initialization or the following expressions:
Assignment
PreIncrementExpression
PreDecrementExpression
PostIncrementExpression
PostDecrementExpression
MethodInvocation
ClassInstanceCreationExpression

[ForUpdate] can be following expressions:
Assignment
PreIncrementExpression
PreDecrementExpression
PostIncrementExpression
PostDecrementExpression
MethodInvocation

ClassInstanceCreationExpression

The [Expression] must have type boolean or Boolean, or a compile-time error occurs. If [Expression] is left blank, it evaluates to true.

All the expressions can be left blank; for(;;) is a valid for loop and it is an infinite loop as [Expression] is blank and evaluates to true.

Multiple comma separated statements are allowed for [ForInit] and [ForUpdate] expressions, where as [Expression] must be single expression which results in boolean or Boolean.

In the given for loop:
[ForInit] = int x = 10, y = 11, z = 12: It is allowed. 3 variables are declared and initialized. x = 10, y = 11 & z = 12.
[Expression] = y > x && z > y = (y > x) && (z > y) [Relational operator has higher precedence than logical AND]. This expression is valid and results in boolean value.
[ForUpdate] = y++, z -= 2. It is allowed. y is incremented by 1 and z is decremented by 2.

Let's check the loop's iteration:
1st iteration: x = 10, y = 11, z = 12. (y > x) && (z > y) = (11 > 10) && (12 > 11) = true && true = true. Loop's body is executed and prints x + y + z = 10 + 11 + 12 = 33 on to the console.
2nd iteration: [ForUpdate] is executed. y = 12, z = 10. (y > x) && (z > y) = (12 > 10) && (10 > 12) = true && false = false.
Control goes out of for loop and program terminates successfully.

Loop's body executes once and prints 33 on to the console.

6.1.69   Answer: A, B, D, F

Reason:
Interface java.util.function.Predicate<T> declares below non-overriding abstract method:
boolean test(T t);

Let's check all the options one by one:

p -> true ✓ Means test method returns true for the passed String. It will print all the elements of the List.

p -> !!!!true ✓ !!!!true => !!!false => !!true => !false => true, means test method returns true for the passed String. It will print all the elements of the List.

p -> !!false X !!false => !true => false, means test method returns false for the passed String. It will not print even a single element of the list.

p -> p.length() >= 1 ✓ Means test method returns true if passed String's length is greater than or equal to 1 and this is true for all the list elements.

p -> p.length() < 7 X Means test method returns true if passed String's length is less than 7 and this is not true for "whether". "whether" will not be displayed in the output.

(String p) -> p.length() < 100 ✓ Means test method returns true if passed String's length is less than 100 and this is true for all the list elements.

String p -> p.length() > 0 X Round brackets or parenthesis are missing around 'String p'. This causes compilation error.

6.1.70   Answer: C

Reason:
calculate method is correctly overloaded as both the methods have different signature: calculate(int, int) and calculate(byte, byte). Please note that there is no rule regarding return type for overloaded methods, return type can be same or different.

`new Calculator().calculate(b, i)` tags to `calculate(int, int)` as byte value is implicitly casted to int type.

Given code compiles successfully and on execution prints 120 on to the console.

6.1.71   Answer: A

Reason:
Few things to keep in mind:
1.
There are 2 rules related to return types of overriding method:
A. If return type of overridden method is of primitive type, then overriding method should use same primitive type.

B. If return type of overridden method is of reference type, then overriding method can use same reference type or its sub-type (also known as covariant return type).

2.

In case of overriding, if overridden method declares to throw any RuntimeException or Error, overriding method may or may not throw any RuntimeException but overriding method must not throw any checked exceptions.

3.

In generics syntax, Parameterized types are not polymorphic, this means even if B is subtype of A, List<B> is not subtype of List<A>. Remember this point. So below syntaxes are NOT allowed:

List<A> list = new ArrayList<B>(); OR ArrayList<A> list = new ArrayList<B>();

Let's check all the options one by one:

abstract List<A> get() throws ArrayIndexOutOfBoundsException; => ✓ It returns the same return type 'List<A>' and it is allowed to throw any RuntimeException (ArrayIndexOutOfBoundsException is RuntimeException)

abstract List<B> get(); => ✗ List<B> is not subtype of List<A>, it is not covariant return type.

abstract ArrayList<A> get() throws Exception; => ✗ As overridden method declares to throw IndexOutOfBoundsException, which is a Runtime Exception, overriding method is not allowed to declare to throw any checked Exception. Class Exception and its subclasses are checked exceptions.

abstract ArrayList<B> get(); => ✗ ArrayList<B> is not subtype of List<A>, it is not covariant return type.

6.1.72 Answer: F

Reason:
Basic/Regular for loop has following form:
for ([ForInit] ; [Expression] ; [ForUpdate]) {...}
[ForInit] can be local variable initialization or the following expressions:

Assignment
PreIncrementExpression
PreDecrementExpression
PostIncrementExpression
PostDecrementExpression
MethodInvocation
ClassInstanceCreationExpression

[ForUpdate] can be following expressions:
Assignment
PreIncrementExpression
PreDecrementExpression
PostIncrementExpression
PostDecrementExpression
MethodInvocation
ClassInstanceCreationExpression

The [Expression] must have type boolean or Boolean, or a compile-time error occurs. If [Expression] is left blank, it evaluates to true.

All the expressions can be left blank; for(;;) is a valid for loop and it is an infinite loop as [Expression] is blank and evaluates to true.

In the given code, for both the loops, `System.out.print(...)` is used as [ForUpdate] expression, which is a MethodInvocation expression and hence a valid statement. Given code compiles successfully.

Let's check the iterations:
1st iteration of outer: i = 0. i < 3 evaluates to true.
   i = 1.
   1st iteration of inner: j = 0. j < 3 evaluates to true as j = 0. Boolean expression `i > ++j` = `1 > 1` evaluates to false. j = 1.
   2nd iteration of inner: `System.out.print(j)` prints 1 to the console. j < 3 evaluates to true as j = 1. Boolean expression `i > ++j` = `1 > 2` evaluates to false. j = 2.
   3rd iteration of inner: `System.out.print(j)` prints 2 to the console. j < 3 evaluates to true as j = 2. Boolean expression `i > ++j` = `1 > 3` evaluates to false. j = 3.

4th iteration of inner: `System.out.print(j)` prints 3 to the console. j < 3 evaluates to false as j = 3. Control goes out of inner for loop and to the [ForUpdate] expression of outer loop.

2nd iteration of outer: `System.out.print(i)` prints 1 to the console. i < 3 evaluates to true as i = 1.

 i = 2.

1st iteration of inner: j = 0. j < 3 evaluates to true as j = 0. Boolean expression `i > ++j` = `2 > 1` evaluates to true. j = 1. ` break outer;` takes the control out of the outer for loop.

Program terminates successfully after printing 1231 on to the console.

Udemy Courses By The Author

Courses for Java 17 Certification:

Topic-Wise Tests:-

Java Certification (1Z0-829) Topic-wise Tests Part-1 [2023]

Assess your preparation of Java SE 17 Developer exam (includes 602 questions)

https://www.udemy.com/course/ocp_java-se-17_1z0-829_p1/?referralCode=7C3BC4B0A074FC5BFCD1

Java Certification (1Z0-829) Topic-wise Tests Part-2 [2023]

Assess your preparation of Java SE 17 Developer exam (includes 610 questions)

https://www.udemy.com/course/ocp_java-se-17_1z0-829_p2/?referralCode=380CD98469BA5D4843DC

Exam Simulation Tests:-

Java Certification (1Z0-829) Exam Simulation Part-1 [2023]

Assess your preparation of Java SE 17 Developer exam (includes 303 questions)

https://www.udemy.com/course/java-11_1z0-829_p1/?referralCode=B84DE9AF0FCC009B726B

Java Certification (1Z0-829) Exam Simulation Part-2 [2023]

Assess your preparation of Java SE 17 Developer exam (includes 303 questions)

https://www.udemy.com/course/java-11_1z0-829_p2/?referralCode=704CEFBDE75B17CB2C2C

Java Certification (1Z0-829) Exam Simulation Part-3 [2023]

Assess your preparation of Java SE 17 Developer exam (includes 303 questions)

https://www.udemy.com/course/java-11_1z0-829_p3/?referralCode=1FDBB124B2F5F8A7EBD6

Java Certification (1Z0-829) Exam Simulation Part-4 [2023]

Assess your preparation of Java SE 17 Developer exam (includes 303 questions)

https://www.udemy.com/course/java-11_1z0-829_p4/?referralCode=0E9648DAD625420184CB

Courses for Java 11 Certification:

Topic-Wise Tests:-

Java Certification (1Z0-819) Topic-wise Tests Part-1 [2023]

Assess your preparation of Java SE 11 Developer exam (includes 535 questions)

https://www.udemy.com/course/ocp_java-se-11_1z0-819_p1/?referralCode=94723C1A0CB233CD799E

Java Certification (1Z0-819) Topic-wise Tests Part-2 [2023]

Assess your preparation of Java SE 11 Developer exam (includes 567 questions)

https://www.udemy.com/course/ocp_java-se-11_1z0-819_p2/?referralCode=0E765C48B618E866CB79

Exam Simulation Tests:-

Java Certification (1Z0-819) Exam Simulation Part-1 [2023]

Assess your preparation of Java SE 11 Developer exam (includes 300 questions)

https://www.udemy.com/course/java-11_1z0-819_p1/?referralCode=360ED8841D658B856247

Java Certification (1Z0-819) Exam Simulation Part-2 [2023]

Assess your preparation of Java SE 11 Developer exam (includes 300 questions)

https://www.udemy.com/course/java-11_1z0-819_p2/?referralCode=9A6070157511183345C8

Java Certification (1Z0-819) Exam Simulation Part-3 [2023]

Assess your preparation of Java SE 11 Developer exam (includes 251 questions)

https://www.udemy.com/course/java-11_1z0-819_p3/?referralCode=019E14731CC414A03B1D

Java Certification (1Z0-819) Exam Simulation Part-4 [2023]

Assess your preparation of Java SE 11 Developer exam (includes 251 questions)

https://www.udemy.com/course/java-11_1z0-819_p4/?referralCode=0876CB0955C2942C81CF

Courses for Java 8 Certification:

1Z0-808:-

[New Pattern] OCA Topic Wise (1Z0-808) [2023]

New questions to prepare for Java SE 8 Programmer I EXAM

https://www.udemy.com/course/java-se-8_1z0-808/?referralCode=76BC955CCA9433B7B81B

[New Pattern] OCA Exam Sim (1Z0-808) [2023]

New questions to practice for Java SE 8 Programmer I EXAM

https://www.udemy.com/course/java-8_1z0-808/?referralCode=DD0A5563E81820B89DC8

Java Certification - OCA (1Z0-808) Topic-wise Tests [2023]

Multiple choice questions covering all the exam objectives of Oracle Certified Associate, Java SE 8 Programmer I

https://www.udemy.com/course/java-ocajp/?referralCode=AAD655BA1CE88EEE7DDC

Java Certification : OCA (1Z0-808) Exam Simulation [2023]

Master the essentials to pass the Oracle Certified Associate(OCA): Java SE 8 Programmer I EXAM

https://www.udemy.com/course/java-oca/?referralCode=2337F77572B062EB41D6

1Z0-809:-

Java Certification - OCP (1Z0-809) Topic-wise Tests [2023]

Multiple choice questions covering all the exam objectives of Oracle Certified Professional, Java SE 8 Programmer II

https://www.udemy.com/course/java-ocpjp/?referralCode=22BEEDC2D666C97BA703

Java Certification : OCP (1Z0-809) Exam Simulation [2023]

Pass the Oracle Certified Professional(OCP): Java SE 8 Programmer II EXAM

https://www.udemy.com/course/java-ocp/?referralCode=13982FCB1E0CAA5B94FB

Other Courses:

Java For Beginners - 1st step towards becoming a Java Guru!

Become a Core Java Expert easily and in step-by-step manner

https://www.udemy.com/course/corejava/?referralCode=831CD22E895230578AF2

Test your Core Java skills

139 multiple choice questions to test your Core Java skills

https://www.udemy.com/course/testcorejava/?referralCode=B8C939C8E3AEDA4EC4FD

Test Java Functional Programming (Lambda & Stream) skills

180+ questions on Inner classes, Lambda expressions, Method References, Functional Interfaces & Stream API

https://www.udemy.com/course/test-functional-programming/?referralCode=6A6A598EDD16CF40AA8E

Java Certification (1Z0-815) Topic-wise Tests [2023]

492 Multiple choice questions arranged in topic-wise manner covering all the exam objectives of 1Z0-815 exam

https://www.udemy.com/course/java-11_1z0-815/?referralCode=B0A027B28ACC27976961

Java Certification (1Z0-815) Exam Simulation [2023]

492 Multiple choice questions covering all the exam objectives of 1Z0-815 exam

https://www.udemy.com/course/java-se-11_1z0-815/?referralCode=F409C96F9DD47698A3AE

Python Quiz - Test your Python knowledge in 1 Day!

11th hour preparation for Python interviews, exams and tests with multiple choice questions

https://www.udemy.com/course/python-test/?referralCode=F070ABFC34905F36FF71

NOTE: Access above links to avail maximum discount on the courses.

OR

You may also send an email to udayan.khattry@outlook.com to request for **MAXIMUM Discount coupon code** for above courses.

www.ingramcontent.com/pod-product-compliance
Lightning Source LLC
Chambersburg PA
CBHW060640060326
40690CB00020B/4465